PROPHETIC REALISM

Beyond Militarism and Pacifism in an Age of Terror

PROPHETIC REALISM

Beyond Militarism and Pacifism in an Age of Terror

RONALD H. STONE

t&t clark

NEW YORK • LONDON

T & T Clark International, Madison Square Park
15 East 26th Street, New York, NY 10010

T & T Clark International
The Tower Building, 11 York Road, London SE1 7NX

T & T Clark International is a Continuum imprint.

Cover design: Wesley Hoke

Library of Congress Cataloging-in-Publication Data

Stone, Ronald H.
   Prophetic realism : beyond militarism and pacifism in an age of terror / Ronald H. Stone.
      p. cm.
   Includes index.
   ISBN 0-567-02641-8 (hardcover)
   1. Christianity and international affairs. 2. Christianity and politics—United States.
   3. Niebuhr, Reinhold, 1892-1971. 4. Nonviolence—Religious aspects—Christianity.
   5. Pacifism—Religious aspects—Christianity. I. Title.
   BR115.I7.S76 2005
   261.8'7'0973—dc22
                                    2005014894

Printed in the United States of America

05 06 07 08 09 10   10 9 8 7 6 5 4 3 2 1

Dedicated to the memory of my teacher,
John C. Bennett,
and to the baby
he baptized, my son,
Randall W. Stone,
now scholar of international relations.

Contents

Preface: After 9/11 ix

Acknowledgments xv

1. Biblical Sources of Prophetic Realism 1

2. Historical Sources of Realism 10

3. The Development of American Prophetic Realism 27

4. A Perspective on International Politics 45

5. Ontology of Power 56

6. On Power and Purpose 72

7. Prophetic Realism and Peacemaking 84

8. Realist Criticism of Just Peacemaking Theory 109

9. Resurgent Pacifist Attack on Realism 122

10. Prophetic Realism, Human Rights, and Foreign Policy 132

11. U.S. Foreign Policy in the Middle East 154

12. The Peacemaking Struggle and Resistance 166

Index. 183

Preface

After 9/11

THREE OF FOUR HIJACKED AIRLINERS found their targets on September 11, 2001. The targets were both real and symbolic. The violence of the hijackers was directed at the World Trade Center and the Pentagon, the economic and military arms of the United States' power. These "successful" attacks followed the failed bombings of the World Trade Center in 1993 and the USS *Cole* in the Aden harbor in 2000. But unless their goal is confined to spreading fear or attracting attention to a cause, single attacks of violence seldom achieve their objective. Modern nation-states do not succumb to random bombings, though sometimes national responses are awesome. For example, the assassination of Austrian Archduke Franz Ferdinand in Sarajevo in June 1914 unleashed events of World War I that are still reverberating today.

The targets of Osama bin Laden's movement were official targets similar to the Sarajevo assassination, though Al-Qaeda used civilians and over Pennsylvania it was thwarted by civilians. On 9/11, citizens rallied aboard United Flight 93, driving it into the ground near Shanksville, Pennsylvania. The passengers' spontaneous reaction was more effective than any intervention by government agencies, whose failures had contributed to the vulnerability of the United States homeland in the first place. Among the losses in New York City were members and offices of the Central Intelligence Agency, whose raison d'être had been to coordinate intelligence to prevent another Pearl Harbor.

The blows on 9/11 were another round of the struggle between Al Qaeda and the United States, a struggle that has its origins in the reaction of Osama bin Laden to the elder President George Bush's response to Iraq's invasion of Kuwait. Bin Laden's offer to defend Saudi Arabia against Iraq at the time of Iraq's invasion of Kuwait was rejected by the Saudi monarchy. That rejection and the presence of U.S.-led forces on Saudi Arabia's perceived "holy ground" were given as reasons for bin Laden's turning against his former ally, the United States. The policy under President William Clinton was to kill or capture Osama bin Laden for his attacks on U.S. forces and interests in Arabia, Yemen, Somalia, Kenya, Tanzania, and the United States. So, while for many U.S. citizens the violence on 9/11 seemed to be the beginning of a new war, to the Arab attackers, particularly Osama bin Laden, it was another round in an ongoing battle.

The 9/11 attacks were either a terrible strategic mistake on bin Laden's part or a failed attempt to draw the United States into a war against Islam that it would lose. Given the advance education and sophistication of various bin Laden operatives, it defies the imagination to believe they thought themselves capable of defeating the United States of America. Like the wiser military leaders of Japan who attacked Pearl Harbor, they must have known they would awaken a sleeping Eagle whose defense of its own would be awesome. U.S. restraint over defeat in Somalia, along with futile responses to the African embassy bombings, may have lured Al Qaeda into a desperate gamble. But despite stirrings, Muslims did not rally significantly to bin Laden's defense, and his Afghanistan corps and allies in the Taliban were unable to withstand U.S. airpower and Afghanistani fighters determined to liberate the country. A consensus justifying a U.S. military response formed quickly among the North Atlantic Treaty Organization, the United Nations, nongovernmental organizations, and churches. All major nations signaled their support of a U.S. military response, which proved more terrible and more effective than many had thought possible. Many Afghans rallied at their liberation by U.S. forces, quickly establishing a pro-U.S. Afghan government.

This conflict in Central Asia and the continental United States has introduced new dimensions of the use of violence in the third millennium. The second millennium closed with the consideration of new forms of counterviolence to be used in interventions for humanitarian rescue; the third opened with religiously inspired terror.

The success of the U.S. intervention in the Afghanistan civil war left the Bush administration with responsibilities of care. The rejection of nation building had been the hallmark of Bush's criticism of President Clinton's foreign policy. Yet the victory in Kabul made it obviously necessary. One form of feminist theory in international relations has emphasized a care-based perspective.[1] After U.S. forces secured victory through military means, a tactic criticized by caring feminism, the need to step up and meet responsibilities of care was forced on the new president and his realpolitik advisors. The burdens that Rudyard Kipling warned the U.S. against assuming in the Philippines in the "white man's burden"[2] were derived from his knowledge of British failures in Afghanistan, and now the United States is not only in the Philippines once again but also in Kabul. The burden is both seized by and thrust upon the United States by a violent response to the 9/11 terrorist attacks and by the virtue of care. The use of power and the demands of virtue become curiously intermingled.

From Kabul to Tel Aviv, U.S. foreign policy reveals a tangle of religious, political, and moral issues. The United States abandoned its hostility toward Pakistan in order to garner Pakistani assistance in defeating the Taliban protectors of Al Qaeda. Claiming fear of Iraq's development of nuclear weapons, the United States invaded that country. A successful blow to change the Iraqi regime required the cooperation of other Islamic nations. The support of Islamic nations depended on progress in thwarting Israel's counterterrorist war against the Palestinians. So the struggle with terrorists, particularly radical-sectarian Muslims, returns full circle to issues raised by Zionist success in establishing Israel. The twentieth-century American realism investigated in this study was Zionist. This study argues that the origins of these realist thoughts were from the Hebrew prophets. These foundations lead to the difficulty of ever really dissolving the religious, political, and moral dimensions of international relations. If even realism has to recognize the connections between religion and foreign policy in the Middle East, will not the other major options of liberalism, Marxism, and international organization have to recognize them also?

To take religion and its social thrust seriously revises the study of international relations even more fundamentally than the dawning realization that ethics is part of the study. Likewise, international relations is a necessary part of the study and practice of religion and ethics. This latter conclusion is not yet appreciated by the religious communities in the United States. These religious communities have responded to the attack on 9/11 more by initiating dialogue with Muslims and by researching Islam than by deepening their study of international relations. Before the U.S. counterattack, bin Laden was even filmed rejoicing at the increased interest in Islam in the Western world. The shattering of the invulnerability of the American homeland by Islamic terrorists has forced American theorists to recognize that international relations needs the study of religion and ethics.

On September 11, 2001, I had just finished a lecture on Christian political ethics at Pittsburgh Theological Seminary when a student, who had been summoned to duty, met me in the hall. He told me we were at war: an airliner was down in nearby Shanksville, Pennsylvania, the Pentagon had been attacked, the World Trade Center was burning, and the president had been diverted from returning to Washington. I spent the next hour and a half watching TV and revising the chapel service in which I was expected to commemorate a former teacher, Robert MacAfee Brown. Many of the readings from Brown's works were to prove relevant to the new chapel service. At the service in Pittsburgh that morning, at least forty people named relatives and friends who were working either in or near the World Trade Center or the Pentagon. Some of our seminary students, trained as paramedics and grief counselors, were already en route to nearby Shanksville. Others were reporting to the National Guard center only a half mile from the seminary. We were involved.

Two weeks later, while in church meetings at the United Nations, the Church Center for the UN, and Pilgrim Church, we adjourned our schedule to make a pilgrimage to the World Trade Center site. There by the smoldering ruins, breathing the smell of the victims, I vowed to deepen my work as an ethicist-theorist of international relations. The ruins confirmed my realism but also cried out for a revision of that realism. This book is a result of those experiences, a career of interpreting Christian realist thought, and a Lilly Faculty Grant from the Association of Theological Schools. Fittingly, most of this book was written in New York City, some of it in Pittsburgh, and the remainder in a cabin in the woods on Laurel Mountain near Shanksville.

This book is for those concerned about U.S. foreign policy who are open to the religious, ethical dimensions of policy making. The argument that prophetic or moral realism is the way to approach foreign policy is developed in twelve chapters.[3] The first chapter traces the development of prophetic realism through biblical sources, and chapter 2 surveys several major realist thinkers of Western history with brief reference to some non-Western parallels. Chapters 3 and 4 explain American prophetic realism and examine the critique of realism. The concept of power in realism is explored in chapters 5 and 6. Chapter 7 revisits arguments over peacemaking and realism, while chapters 8 and 9 criticize the newer just peacemaking strategy of Glen Stassen and the pacifism of Stanley Hauerwas. The final three chapters discuss contemporary issues in ethics and foreign policy: human rights, terrorism, and resistance to militarism.[4]

The goal of this book is to explicate the religious roots of a certain form of realism that I call prophetic realism. I argue that its deep understandings of flawed human nature and ambiguous history provide a wise foundation for the formation of U.S. policy when combined with the study of international politics. U.S. policy needs a limiting philosophy, and prophetic realism provides it. The entire book is a presentation of prophetic realism's case as a form of political realism, which has been so dominant in recent U.S. policy formation.

The practice of international politics is ultimately grounded in assumptions about values, human nature, and the meaning of history and ethics. For most of human history, these assumptions have been known to be religious. Prophetic realism refuses to neglect these assumptions. But it does not impose answers from ancient religious books on political reality. It respects politics. It knows that politics is about national goals and the struggle for power. Yet it is concerned about the religious meanings and the limitations they impose on the tendency toward national aggrandizement. It maintains the quest for peace, and it seeks the promotion of the common good. It tries to steer nations between unilateralism and universalism. It does this because it respects that the nature of international politics is both relational and self-serving. While seeking peace, it knows the folly of refusing the responsibility for national security. The quest for national security must be guarded against imperialist motivations. The nations need to seek to understand common ethical values. Universal standards such as human rights are perceived to have their origins in particular religious traditions. In its own Jewish-Christian sources, realism turns not primarily toward biblical laws, apocalyptic chapters, pastoral letters to the churches, or the teaching of the earliest disenfranchised church, but to the biblical books fascinated with international politics. Biblical guidance for international politics is found mostly in the prophetic books. The New Testament contains the Christian message of salvation and the witness to Jesus Christ, but it contains very little of relevance to international politics. Neither Jesus nor Paul advised the empire of his day. The Revelation of John does not discuss politics of our day, and it hides the discussion of the Roman Empire in apocalyptic imagery. The prophets, particularly Amos, Isaiah, and Jeremiah, are the best guides to biblical wisdom about international politics.

In the history of Western thought, not all forms of realism can provide what we need. The cynics mislead us, as do the idealists. Neither group represents the dual reality of morality and politics we need. For the West to meet the challenges of religious fanaticism and cynics, wise moral responses related to the depths of our religious traditions are needed. It is not enough to know that some Islamic militancy is religiously based; our response must be in terms of our own wisest religious resources guiding wise political responses. Prophetic realism is a practical philosophy of international relations conceived to provide advice to policy makers and to inform the public interested in foreign affairs. It utilizes empirical data and historical resources as well as political philosophy to help formulate policy. The perspective contains a large amount of normative theory drawn both from Scripture and from the history of moral philosophy. The normative aspects of the approach are always in tension with the power struggles of international politics. Prophetic realism in its relationship to American foreign policy promotes certain long range goals of peace, justice, and human development, but it emphasizes the competitive forces which resist those goals.

I wish to thank Pittsburgh Theological Seminary for the sabbatical permitting the writing of this book. The school nurtured my scholarship for thirty-four years and encouraged the Association of Theological Schools to award me the Lilly Faculty Fellowship, which funded the travel for research.

Mrs. Sheryl Gilliland, the faculty secretary, and Ms. Christine Wissner, a graduate of the school, together helped prepare the manuscript from my handwritten yellow tablets. This book would not exist without their help, and I am thankful for their assistance.

Notes

1. See Kimberly Hutchings, "Ethics, Feminism, and International Affairs," in *Ethics and International Affairs* (ed. Jean-Marc Coicaud and Daniel Warner; Tokyo: United Nations University Press, 2001). Her discussion of Susan Ruddick (pp. 203–15) is particularly insightful.

2. Rudyard Kipling, "The White Man's Burden" in *Kipling: A Selection of His Stories and Poems* (ed. John Beecroft; Garden City, N.J.: Doubleday, 1923), 444–45.

3. At the secular level of international relations theory, Roger Spiegel makes a similar move. His "evaluative political realism" corresponds to my term *moral realism* and to the further specification I give to my particular form of it as prophetic realism. This is a reformation of the classical realism of E. H. Carr, Hans J. Morganthau, Reinhold Niebuhr, Herbert Butterfield, George Kennan, Kenneth Thompson, and others and is distinguished in Spiegel's work from positivist empiricism or scientific theory and from emancipatory or liberation theories of international relations. See Roger D. Spiegel, *Political Realism in International Theory* (Cambridge: Cambridge University Press), 3–21, 191–244.

4. The Jean-Marc Coicaud and Daniel Warner volume *Ethics and International Affairs* also lists sustainable human development and humanitarian intervention as emerging ethical issues for international relations (p. 12).

◖◗ Acknowledgments ◖◗

Portions of chapters 3, 4, and 6 were previously published in Ronald H. Stone, *Realism and Hope* (Washington: University Press of America, 1977).

Chapter 5 written for this volume was also published in Mar Dumas, Francois Nault, et Lucien Pelletier, *Theologie et Culture: hommages a Jean Richard* (Laval: Les Presses de l' Universite Laval, 2004).

Portions of chapters 7 and 10 were previously published in Ronald H. Stone, *Christian Realism and Peacemaking* (Nashville: Abingdon Press, 1988).

Chapter 12 is an edited version of a chapter published in Ronald H. Stone and Robert L. Stivers, eds., *Resistance and Theological Ethics* (Lanham: Rowman and Littlefield Publishers, Inc., 2004).

Chapter 8 written for this volume was published in *Journal of the Society of Christian Ethics* 23, no. 1 (Spring/Summer 2003): 255–67.

1

Biblical Sources of Prophetic Realism

CONTEMPORARY ACADEMIC POLITICAL THOUGHT has been neglectful of the biblical basis of much of Western political thought. Popular movements from the right wing of Protestantism have reinserted biblical language into political debate. This popular upsurge of biblical language has disregarded much of what the academy has learned about the Bible. This study explicates biblical realism as foundational to the wiser dimensions of Western thought and attempts to appropriate that realism critically.

The Bible presents an epoch of human life from its origins to its fulfillment. This epoch from Eden to the Heavenly City is composed in a political-international context of at most 1,450 years. Both in Eden and in the Heavenly City, peace reigns, but within this end and this beginning, violence, disorder, and group conflict dominate. The story is set in the conflictual crescent sweeping from Mesopotamia to Egypt and is focused on the besieged and dependent people of Judah and Israel.

Biblical human history begins with self-consciousness emerging in Adam and Eve, who seek to distinguish between good and evil. They leave the sleeping innocence of Eden, and their progeny plunge into killing each other. Brother Cain, the farmer, kills Brother Abel, the sheepherder, over a dispute about religious sacrifice. This conflict is played out in the Middle East even today. The murderer who refuses security from God builds a city or a fort for security. Among Cain's descendants, the city and military technology grew together.

The Old Testament roars on through its history of tribulation and conflict. Israel's faith and nationhood begin in a slave revolt. God uses Moses, a murderer of an Egyptian officer, to lead a revolt disrupting Egypt's plans

1

for city building, to destroy the pharaoh's army, and to initiate a people of faith who conquer the peoples of Palestine.

The Bible is filled with stories of Yahweh, the Hebrew God, trying to retain the people's loyalty to the covenant. The people's political loyalties, alliances, and wars continually lead them to serve other gods in their worship and to create oppressive social systems modeled after those in other societies. The various expressions of covenant in Exodus, Leviticus, and Deuteronomy, reflecting six hundred years of social development, all use divine and mosaic authority to order a society.

The covenant as a document binding together disparate people to a central loyalty reflects the moral achievement of the Hebrews and also calls them to a higher loyalty. Society was not far from chaos, but the covenant represented emerging moral order.

The early history of the tribes reads as a period of leadership under charismatic leaders. The charisma is institutionalized by Samuel, whose sons are inadequate to lead the chaotic society. First Samuel 8 describes the people as sinners and the kings as sinners with power. Samuel promised the king would tax them, take their children, and reduce them to serfdom. The benefits the people wanted were military leadership and government. The writer of 1 Samuel 8, looking backward from several centuries of misrule by the kings of Israel and Judah, is utterly realistic. The books of 1 and 2 Samuel and 1 and 2 Kings continue the history of sorry misgovernment and failed wars. Only occasionally does a king emerge who can be compared to the anointed King David. One who does emerge near the end of Judah's history, Josiah, finds the Deuteronmic covenant but is soon killed by the Egyptian pharaoh near Megiddo. The prophetic strand emerges against the royal prerogatives, announcing that the poor should be protected and that even kings should not take others' property or families. The turmoil of the Bible is also the story of priests and prophets being plowed into the political conflicts of a small land beleaguered by great powers on both flanks. While there is no escape for the religious leaders from politics, the Bible resists portraying the kings as divine, and the prophets' capacity to criticize the kings' injustices is retained.

After Solomon's grand and wasteful reign, God and people work together in a tax revolt against Rehoboam to bring Jeroboam out of exile from Egypt to found the northern kingdom of Israel. Divided, the tribes are even easier prey for neighbors. Political commentaries of the West remembered this revolt so that even John Calvin twenty-five centuries later could advise princes to read the story and tremble. Stories of political-religious resistance in Daniel and Esther would add to the capacity of biblically formed people to resist unjust rule in different ages.

A main theme of the whole Old Testament is Yahweh's seeking true worship and a just order for a people bound together in their identity in a covenant. The books of prophecy never get far from the task of criticizing worship or politics for their injustices.

The Hebrew Bible reaches lyrical heights in expressing God's love for the homeland and for Zion, or Jerusalem. Yet Hebrew nationalism is transcended in Israel's housing a mission of salvation for the world's nations. This mission in Isaiah and other prophets reaches quite specifically into eschatological visions of peace in which the nations will meet in council under God's law. All of the ingredients needed for peace are present in the Bible—just government, conciliar decisions, right religion, human rights, fruitful agriculture, provision for all, righteous people—but the actual history is of conflict even today.

Prophets and International Relations

The prophets of Israel were crucial for the political thought of three religiously based political philosophers of the third quarter of the twentieth century. Two were very explicit in their debt: Reinhold Niebuhr, and Paul Tillich. Hans Morgenthau's debt is seen in his youthful Jewish studies, in his support of Israel, and in his old-age return to practicing Judaism. The contours of his morality regarding international relations reflect the prophet's demand for justice and the transcendence of the source of morality.

Amos represented God's voice to the northern kingdom of Israel during the prosperity of the reign of Jeroboam II, 786–746 B.C.E. Amos detailed the relative richness and luxury of the establishment during this time. But his eye was also on the suffering of the poor, and one of the most outstanding characteristics of his prophecies is the demand for justice. As the earliest of the prophets whose oracles are extant, he stamped the demand for justice on the very meaning of the role of the prophet. Twenty-eight centuries later, the same words of justice would be used by the prophetic realists and forever connected to the civil rights movement of the 1950s and 60s by their friend Martin Luther King Jr.[1]

For Paul Tillich, this emergence of the union of justice and universal monotheism was the deciding characteristic of prophetic consciousness. The prophets demanded justice in both of its expressions: as the correctness of the legal system, including the structures of society, and as the more personal righteousness that makes for correct and fulfilling relationships. This twofold justice includes not only the formal requirements of society but also the pursuit of right relationships and actions. The terms *justice* (*mishpah*) and *righteousness* (*tsedeqah*) are used in parallelisms to reinforce the demand of the prophet, who speaks for God for right behavior.[2] Justice included obedience to the codes of Israel, but it was more than that, pointing to God's requirements for correct conduct in regard to economics, sociopolitical issues, cultic issues, care for the poor and defenseless,[3] and international relations, particularly diplomacy and war. For these three contemporary realists regarded here as prophetic, the central social-moral issues are economic justice; race relations, including protection of Jews; the state of democratic politics and government; and international relations, particularly issues of diplomacy, war, and nuclear weapons. The continuity between the macro concerns of the eighth century B.C.E. and the twenty-first century C.E. is remarkable. To some degree, the issues are simply major issues; but at another level, the impact of the morals of Amos, Hosea, and Isaiah has been communicated through Scripture, the church, Judaism, and teachers to morally concerned exponents of those traditions in the twenty-first century.

Old Testament scholar James Muilenburg reminded his readers that the demands of the prophets were concrete and particular.[4] The book of Amos begins its account with "The words of Amos, one of the shepherds of Tekoa—what he saw concerning Israel . . . when Uzziah was king of Judah and Jeroboam son of Jehoash was king of Israel" (1:1 NIV). Amos and those who follow in the school of prophetic religion are very specific; they do not generalize. Amos spells out the historical destruction to be directed at Syria, Gaza, Ashkelon, Philistia, Tyre, Ammon, and Moab. In each case, the victims of Assyria's wrath are indicted for war crimes. Judah's crimes are rejection of the law, mistreatment of the poor, misuse of the cult, and sexual malpractice. Israel's crimes are desertion of justice, mistreatment of the poor, and fraudulence in trade; its fate was to be destroyed. A gloss in the last chapter of the book promises the redemption of a remnant and an eventual rebuilding of ruined cities.

Amos detailed war crimes before there was international law. His book portrays a judge who mysteriously weighs the lives of the nations and uses war and the destruction of cities to carry out the divine will.[5] Hope here, in view of a God whose will surrounds all nations, is only in the remnant and future rebuilding. The Lord is like a lion devouring prey. Israel has been saved before "like a brand snatched from the fire" (4:11), but this time the hope of any salvation *follows* the destruction. Very little hope is given for international relations. Israel is a minor player in the world of nations, and her days as a player are about to be suspended by Assyria: "Prepare to meet your God, O Israel!" (4:12).

But Assyria also will meet judgment. She has always been a pawn in the hands of the God who determines the fate of his people Israel. The breaking of Assyria is a theme of the later prophet Isaiah: "I will break the Assyrian in my land" (Isa 14:25). By this time Israel is gone, and the hope is in Jerusalem as Zion. The reader must wait for the opening of Isaiah's prophecies to see hope for history.

In days to come the mountain of the LORD's house shall be established as the highest of the mountains, and shall be raised above the hills; and all the nations shall stream to it. Many peoples shall come and say, "Come, let us go up to the mountain of the LORD, to the house of the God of Jacob; that he may teach us his ways and that we may walk in his paths." For out of Zion shall go forth instruction, and the word of the LORD from Jerusalem. He shall judge between the nations, and shall arbitrate for many peoples; they shall beat their swords into plowshares, and their spears into pruning hooks; nations shall not lift up sword against nation, neither shall they learn war any more. (Isa 2:2–4)

Even this hope has an eschatological quality, for it requires the nation's obedience to the moral law of God, who will rule the nations from Jerusalem. Then disarmament can be real as well as conversion of arms to peacetime uses, and with law established, the learning of war can be abandoned.

In Amos a radical monotheism emerges that is expressed even more strongly in Hos 13:2, which draws a connection between sin and idols, and in Hos 13:4, which asserts that there is no God but the Lord and no savior besides God. The demands of social justice and international justice are clearly explicated, as is the characterization of this God as the universal ruler of all nations. Max Weber probably had Amos in mind when he called Yahweh a specialist in international relations.

The prophet proclaimed that the day of the Lord is "darkness, not light" (Amos 5:18). Except for the editorially disconnected hope for a remnant rebuilding at the end, the book is one of unrelieved pessimism. Realistic polemics in the second quarter of the twentieth century needed to provide historical hopes to save them from the charges of unrelieved pessimism. Neibuhr and Tillich's commentaries on European descent into evil from 1932 to 1945 were quite pessimistic. But in that pessimism was accuracy, as Berlin, Brussels, Amsterdam, Kiev, Paris, Rome, and Tripoli had their lights extinguished. The fascist terror and punishment were no less than the Assyrian terror that swept down the Mediterranean coast, crushing Gaza, Ashkelon, the remnant of Philistines, and Tyre. As Japan threatened Hawaii, Midway, Burma, Thailand, Hanoi, and Jakarta, so Amos prophesied the destruction of Edom, Damascus, Samaria, and Jerusalem. Both periods were times of international terror. The realists found strength in God's strengthening of democratic forces in Britain and the United States and authoritarian forces in Russia and China. Likewise, in the third quarter of the twentieth century, they found hope in deterrence, industrial strength, democratic government, shared responsibility with Russia for avoidance of nuclear war, and God-inspired human striving in the long travail toward freedom and responsible government. Still, as with the eighth-century prophets, there was much to condemn on both sides of the Cold War.

Isaiah 52–54 portrays the promise of the Lord's Servant to be in the bearing and redeeming of the world's suffering as revealed in the great eschatological council of nations. So in the gospel of the Servant as reinterpreted by Matthew, the secret of salvation in Matthew 25 is revealed as the nation's representatives caring for prisoners, feeding the hungry, and watering the thirsty.

But even more hopeful is the vision of a common moral law, nations reasoning together, the conversion of weapons to tools, and finally the unlearning of war. In Isaiah it is an eschatological vision, and while we cannot rule our nations with eschatological vision, this one provides a sense of direction. Policies may be eschatologically inspired while ethically informed. Law, council, disarmament, and the disestablishment of war are both prophetic and relevant policy goals.

These goals place prophetic realists who embrace them in conflict with the U.S. government. One of the most famous of these conflicts was based explicitly on Amaziah's denunciation of Amos in Amos 7. In this chapter, Amaziah, the chaplain of Jeroboam II, denounces Amos and expels him from the capital city. Amos denounces the king's chaplain and proclaims the end of Israel. The Protestant social ethicist Reinhold Niebuhr used the story to denounce the preaching of sermons at the White House Chapel that supported President Nixon and shielded him from anti-Vietnam religious criticism. Niebuhr compared J. Edgar Hoover to Amaziah, who served to protect the king in the king's court. Niebuhr's adoption of Martin Luther King Jr.'s cause and his critique of the war policy earned him much assault from the religious and political interests supporting Nixon and the Vietnam War. In America, Niebuhr could not be easily silenced. But the White House could and did intensify the FBI's investigation of the aging prophet as John Ehrlichman was the last Nixon official to examine the lengthy FBI file (more than six hundred pages). Again, domestic justice, international war policy, and the king or president's chapel were all integrated in prophetic critique of official religion and policies.

Abraham Heschel regards Isaiah (1–39) as more concerned with domestic injustice and idolatry than with international relations. Yet Heschel's book *The Prophets*[6] was published before the heat of the Vietnam War overshadowed, for a time, attention to the corruption of American domestic politics. Still within the totality of Isaiah 1–66, Israel is a pawn of the superpowers, achieving autonomy and some international standing only in the southern kingdom under Uzziah. Assyria stands astride Palestine, destroying the northern kingdom and subjecting the southern kingdom. Isaiah's polemics against treaties aside, Assyria, Egypt, Babylon, and Persia all play with Israel. She has to learn her survival at the hands of the superpowers regarded by the prophets Amos, Hosea, and Isaiah as being used by God to punish the faithless Israel. There is little doubt that God is in control in those prophets. Yet the Lord's punishment is indistinguishable from the policies of the nations. Israel, the home of these prophets, is chosen to witness to Yahweh, whose will is expressed internationally. Nations fall because of internal corruption, unfair business practices, cruelty to the poor, the pride of the inhabitants, and unethical and idolatrous religion. Pride leads to destruction. Could moral conduct, recognition of international standards, humility, fairness, and ethical religion have prevented destruction? Perhaps! Yet in Isaiah 2 and 66, the prophet pointed to the need for a religiously based international law, an international council, disarmament, and the learning of ways other than war.

New Testament

The witness of the New Testament depended on the Old. The writers found in the prophets specific references that they could apply to the drama of Jesus' life. They found in him the fulfillment that the prophets had sought. Of course, the fulfillment was of a different sort.

The Old Testament makes up more than 75 percent of the Christian Bible. Still, for Christians, the New Testament is the bridge by which the Hebrew traditions are given to the Gentiles. In the New Testament the promises of Israel's becoming a light to the nations are opened. Here the particularities of a faith recorded in Hebrew are overcome with a faith testified to in Greek, opening the essential message to the Mediterranean world of the Roman Empire.

Jesus, whom Christians confess as the Christ, lives his life in this narrow area of the Roman Empire. His life is surrounded by domestic and international politics. His death is a political-religious act apparently shared by Romans and Jewish temple collaborators. His message of the reign of God for his followers is easily mistaken for a rebellious, theocratic regime turned against Rome. The sources of the drama of his ministry, death, and resurrection proclaim him as born lowly but descended from kings. The Scriptures affirm that he is worshiped by representatives from the east, that his birth is followed by Herod's butchery of potential Hebrew kings, and that his family has to flee to Egypt. The one who ordains him is beheaded by the political authorities. Jesus avoids the temptation of political power as he dodges overly zealous political commitments throughout his life and work. Finally, his disturbances of the peace and his challenges to the religious leadership of his day result in that religious leadership conspiring with Roman political leadership to kill him. The gospel writers, however, don't regard him as deeply politically involved, and there is little evidence that either Rome or the temple authorities would have hunted him down in Galilee.

Jesus was critical of the immorality of his day and sought to teach a more perfect way of love and the reign of God. He organized his followers so well that despite betrayal by Judas and his execution, they could experience him alive and initiate the church. Through the church, power to become whole, free, and loving would extend through the ages in his name. He healed, taught, organized, and provoked. If he preached an apocalypse, he was mistaken, but it is more likely that the apocalyptic imagination of his time put that twist on his message.

Crucial to our search for a prophetic realism is the question, did Jesus teach an alternative politics? The Gospels portray him as charged, as a rebel seeking a new political order, but they also regard him as innocent of the charge. Matthew 21:46 depicts Jerusalem as seething with trouble, and Jesus' entry and cleansing of the temple certainly contributed to the commotion, but this does not mean historically that he was seeking a revolt. The fact that Revelation sees an apocalyptic end of Rome and the victory of the redeemed does not mean these happenings were on Jesus' mind.

There is very little in Jesus' teaching to suggest he recommended pacifism to soldiers or particular styles of diplomacy to rulers. History in its political manifestations continued its bloody story before, through, and after the life of Jesus. In a few instances, he seems to urge cooperation with Rome, and he warns against taking up the sword against it, or so interpreters of the gospel interpreted him after the fall of Jerusalem. His was a nascent sectarian movement within Judaism that at the time avoided the big political questions and even avoided suggesting policy to Caesar.

The text attributed to Jesus about negotiating if your enemy has twice your strength (Luke 14:31–32) seems in context to have more to do with prudence in calculating the cost of a movement than with international politics. The blessings of peacemakers, the taking of only two swords, the lack of defense in Gethsemane, the faith of the centurion, the silence before Pilate all seem congruent with the message that there will be wars and rumors of war. The ethic of demonstrating love and seeking peace seems well established for Jesus, but the attempts to portray him as having a particular political program seem exaggerated. The New Testament, like the Old, presents a history in which prophets are disbelieved and martyred and historical existence is characterized by conflict even until the end in Revelation. In such a world, Jesus' advice to love your neighbor, as well as Paul's advice, "If it is possible, so far as it depends on you, live peaceably with all" (Rom 12:18), rings true.

Notes

1. Amos 5:21–24: "I hate, I despise your festivals, and I take no delight in your solemn assemblies. Even though you offer me your burnt offerings and grain offerings, I will not accept them; and the offerings of well-being of your fatted animals I will not look upon. Take away from me the noise of your songs; I will not listen to the melody of your harps. But let justice roll down like waters, and righteousness like an everflowing stream."

2. Bruce Birch, *Let Justice Roll Down* (Louisville: Westminster John Knox, 1991), 259.

3. Ibid., 261–69.

4. James Muilenberg, *The Way of Israel* (New York: Harper & Brothers, 1961), 76–77.

5. Walter Bruggemann, *Theology of the Old Testament* (Minneapolis: Fortress Press, 1997), suggests that the judgment is like a treatise on human rights or in international standards of conduct.

6. Abraham Heschel, *The Prophets* (New York: Harper & Row, 1962).

Historical Sources of Realism

THE REALISTS' USE OF BIBLICAL REALISM moved through sources of historical wisdom. They did not jump directly from the Bible to contemporary
historical politics. Hans Morgenthau taught Aristotle's politics and wrote a
book on Abraham Lincoln's political mind. Reinhold Niebuhr wrote and
rewrote the history of social theory several times. Paul Tillich wrote *A
History of Christian Thought* and moved comfortably in and out of the history of political philosophy. Niebuhr probably drew more from the history
of political thought than the other two. Morgenthau and Tillich were more
inclined to organize their thought philosophically while using history.
Niebuhr organized his political thought historically while reflecting philosophically. Still, these scholars represent an older approach to political
thought in their insistence that it be historically grounded. The history of
politics and the ideas about politics were together secondary only to a grasp
of human nature in controlling and defining their perspectives on politics.

The Realism of Thucydides

The realism of the Bible is under the providence and control of God.
Throughout the detailed histories of Israel's fallen rulers and prophets,
God remains in control. The wars and punishments from God and the
realization of peace will be through God's intervention. In Greek
thought, the contentious gods work their wills in Homer's epic of war on
the plains of Troy. In the writing of the exiled general of Athens,
Thucydides, secular realism emerges. By the end of fifth-century B.C.E.
Greece, human explanations for the war that ruined Greece would suffice
for Greek political philosophy. Athens reached its intellectual, artistic,

and political height in the age of Pericles, preceding the disastrous war into which he led the Athenians.

Modern scholarship on war is at home with Thucydides' secular realism. Most theologians of modernity will not place the blame for war on God. Ordinarily no modern prophetic realist would claim God's will for the outcome of a war. As recently as World War I, however, churches took opposite sides in blessing or condemning the Triple Entente and the Central Powers. World War II was less of a crusade, but an exiled German theologian, Paul Tillich, certainly saw God in opposition to the evil of the Hitler regime. He could interpret the destruction of Germany as God's judgment. In so doing he identified with the prophet Jeremiah.

But ordinarily modern thought is more cautious, more secular. Christian ethics has to risk judgment, though, on the justice or lack of justice regarding a war. The claims of ultimacy echo in proscription against needless or deliberate killing of noncombatants. For many the struggle against militarism and nuclearism becomes an absolute issue. Also, church support, such as advocacy against terrorism, the approval of some wars, and the aid and preparation of chaplains, reflects the deep conviction that though God may not cause wars, God's will against the evils of war is still relevant. So churches, when they realize what is important, promote peace, prepare their members' minds, and make judgments regarding war. At a more absolutist level, some fundamentalists and some religious devotees in most religions can be very dogmatically for or against war.

Thucydides, as a general, wrote about a war from which he was an early exile. His perspective is therefore unusual. He died before he saw the final defeat of Athens by the Spartan alliance. But he was able to record most of three decades of the wars in *The Peloponnesian War*. The book is a narrative history of conflict rather than an explanation of all Greek city-state relationships. Its tone of realism is partially due to the fact that it is describing a particularly destructive war by one whose city was sliding into defeats, plague, and finally ruin.

The primary cause of the war, according to Thucydides, was Sparta's fear of the growing power of Athens. Yet Donald Kagan,[1] following Thucydides' history, is able to explain the slow process by which the Greek peace broke down into two contesting antagonists. The Spartans did not rush to war but were dragged in by Corinth's ambition to control a colony sought by an ally of Athens. Athens sought peace also, but in the end Athens would not agree to the terms of appeasement demanded by Sparta, and so arbitration was suggested. Athens' intervention to protect allies was hesitant. It tried to find a middle path. Sparta seemed to want to avoid the war by negotiation. Yet the relative autonomy of the Greek city-states, buffeted by passion, greed, and fear, led to the war. Given the disastrous consequences of the war, it cannot be regarded as rational. It was irrational and evil, but despite the best efforts of some seeking peace, the collapse into war came.

For Thucydides the rivalries among the city-states were fueled by fear, honor, and self-interest. All three led toward Sparta's demands of Athens. Yet Sparta reduced its demands to the point at which Athens only had to give up its economic boycott of relatively insignificant Megara. Fear, honor, and the interest of holding alliances together finally led Sparta into a preventive war following the precipitous actions of its ally Corinth. Michael Doyle regards the realism of Thucydides as a "complex realism"[2] because of the realities of relative anarchical systems, the particularities of city-states, and the passions of the human actors.

Probably the best-known passage from *The Peloponnesian War* regards the Athenian boasts before the slaughter of the Melians: "The strong do what they have the power to do and the weak accept what they have to accept."[3] Yet Thucydides did not approve of this unnecessary slaughter nor of the other massacres he recorded; what he approved of is detailed in the second most famous section of the work, "Funeral Oration by Pericles."[4] Here the virtues and sacrifices of the Athenians who had defended Athens were praised for their contributions to the quality of Athenian life and its democracy. Thucydides found in Pericles' speech praise for Athens both for taking care of itself and for "doing good for others."[5]

In the realism of Thucydides, people make moral choices in a world of conflict. Their range of choices is narrowed by the need to choose the interest of the city-state in which they live. They must apply abstract moral principles prudently within the constraints of self-protection. And they are to pursue the good of the community, not personal gain, while limiting harm to necessity.

Finally, Thucydides is writing a history of war, not a history of morals. Students of politics must keep in mind the context of a war in which democracy is lost, a war recorded by a losing, exiled general. The volume is to be praised for its understanding of diplomacy and not for a resolution of morality and power politics. Thucydides comes alive in British politics after Thomas Hobbe's seventeenth-century translation. His complex realism resurfaces again in Hans Morgenthau.

The Comparative Politics of Aristotle

Even though his major work, *Politics*, remains unfinished, Aristotle deserves recognition as the founder of political science. His dominant method is that of comparing political orders and applying reason to these diverse orders to seek out the meaning of politics. His school had assembled data in politics as it had in biology and physics. The data consisted of reports on 150 to 158 constitutions of Greek states. Apparently he wrote *The Constitution of Athens* himself, and his major work draws on these studies in a comparative way. The formal nature of constitutional analysis is supplemented by historical reflections on those city-states. While *Politics* lacks much that contemporary comparative politics would require, the foundations of contemporary comparative politics are apparent in Aristotles' work.

Plato seems to have abandoned some of his political realism after his unhappy venture in Syracuse. Aristotle knew this older, more realistic Plato of *Laws*. So although Aristotle's own lecture notes as found in *Politics* begin to seek an ideal state that is abandoned, he realistically argues that the existing state for a people is relative to the condition of that particular people. Reflection on all of these differing political orders drove Aristotle toward relativism. But Hans Morgenthau argued that Aristotle never got there, as he continued to argue for truth in political thought.[6] Much political knowledge derived from reason, common sense, history, and the study of comparative constitutions was universally true for Aristotle.

Besides criticizing Plato's utopianism and lack of reflection on foreign policy, Aristotle borrows many categories and much insight from Plato. But his shift from the quest for the ideal state to empirical observation and deduction moves toward realist traditions in method. In book 5 of *Politics*, in which he gives advice for how a tyrant should rule, he is as brutal as Machiavelli would be eighteen centuries later. His own political-educational career had allied him with the tyrant Hermias of Atarneus and with the most important figure of his day, Alexander the Great, whom he tutored. George H. Sabine has pointed out that Aristotle did not reflect much more on foreign affairs than had Plato.[7] If he had, he might have made more of a contribution from his association with Alexander. After tutoring Alexander, he returned to Athens to found his Lyceum, teach, and write, living the good life of reason, which was the highest existence for the human in his view. *Politics* seems innocent of any reflection on the significance of Alexander's empire, which effectively ended the city-state system. Still, it is probable that he left Athens shortly before his death because of his Macedonian connections with imperial power, for which he seems to have written three manuscripts, which are not extant. He and his teacher, Plato, brought the reflection on the city-state to its highest form as it gave way to imperial rule. It would be later in Rome that his lectures would be published. There his influence would be felt in Roman reflection, but it became crucial for the extension of Roman forms and thought into Roman Catholicism, in which Thomas Aquinas would make his thought decisive for European civilization. But in regard to Aristotle's contribution to political theory, Sabine sees his method of observation, organization, and historical reflection as foundational to political science: "Aristotle was the founder of this method, which has been on the whole the soundest and most fruitful that the study of politics has evolved."[8]

Aristotle pitied the "resident alien"[9] for the lack of citizenship and believed happiness is found in the life of virtuous action of the citizen.[10] In *Nicomachean Ethics* he concludes that contemplation is the best life for humanity or its highest goal: "For man, therefore, the life according to reason is best and pleasantest, since reason more than anything else is man. This life therefore is also the happiest."[11] But in the very next pages he argues for virtuous action and notes the need for education in virtue and the need for good laws. Our natural existence leads to activity, and according to Aristotle, "the life of the man who is active in accordance with virtue will be happy."[12]

These ideas led directly into Aristotle's outline of *Politics*. The good life requires a good polity, and Aristotle decried Sophists who wrote about politics with no experience of it. Similarly, he found the statespeople not writing about their art. Concluding that those who would know about politics "need experience as well,"[13] he set out to outline his work on political theory at the conclusion of his *Ethics*.

In the heart of *Politics*, Aristotle seeks to explain what can be done under various polities to govern well. The two most dominant reflections are under what he regards as compromised governments: oligarchy and democracy. In page after page the reader finds a sense of realism; knowing that good government is not certain, Aristotle desires a better government for the virtuous. Of course, he neglects the happiness of the noncitizen. He does not regard it possible for women or slaves to have political rights or social happiness. His view is elitist, even though he writes pages about equality. The vast population of slaves in Attica is not the subject of his treatise; he thinks they are by nature slaves and unfit to govern. Likewise, his organic view of the family and its contribution to the society is patriarchally oppressive. His opinions here were based on empirical observation, but here he was inclined to turn an "is" into an "ought." The effect of these confusions would be to help enslave workers and women wherever his political writings had influence in Western history.

Yet despite his tutoring of Alexander, his mistakes vis-à-vis the potency of women, aliens, and slaves, and his lack of foreign policy, Aristotle makes a contribution in methodology. Despite his realpolitik advice to the tyrant in book 5, his politics has a moral seriousness that contemporary political science needs. In fact, his *Politics* ends in a discussion of education and a plea for understanding what it is capable of achieving: "Thus it is clear that education should be based upon three principles—the mean, the possible, the becoming, these three."[14]

How much better would American life be if our political science aimed for the correct balance in educating our children to be virtuous? The end of politics, for Aristotle, in this reading is the virtuous education of children. Before turning to his conclusion regarding the education of children, he had pointed out that both war and peace come and that it is the responsibility of the legislator to find the way of peace and to teach it. He explicitly rejected the study of war to enslave other people; rather, he taught that the legislator's goal was to provide leisure and peace.[15] Aristotle's philosophy holds as much realism as the American hegemonic republic needs, but it also needs his goals of education, leisure, and peace.

Christian Realism

Niebuhr could have been more appreciative of Aristotle's realism,[16] but he found the philosophy of humanity too simple. He could not accept as real the domination of human life by reason. He needed a more dynamic view of humanity, which the moral realists found in Augustine.[17] In turning to Augustine, we see the contours of Christian realism emerge. Morgenthau lectured on Aristotle's politics, but to the extent that he learned his doctrine of man from Niebuhr and some of his ontology from Tillich, he too had turned toward Augustine. Tillich confessed his dependence on Augustine: "I will say, almost unambiguously, that I myself and my whole theology, stand much more in the line of Augustinian than in the Thomistic tradition."[18]

What did these realists find in Augustine's politics? He wrote perhaps the first Christian autobiography in *The Confessions* and a great theology of history in *The City of God*, but he never wrote a treatise on political theory.

The outlines of Augustine's politics, which he exercised in an eclectic-pragmatic way as a Roman Catholic bishop in North Africa, can be deduced from his theology. The realists found in his doctrine of human nature and his theology of history their support for a non-utopian realistic-pragmatic politics. To the degree the realists were Augustinian, they would not dream of a world of nations without war or a just economic order. Like Augustine they sought peace, but they knew it would always be an uneasy peace rooted in unjust economic structures.

Augustine has been misrepresented as teaching a doctrine or theory of just war. No developed doctrine or theory of just war appears in his writing. Like Plato before him, he used the phrase, but he did not organize his thought into a theory. Like all major theologians since Constantine, he was not a pacifist. He recognized the necessity of war for defense or to punish evil. He knew governments have such responsibilities and that Christians are called to participate in government. He recognized that the establishment of peace sometimes requires war, and he urged his friend Count Boniface to defend Africa.

To Boniface he wrote: "Peace ought to be what you want, war only what necessity demands. . . . Be a peacemaker, therefore, even in war so that by conquering them you bring the benefit of peace even to these you defeat."[19]

While not expecting earthly peace, he built his great apology for Christianity, *The City of God*, around the two kinds of peace, earthly and heavenly, and as a bishop with earthly powers, he worked for the establishment of peace. In the last years of his life, Reinhold Niebuhr criticized Augustine's stark realism for not having enough of the reforming drive that democratic society requires.[20]

The Augustinian dualism between the two cities of those who follow heaven and those who follow earth owes its origins to the Manichaeanism that Augustine overcame, to the horrid realities of a failing Roman Empire, and to his skills in rhetoric. According to Niebuhr, Luther's two kingdoms followed from Augustine, and to interpreters of Niebuhr, the division between personal and public morality originated from Augustine and Luther. The distinction was, of course, widespread in political theory and particularly so in German thought. The distinction was important to Niebuhr, Morgenthau, and Tillich.

This short discussion of Augustine does not imply that Augustine proposed a distinction between personal and public morality. His distinction is more obviously located between the requirements of ascetic Christian communities and the public role of Christians. He can be seen as the major voice in articulating early Christian realism, but probably not as one who radically separated personal and public morality for Christians.

The Christian ethic for Augustine is for those who would love rightly and not for those committed to the dying world. The goal of the Christian life is to participate in God through knowledge of God and to participate in the divine love, thereby finding eternal happiness. Faith, hope, and love are the summary virtues of Christian faith that are expressed in the classical virtues of courage, wisdom, temperance, and prudence, making these virtues expressions of love.

Augustine's distinction between the two cities is a distinction between archetypes: "The one consists of these who wish to live after the flesh, the other of these who wish to live after the spirit, and when they severally achieve what they wish, they live in peace, each after their kind."[21] The city of God is of those who seek the peace of God according to God's way; the city of earth is of those who seek the peace of the world in the world's way. A Protestant reading of Augustine stresses that the cities are not exactly historical institutions but that the types are reflected in the institutions of the church and the state. The Christian, for example, Count Boniface, is

criticized for not fulfilling Christian sexual morality but is enjoined to protect the peace of earth through the use of the sword and state power.
Augustine has political ideas but not a political theory. His eye is on the
city of God. In society, human beings, not structures, are the focus. The
state originates in sin, and the history of human beings in the state is
bloody. The governor of the state should serve as a Christian in two ways
that are denied as a private citizen: the ruler must govern for the protection
and mutual welfare of the citizens and use force to punish evil and maintain the earthly peace.

Christians live in the city of God but are in pilgrimage through the city
of earth. In this pilgrimage the goals of the economy can be accepted. The
aims of the two cities are different. The city of God has a more other-
worldly focus with little emphasis on working for earthly peace, about
which Augustine is pessimistic. The church is not against society, but it has
a different aim. Augustine is something of a cultural relativist, sensing that
people are governed by diversity of laws and institutions, and he has few
moral absolutes for human society. He does not expect much improvement in society. Society could be improved if all were Christian, but since
that is not the case, he does not place much emphasis on social reform.

Garry Wills' delightful, if defensive, book on Augustine emphasizes the
importance of Matthew 13:30, which holds that the wheat and weeds will
grow and develop together until the end.[22] Wills sees this text as the thesis
of *The City of God*. Such an interpretation that saints and sinners dwell in
the church and world together is a great help in dealing with purist fanat-
ics in the church. It is, of course, foundational to realist thinking, but
Niebuhr found it inadequate anthropologically. The split between good
and evil in his view was not between different types of people but within
each person. The depiction of two types of humans, with one type loving
God and the other loving the world, is overly simple; it can and has encouraged later moralism.

Augustine praised Christian rulers for ruling with justice, remaining
humble, promoting right worship, mitigating necessary punishments,
defending the empire, restraining their luxury, governing their desires, and
doing all these things for the love of God and not for glory.[23] Through giving advice, writing, and lobbying, he acted as a bishop to promote these
values. Herbert Deane has pointed out that Augustine's praise for just
Christian rulers was not an attempt to say that all Christian rulers are just;
rather, it was of the genre of "mirror of princes" literature, which held up
an ideal of the Christian ruler.[24] Stoic philosophers preceded Christian
authors in this form of political writing. An even more ancient model, of
course, is that of Old Testament history, in which each king is judged in reference to David. The short summaries of the next two chapters in *The City*

of God following the "Mirror of Princes" chapter evaluate Constantine and the emperors following him.

Augustine had to scrap what may have been a classical tendency to idealize the political order of Greek city-states, but the Greek city-state was more ideal than the Roman Empire. He saw clearly the moral ambiguity of politics, even if he overidealized pure Christian contributions to political order. His sense of history and his willingness to read it and write it prevented him from much overidealization. Yet in his realism, he sought justice. Without justice, a political order was little more than an organized circle of criminals. The Christian ruler was to seek justice while keeping an eye on the true eternal home.

Augustine blurred distinctions between church and government as he gradually moved from a freedom of religion position to a government suppression of heresy position. He finally used Old Testament texts and the New Testament references to compel people to join the feast of the Lord to reinforce his own observations about the successful persecutions of the African Christians who threatened the Roman Catholic Church. His earlier insight in *De Vera Religions* that Christ did nothing by force seems, of course, from our perspective superior to his later hardening.

Many of Augustine's references to government are overly pessimistic for the formation of Christian social theory. Perhaps he was misled by the Stoic myth of a golden age. His insight that "righteous men of previous times were made shepherds of cattle rather than kings of men"[25] blurs some distinctions between animals and human subjects. He needed more insight on limiting and regulating rulers and a more fully developed sense of justice. A social hermeneutic of the New Testament could have led him to find resources that he did not utilize. Our social ethics might better turn to the "mirror of princes" insight than to the dualism of the two cities or to his views on persecution of heretics. Whatever our contemporary criticism of Augustine's political perspective, it was foundational for Thomas Aquinas, Martin Luther, and John Calvin and therefore for the Western world.

Thomas Aquinas united Aristotle and Augustine in the thirteenth century in a synthesis that still endures in Roman Catholic political theory. His synthesis represented the church position in a politics for Christian European civilization. Thomas's creative work was not determinative for the realist theory under examination here, though Aquinas and Roman Catholicism have presented a realist social philosophy. Augustine's own creative perspective without much of Aristotle took root in Martin Luther and John Calvin in the sixteenth century, and our thinkers Niebuhr, Tillich, and Morgenthau find their roots there. An alternative empirical realism appeared in Niccolo Machiavelli in the same century. Luther lacked a political philosophy, though the expression of his personal religious insights into active politics broke the political order of Europe. Luther's impact was to revolutionize a significant part of Europe, giving Germans a new Bible, new hymns, and new language and breaking the economic-political power of the Roman Catholic Church north of the Alps. His genius in personal religion was not matched by insight in social religion, and his ecclesiology could not control the princes who became both religious and secular authorities. In saving his religious revolution from being captured by rebellious peasants, he became extreme in his polemics, urging the peasants' utter defeat. His pronouncements were as bloody realpolitik as Machiavelli's strategies. Despite all Germany owes to Luther, his political legacy was not a blessing to that country's history. Machiavelli's politics failed, and his schemes to unite Italy, whether under the leadership of the papal family or in a more secular republic, had to wait four centuries for realization. The separation of the political realm from religious social ethics in the fashion of Luther remains a contemporary option. The cynical realist politics of Machiavelli remains a contender for dominance in the American republic. But it was the relative success of John Calvin's politics in Geneva and the institutionalization of his ideas in the Netherlands, England, and Scotland and finally in the United States Constitution that had the healthiest influence, an influence that needs nurturing today. Noting the contrast between Calvin and Machiavelli is a useful way to illuminate the distinction between a moral realism and an amoral realism.

John Calvin and Niccolo Machiavelli

Calvin and Machiavelli helped lead their two republic city-states in the sixteenth century. Machiavelli was secretary to the Council of Ten in Florence and an aspirant to serve the Medici; his politics succeeded those of the religious rule of Savonarola. Calvin finally succeeded in establishing in Geneva a rigorous religious rule that won Geneva a reputation as a good, if serene, city.

Both Calvin and Machiavelli flourished at a young age and sought the good of their cities. Both experienced exile and defeat as well as the exercise of power. They excelled in classical studies, though John Calvin's conversion to Protestantism led him to turn his attention to biblical texts, while Machiavelli's secular historicism kept him commenting on classical texts. Machiavelli's death preceded Calvin's influence in Geneva, and therefore there is but one possible reference in Calvin to Machiavelli and no mention of Calvin in Machiavelli, who was aware, however, of religious stirrings in Germany.

Though their political lives were circumscribed by their city-states, they both aspired to improve the welfare of their whole country. Calvin wanted to convert France, and Machiavelli wanted to unify Italy. Calvin's realism would have appealed to Machiavelli, and Calvin fulfilled the rigorous demands of virtue that Machiavelli sought in statesmen. Their similarities extended to their expertise in foreign affairs, which was a condition of the survival of their respective city-states.

Their great difference is what this whole book is about: the relationship of morality to international policy. Calvin was a moralist who as a doctor of law insisted on the importance of the prescriptive. Machiavelli tried to turn away from moralism toward reality. He prided himself on the attempt to remain descriptive, or to tell political history as it actually happened, not as it should have happened. Calvin's politics are filled with the injunctions to fulfill the law of God, natural law, and the law that instructs the conscience. In obeying the law, Christians can find a regulated liberty. Machiavelli wanted to achieve the political liberty of Florence or all of Italy, and to fulfill this goal, he focused on strategy. Calvin was not oblivious to strategy, but his writing is focused on the morality of the political order. Machiavelli is not within the central trajectories of European political history. He does not bother to define his terms, and he is anti-theological in method. He does not reason like Aquinas, Hobbes, Bodin, or Locke; rather, he appeals to historical examples. He does not provide any way of testing his use of history. He is a realist in his fascination with history and in his polemics against idealism, but he can hardly be considered a political scientist because of his lack of rigorous method. The heavy reliance on Machiavelli in American colleges seems to provide a disservice to the students by separating morality from politics. His focus is on political power; Calvin's focus is on God's power as good. Both Calvin and Machiavelli would likely in practical matters regard human beings as equally sinful, but Calvin provides safeguards in balanced governmental recommendations, whereas Machiavelli seems ready to tolerate or even serve absolute political rulers. Calvin, thinking prescriptively, wants more republican-oligarchic safeguards. While prospering in a republic of Florence, Machiavelli will serve a prince. Contemporary commentators reflect different judgments on Machiavelli's morality.

My former teacher John Plamenatz believes Machiavelli had different moral concerns than most moral philosophers and suggests that he was looking for strength and courage and political acumen to succeed. Max Lerner regarded him as expressing the reality of sixteenth-century Italian politics. J. W. Allen finds him to be immoral with an eye to the common good but without ethical feeling. Herbert Butterfield regarded him as immoral, pursuing private interests with an eye toward strategy for those interests. Hans Morgenthau found Machiavelli's focus on seeking power to be self-defeating. An apology for his morality would need to build a case on his *Discourses* and emphasize that he was advocating liberty and unity for Italy. His picking Caesar Borges as his approved model suggests that neglect of moral consciousness was not a disqualifying characteristic for his political leadership. As a Florentine, he curried favor with papal politics and dreamed of the pope's nephew unifying Italy. His hopes for a restoration to a position in Florence depended on a papal pardon, and his brother was a priest. So though Machiavelli seems to have been non-theological, he was Roman Catholic and deeply involved in commenting on religious politics in a secular manner. In the sense of being antimonarchical, he was a liberal. But it was the restored republican council that rejected him after his treatise *The Prince* was ignored by the house of Medici.

Near the end of his *Institutes*, in a major treatise on the liberty appropriate to government, Calvin writes, "I have promised to share by what laws a Christian state ought to be regulated."[26] Law, not the struggle for power, is preeminent in this biblical theologian who was trained as a lawyer. Calvin goes on to expound the moral law that undergirds the whole political system as the command to love both God and neighbor sincerely. Despite Calvin's social relativisms in which he recognizes that different societies will necessarily follow different laws, his thought, as well as the practice of his followers, is tinged with biblicism and legalism. A free society, though, can better risk biblicism and legalism than it can the amoral or immoral pursuit of power.

Thomas Hobbes

The first time I taught international relations to college students, my opening lecture was on the Hobbesian situation among the nation-states. Several of the students were Rhodesians suffering from the unilateral declaration of independence of Rhodesia by the white nationalists; others were Americans trying to understand the Vietnam War. Hobbes's description of international politics as a struggle for power without many institutional or moral restraints seemed a priori to be accurate. That politics in the international realm with no effective sovereignty above the nation-state was a war of all against all seemed potentially true. Hobbes's belief that politics with no sovereign is conducted in a state of fear resonated in the consciousness of both the black Rhodesians and the draft-anxious American students.

Now international politics seem more complicated; there are many restraints on nations. Many types of governance are exercised by transnational corporations, international governing institutions, and nongovernmental organizations. Often moral principles are relevant and sometimes constraining. One would not describe today's international politics as conforming to Hobbes's view, because today there is too much governance and control. But in a world where alliances shift, as in U.S. Middle East policy— for example, arming Iraq in one decade and going to war in the next, or supporting and arming mujahideen in Afghanistan in one decade and bombing them in the next—a state of potential war does exist, and lasting sovereignty is rare. Post–9/11 international politics reveals the presence of fear, particularly on the part of the United States. International organizations exist, but their direct influence in restraining major powers is meager. Probably Hobbes's vision of the state of nature was more relevant to his seventeenth-century Europe or even to the Europe of the early twentieth century than it is today. Yet he made several contributions to modern political theory.

Thomas Hobbes's great work of translating Thucydides' *The Peloponnesian War* acquainted him in detail with the cost of Greek civil war. In England, where he served Charles II as tutor and wrote *Leviathan* to justify Cromwell's reign, he knew the price of disorder. Never praising his own courage, he portrayed himself as fearful. His early self-exile during the English revolution confirms this self-description. Out of civil war he reflected on order and its emergence. Abandoning the historical approach of Thucydides, he gave European thought its first version of the social contract. In Hobbes's view, human life in the state of nature is short, brutish, and vulgar. He recognized that natural laws governed humanity; thus, he argued for a political creation of social order. In the background were reports of states of nature in the Americas and the need to justify Cromwell's governing of the Commonwealth. His state of nature, of course, was an illusion, for humanity is inevitably social; and while selfish and brutish, humanity is also by nature semicooperative. But like John Locke, Jean Jacques Rousseau, and John Rawls after him, he had an imaginary moral construct to justify the emergence of government of a certain type. The dialectic between his version of human nature and the human creation of a state is fascinating. But Hobbes's human psychology is rather thin, with reason controlling the passions, and his state is rather simple, based on absolute rational state. The imaginary constructs of social contracts may have misserved political philosophy. We have no records of their historical reality, and their articulation obscures the slow creation of political order that humanity has actually experienced. Despite the power of the notion of an ideal or mythical social contract, it obscures the historical realities of making actual constitutions.

War, for Hobbes, came from anarchy. The overcoming of it required a sovereign power. He thought that such a sovereign would be a source of terror like the biblical Leviathan. His sense that sovereignty needs to be absolute and monolithic reflects his own experience of governments dividing and falling into chaos. Such unitary government is not necessary, as Montesquieu theorized a century later and the American republic realized. Realism continues to hold that the lack of sovereignty given personal and national egoism is a continual source of discord, creating what Hobbes called the season of war. "For as the nature of foul weather lies not in a shower or two of rain but in an inclination thereto of many days, so the nature of war consists not in actual fighting but in the known disposition thereto during all the time there is no assurance to the contrary. All other time is peace."[27]

The inclination to establish an orderly government to produce peace rests in human nature. Human nature is inclined toward peace in the first rule of natural law for Hobbes. He views this and the other principles of natural law, including the Golden Rule, as principles of morality, guidelines of prudence, and in fact the very law of God. He also argues that the rules of natural law are guidelines derived from human self-interest. Many different theories are mixed together here, but it is not contradictory to assert that human interest, the will of God, and natural law all advocate the same principles.[28] Hobbes sees that though people may agree on these universal rules, in their application there will be many divergences.

Part 3 of *Leviathan*, "Of Christian Common-Wealth," is seldom read. Part 3 is Hobbes's political theology. It contains detailed exegetical work revealing Hobbes's own knowledge of the state of biblical scholarship of his day. He is quite knowledgeable about church history and fiercely anti–Roman Catholic. His theology is that of a Calvinist member of the Church of England. From beginning to end, the text enjoins obedience to the national sovereign, who is head of the church. The argument is scriptural, but the conclusion is the same as the arguments from natural law and prudence: obey the sovereign. From Scripture Hobbes deduced the responsibilities of the rulers of the several Christian commonwealths, staying at a general enough level to have included both monarchs and Cromwell. The book did, however, contribute to his expulsion from the exiled court of Charles II, who had been his student.

The theology is that of a high but critically appropriated Scripture with the major emphasis on the sovereignty of God and the corruption of humanity. Salvation is attained by faith in Christ and obedience to the laws of Christianity. Interpretation of these laws is mostly the responsibility of the national sovereign, and individual or sectarian interpretations are united. Idiosyncratic interpretations ought not in his view be allowed to disturb the order or ferment revolution. One would not be damned for following the Christian obligation to obey the sovereign.

Both his times and his nature inclined him to seek security, which he regarded as the first requirement of reason. He was fearful as well as extraordinarily brilliant. A philosopher in a turbulent time of many martyrs, he recognized the need to accept martyrdom for the faith,[29] but he kept his head and preached obedience. If guided by his principles of natural law and scriptural principles, his Christian Commonwealth could be well governed. Without such ethics, his doctrine of unified sovereignty, whether king, assembly, or dictator, is inadequate for good human life or a peace that includes justice.

Modern Elaborations

The restoration in England of the Stuarts, Charles II (Hobbes's student), and James II tested England's toleration of absolutism. The Glorious Revolution of 1688 saw William and Mary installed by an act of Parliament. The philosopher of that revolution, John Locke, opened up governance to pluralism while insisting on majority rule. He continued Hobbes's fiction of a social contract legitimating revolution against absolutism. While characterizing Locke as among the idealists, Reinhold Niebuhr saw him adding democratic principles to the dominant realism.[30] In France the social contract as seen by Rousseau and the right of revolution would unleash the fanaticism of the righteousness of the "Terror." The dangers of idealism or social utopianism were avoided in England, Niebuhr thought, by the empiricism of David Hume and the moderate conservatism of Edmund Burke, who approved of the American Revolution while deploring the French. Another realistic religious thinker of England's eighteenth century deplored both the revolutions of France and America while standing on the settlement of the English. John Wesley's realism about society was grounded both in his study of history recorded in his book *A Short History of England* and in his study of Scripture.

The Lockean optimism bore fruit in the American Revolution and constitutionalism, which resembled social contract ideology. After all, the revolution was fought partially over property rights, and Locke had insisted on the protection of property in the social construct.

Enlightenment optimism, however, never prevailed in America. By the time the presuppositions of Baron Montesquieu were expressed in the U.S. Constitution, they had been muted by the Calvinist tutoring of its author, James Madison, by the Scot divine John Witherspoon.[31] *The Federalist Papers* of Madison and Alexander Hamilton provided the realism for the American experiment and also expressed illusions about new beginnings and virtue grounded in victory against monarchical Britain and the old empire. Some of the idealism of the new republic was due to illusions, but some of it was just the reality of morality expressed by all of the prophetic realists we have studied. American politics would continue to express a dialectic between morality and realism even when idealism seemed to be driven out of the contest. Sometimes realist polemics, as against Woodrow Wilson and John Foster Dulles, also obscured the realism of the figures criticized. Wilson and Dulles, so often the caricatured targets whom realists criticized, were using ideals and legal language to advance their Calvinist understanding of American long-range interests.

Through the competition of labor and capital, the civil rights struggle, international wars, and the struggle for women's rights, gradually a "democratic realism" emerged. The "democratic realists" were progressives in domestic politics but quite willing to engage in competition or war against Fascism and Communism to protect this synthesis of history and thought that had evolved.

The German inheritance in Niebuhr, Tillich, and Morgenthau meant that the context of influence of German realpolitik was not lost upon them, as they knew of Treitschke and Clausewitz. Even the influence of Bismarck's liberal imperialism was not absent; Tillich's father was chaplain to William II. But they expressed in their own way and most impartially in an American context the insights from Max Weber's work *The Vocation of Politics* that there is a significant difference between the politics of responsibility and the politics of absolute ends. While all of them were aware of absolutes from their religious traditions, they sought to guide U.S. foreign policy in terms of a politics of responsibility.

These accents of German realism were absorbed into the American constitutional republic. That constitution had been drafted in large part by James Madison, an early Christian realist statesman tutored in Calvinistic realism about the human condition. It was not Hobbes but an Augustinian realism that John Witherspoon had taught him at Princeton. It was a realism that fought against the Alien and Sedition Acts in terms of the rights of Americans. While crafting the U.S. Constitution to protect human rights through a strategy of balancing structures, interests, and powers, it also expressed a willingness to strengthen the young republic. Madison was willing to fight Britain in 1812 to guard the republic from imperialism. He was also ready as secretary of state to support Thomas Jefferson in buying the Louisiana Purchase from Napoleon. The Purchase shielded the republic from designs from either France or Spain and laid the foundation of an emerging American empire.

Notes

1. Donald Kagan, *On the Origins of War and the Preservation of Peace* (New York: Doubleday, 1995).

2. Michael W. Doyle, *Ways of War and Peace* (New York: W. W. Norton, 1997).

3. Thucydides, *The Peloponnesian War* (trans. Rex Warner; London: Penguin Books, 1988), 402.

4. Ibid., 145.

5. Ibid., 373.

6. Hans J. Morgenthau, as found in John Cotton Brown, *Notes on Lectures* (Manuscript Division of Library of Congress), January 7, 1947, and January 30, 1947.

7. George H. Sabine, *A History of Political Theory* (3rd ed.; London: George G. Harrays, 1968), 126.

8. Ibid., 122.

9. Richard McKeon, ed., *The Basic Works of Aristotle* (New York: Random House, 1941), 1176.

10. Ibid., 1282.

11. Ibid., 1105.

12. Ibid., 1179.

13. Ibid., 1111.

14. Ibid., 1316.

15. Ibid., 1299.

16. See Reinhold Niebuhr, *Man's Nature and His Communities* (New York: Charles Scribner's Sons, 1965), 32–37.

17. See Ernest Barker, *The Political Thought of Plato and Aristotle* (New York: Dover Publications, 1959), for a thorough treatment of Aristotle's political theory.

18. Paul Tillich, *A History of Christian Thought* (New York: Simon & Schuster, 1967), 104.

19. Augustine, "Letter 189," in *Augustine Political Writings* (ed. E. M. Atkins and R. J. Dodaro; Cambridge: Cambridge University Press, 2001), 417.

20. Niebuhr, *Man's Nature*, 44–46.

21. Augustine, *The City of God* II, 14.1 (ed. Marcus Dods; Edinburgh: T&T Clark, 1872), 2.

22. Garry Wills, *Saint Augustine* (New York: Penguin Putnam, 1999), 83.

23. Augustine, *City of God* I, 5.24, 323.

24. Herbert Deane, *The Political and Social Ideas of St. Augustine* (New York: Columbia University, 1963), 131.

25. Augustine, *City of God*, II,19.15, 324.

26. John Calvin, *The Institutes of the Christian Religion*, II, 4.20.14 (ed. John T. McNeil; Philadelphia: Westminster Press, 1960), 1502.

27. Thomas Hobbes, *Leviathan* (ed. Herbert W. Schneider; New York: Bobbs-Merrill, 1958), 107.

28. My professor found Hobbes's thought to be quite confused. See John Plamenatz, *Man and Society* (vol. 2; New York: McGraw-Hill, 1963), 145–54.

29. Thomas Hobbes, *Leviathan* (ed. Richard Tuck; Cambridge: Cambridge University Press, 1991), 414.

30. Niebuhr, *Man's Nature*, 61.

31. Among several studies noting James Madison's Calvinism and sober view of humanity's sins, Garrett Ward Sheldon, *The Political Philosophy of James Madison* (Baltimore: Johns Hopkins University Press, 2001), is particularly thorough.

3

The Development of American Prophetic Realism

GERMAN REFUGEES FROM HITLER brought their developed ideas with them to America. In the cases of Hans Morgenthau and Paul Tillich, these ideas were merged into Protestant social ethics. Tillich joined Reinhold Niebuhr in the Fellowship of Socialist Christians. Morgenthau joined with the heirs of the Fellowship and others in Clergy and Laity Concerned about Vietnam in the 1960s and contributed to its distinctiveness.

The socially reforming Protestant movement known as the social gospel had arisen as a response to industrialism and urbanization in the 1880s. In the 1930s many of its distinctive reforms were implemented by the New Deal. Though Norman Thomas would continue its socialist politics, Reinhold Niebuhr came to appreciate the politics of mixed economic solutions, affirming the New Deal and moving his political allegiance to the Liberal Party.

John C. Bennett, a younger colleague and friend of Niebuhr and heir to Niebuhr's mantle, wrote several books on foreign policy, Communism, and nuclear weapons, continuing the movement they called Christian realism. Paul Tillich, dismissed from the University of Frankfurt in 1933, was very active in World War II, founding the Council for a Democratic Germany and broadcasting propaganda to occupied Germany.[1] Hans Morgenthau was a favorite political theorist for Niebuhr and Bennett. His writings were assigned in their course on moral issues in international relations and reflected in their writings. Abraham Heschel, who was not so politically active earlier, joined them in the civil rights movement and Clergy and Laity Concerned about Vietnam in the 1950s and 60s.

All three of the refugees knew the power philosophies of Germany. Tillich and Morgenthau both at an earlier stage had been influenced by

Friedrich Nietzsche. But in the United States, their previous work was melted into this reforming philosophy led by Niebuhr and continued by John C. Bennett. They contributed beyond this school. Paul Tillich led in systematic theology and theology of culture, Abraham Heschel made his contribution to biblical studies and Jewish mysticism, and Hans Morgenthau defined the study of international relations; but here I emphasize their contribution to Christian social ethics. They sought a realistic perspective to overcome an idealism in both church and public discourse in America for the sake of reform.

Reinhold Niebuhr

Niebuhr inherited the social gospel and then criticized it to find a more adequate basis for Christian social ethics. The social gospel combined sectarian and Calvinist motifs with a good deal of secular optimism to advance Protestant ethics beyond individualism. The social gospel took institutions and economics seriously and called for their radical reform, but at the same time it remained somewhat naively optimistic and largely pacifist. The movement reached its zenith in the years immediately following World War I in the celebration of the victories of Versailles and prohibition and the expansive spirit of Protestantism. It was the articulate minority within the mainstream of American Protestantism, and even at its height, it could not count a majority of the members of any Protestant church within its ranks. It quickly collapsed, and by 1933, former followers of the social gospel regarded it as dead. Many historical factors contributed to its decline; Reinhold Niebuhr's polemics against its ideology are of particular interest here because they contain many of the ideas of political realism.

Against its optimism about reforming institutions to express the Kingdom of God, Niebuhr emphasized a dualism that consciously owed much to Augustine and unconsciously was derivable from Luther. One could fulfill the law of love directly in personal life but not in social life. Sin or prideful egoism was exaggerated in the social arena to the point at which the best that could be hoped for was justice, understood as a tolerable balancing of the claims and counterclaims of various groups. The Christian virtues were directly relevant to personal life but were relevant to social life primarily as ideals that, while impossible to fulfill, revealed the relativity of all social achievements. Moral judgments in the political arena involved a heightened degree of ambiguity because of the need to balance the competing claims of groups that could not be expected to renounce their group interest. Whereas the social gospel had attempted to realize directly the will of God in the common life, the political realists regarded this as impossible because the structure of the common life involved competition, rough justice, and coercion.

Over against a social gospel assumption that humanity was creating a more moral social order, Niebuhr argued in the 1930s that (1) there was no historical evidence for a doctrine of inevitable progress; (2) the Christian doctrine of history was one of tragedy, not inevitable progress; (3) the history of the interwar period revealed little progress in international politics; and (4) the Marxist analysis of the capitalist economic collapse was essentially correct.

Niebuhr stated the ethic of Jesus in more extreme terms than had the social gospel. For him, the ethic of Jesus was one of nonresistance, not one of nonviolence. This analysis relegated the ethic of Jesus to a more transcendent position than it held in the social gospel, but it also cut the support from under those who were proposing nonviolence as the Christian ethic. Niebuhr broke with the Fellowship of Reconciliation (FOR) over the use of violence by strikers. The majority of the FOR held to the position that strikers ought not resort to violence, whereas Niebuhr sanctioned the discriminate use of violence. He came to believe, for reasons of Marxist class analysis, that nonviolent teaching would support the foes of reaction against the just demands of the proletariat. Violence was wrong according to the ethic of Jesus, but so was resistance. Justice, not the ethic of self-sacrificing love, was immediately relevant to the domestic struggle, and justice demanded the use of violence. Niebuhr held out against sanctioning international war after his Christian pacifism had been refuted by his analysis of Jesus' ethic and the requirements of his analysis of the class structure. Once the ethical distinction between nonviolent coercion and violent coercion was blurred, the outlines of the realist position sanctioning the use of discriminate force on the international scene began to appear. Niebuhr's own first post–World War I approval of international force was the hope that Great Britain would compel Italy to stop its invasion of Abyssinia. The enforcement of a League of Nations oil embargo against Italy would have required the British navy's enforcement of it in the Mediterranean. Such enforcement, though sanctioned by international authority, would have required armed forces.

Niebuhr regarded much of the optimism of the interwar period of the United States as due to oversimplified doctrines of humanity. He wanted to emphasize both the grandeur and the misery of humanity and to insist that both the extreme optimists and the extreme pessimists were wrong. Human freedom violated doctrines of humanity that attempted to understand humankind in terms of either rationality or nature. Both the social sciences and philosophy were necessary to understand humanity, but they necessarily erred if they tried to comprehend humanity solely in terms of either logic or nature. One was free to make moral choices and to choose ultimate ends, but misery arose from the inevitable choice of selfish egoism. The self promoted its own interest, heedless of the interests of others, and thereby corrupted its understanding of itself and the common life. For Niebuhr, politics had to start with the desire to control and balance common egoism drives, not with schemes for the elimination of egoism.

Political realism grew out of this protest against the optimism of both secular and religious forces in the post–World War I period, and it attacked this optimism with an ethical dualism, a tragic view of history, an antipacifist interpretation of a social ethic, and a doctrine of humanity that insisted that insofar as politics was concerned, the self remained a sinner. In Niebuhr it was an attempt to find a Protestant ethic adequate to deal with American social problems that were partially analyzed in the 1930s in Marxist terms.

Hans Morgenthau did not take up political realism in an attempt to reform the Protestant ethic, but he inherited much of Niebuhr's teaching. He has repeatedly acknowledged his debt to Niebuhr, and his *Scientific Man vs. Power Politics* reflects much of the argument of Niebuhr's *Moral Man and Immoral Society* and *The Nature and Destiny of Man*. Morgenthau joined with Niebuhr in combating American political optimism as symbolized by the creation of the Carnegie Endowment for International Peace; after the war problem had been resolved, the funds were to be applied to the resolution of other social problems. With Niebuhr's and Morgenthau's biblical doctrines of humanity and their recognition of the essential anarchy of international politics, they repeatedly joined in attacking simplistic schemes for the elimination of the struggle from international politics. They also exerted a common critique of American politicians who obscure the nature of the struggle through moralistic sloganeering. Woodrow Wilson's war to make the world safe for democracy is perhaps their favorite example of an American politician conducting a moral crusade when he should have stayed within the bounds of traditional diplomacy. Niebuhr particularly resented Wilson's idealism because he personally joined in supporting World War I for a mixture of reasons, including Wilsonian idealism and American nationalism. Morgenthau finds nationalism's capture of morality, which characterized Wilson's policy, continued in the self-righteousness of American policy under John Foster Dulles and in the globalism of Lyndon B. Johnson's policy, which assumed the role of an anti-Communist crusade in the third world.

Hans J. Morgenthau

Morgenthau understood politics as a realm where the ideal confronts the real. There is an absolute realm of transcendent values or ideals that we grasp dimly. The world of politics was judged by those ideals, but often politics was only a choice between greater and lesser evils. In Germany Morgenthau had written essays and volumes on international law and its limits, the criticism of pacifism and the philosophy of war, the reality of the state, the philosophy of politics, the reality of norms, international sanctions, and the crisis in ethics from Kant to Nietzsche, and he projected his major work on the theory of international politics. He drew on all of this work, first as he argued for political realism, and later as his ethics became more pronounced in his critique of American foreign policy.[2]

Within Morgenthau's system, morality, as well as the balance of power, is regarded as one of the limiting factors of national ambitions. The relationship of morality to international politics is threefold:

> First, morality limits the interests that power seeks and the means that power employs to that end. Certain ends cannot be pursued, and certain means cannot be employed in a given society within a certain period of history by virtue of the moral opprobrium that attaches to them. Second, morality puts the stamp of its approval upon certain ends and means which thereby not only become politically feasible but also acquire a positive moral value. These moral values, then, become an intrinsic element of the very interests that power seeks. Third, morality serves interests and power as their ideological justification.[3]

In the domestic sphere, morality influences power relations by fulfilling all three of the above functions. But in the field of international politics, morality is used primarily as the ideological justification of power interests. The nation-state, which is the final element in the field of international politics, has been able to proceed relatively unlimited by morality. Nations have equated the interests they seek with the claims of professed moral principles.

Morgenthau is aware that his own philosophy of international politics is built upon a particular worldview. Particular doctrines of political science have their roots in assumed conceptions of morality, purposes, and goals, and it is not the task of political science to question these conceptions. The particular worldview and mores of a nation shape and limit that nation's foreign policy.

The pursuit of power needs to be limited by the claims of ethics. The Bible, ethics, and the constitutional structure of American democracy have emphasized keeping the drive for power within limits. All of the dominant systems of Western ethics have recognized the universality of the drive for power and have sought to limit it. The political systems and philosophies that have exalted the struggle for power have become self-destructive, Morgenthau claims.

There is abundant evidence witnessing to the relevance of morality as a limiting factor of political means. The influence of moral principles is most obvious to Morgenthau in peacetime, when ethical inhibitions prevent executions that would be politically expedient. Morgenthau regards the decline in the once-common practice of assassinating military and political leaders as indicative of moral influence. Bismarck, in contrast to Hitler, though vicious enough in individual moves on the political chessboard, honored and did not attempt to eliminate his opponent, France. Churchill demonstrated the difference between a moral realist and an amoral one at Tehran when he refused, in the name of British honor, to concede to Stalin's plan to execute 50,000 German officers after the war. Morgenthau writes, "The fact of the matter is that nations recognize a moral obligation to refrain from the infliction of death and suffering under certain conditions despite the possibility of justifying such conduct in the light of a 'higher purpose' such as the national interest."[4] All of the conventions and treaties regarding the conduct of war, though often violated, bear witness to a growth of moral reluctance to use unlimited violence as an instrument of foreign policy. Only in the last half-century has the avoidance of war per se become an object of statecraft. No longer, Morgenthau argues, can the initiation of a war be declared a foreseen and directed culmination of a nation's foreign policy. War must now be interpreted as a natural catastrophe or as an evil act of the enemy. The propaganda campaigns to justify national actions, and national protestations of innocence are indirect recognition of moral norms that nations often violate and sometimes completely overthrow.

The Decline of Morality in International Politics

Morgenthau argues that the limiting force of morality has declined in international politics since the seventeenth century. As evidence of the decline, he cites the failure of the world's decision makers to acknowledge a common standard of values, the elimination of the old international society, modern warfare against civilians, and the breakdown of traditional means of diplomacy. Viewing international morality as an effective restraint on politics as impossible, he approvingly quotes Dean Roscoe Pound: "It might be maintained plausibly that a moral . . . order among states was nearer attainment in the middle of the eighteenth century than it is today."[5]

The cause of morality's failure to fulfill its rightful place in international relations is the people's disbelief in objective standards of morality. Morgenthau bemoans modern humanity's loss of religiosity, that is, a "dependence upon a will and a power which are beyond his understanding and control."[6] People's loss of a sense of mystery, tragedy, and guilt has dehumanized them. In "Reaction to the Van Doren Reaction," Morgenthau attacks the moral obtuseness of America and affirms his belief in moral truths that people do not create but find in the nature of the world.[7] He is profoundly aware of the skepticism that allows one to fulfill the cultic acts in the midst of one's unbelief. He writes, "Religion has become an organized social activity and the public demonstration of official piety, permeated with doubt and disbelief."[8]

The democratization of the conduct of international politics has also dealt a blow to international morality in Morgenthau's view. Reference to a rule of conduct presupposes an individual conscience that responds to the rule. When the conduct of foreign policy was definitely traceable to the monarch or his representative, these individuals could hold themselves morally accountable for the actions of their governments. Today the vast bureaucracies of the world hold no common consensus as to moral requirements, and no individual conscience is responsible for governmental actions. It is one thing to say that George III of England and Louis XVI were subject to moral restraints in their dealings, and quite another to say that Great Britain or France today has moral obligations one to the other. Even the vast turnover in the upper echelons of the U.S. Department of State reveals how nebulous any consensus of an international moral order is today.

Morgenthau's argument that no one can be singled out who is morally responsible for the conduct of foreign policy ignores a significant amount of evidence: DeGaulle dictated French policy; Johnson was constitutionally responsible; Eden resigned following the failure of his foreign policy. Morgenthau is correct in his claim that there is no consistent interpretation in the United States as to the demands of morality in international relations, but there are individuals who are morally responsible for the conduct of U.S. foreign policy. Two cases in point are Eisenhower's assumption of responsibility for the U-2 incident and Kennedy's acceptance of the Bay of Pigs invasion as his mistake. President Johnson's resignation of the presidency personalized responsibility for failure in Vietnam. Carter too accepted responsibility for foreign policy failures vis-à-vis Iran.

Morgenthau feels that the influence of morality on international politics has decreased with the destruction of the old aristocratic set that ran the political affairs of Europe in the seventeenth and eighteenth centuries. The aristocrats shared family ties, a common lifestyle, the French language, and common moral values with regard to how the political game was to be played. The attempt of the czar to hire Bismarck to work in his foreign service is an example of the cordiality in international politics of a past age. Though Morgenthau may overemphasize the graciousness of previous European politics, he makes his point that the contending powers of the twentieth century were less limited by common values than their predecessors.

There are signs, however, of a developing moral consensus that Morgenthau overlooks. The United Nations is serving to bring together diplomats and to create shared values, customs, and morals. UN diplomat

Andrew Cordier has pointed out how quickly the representatives of the new nations matured; he saw one of the more important functions of the United Nations as training the world's diplomats. Hammarskjöld emphasized the importance of "corridor diplomacy," which, through informal contacts, tends to form a community of diplomats. The decline in "supranational moral rules of conduct" may be at an end, and the present trend may be toward a more universal recognition of principles of international conduct as represented by the United Nations Charter, UN resolutions, and the UN community of diplomats. The moral authority of UN resolutions varies with the degree of unanimity achieved in the voting, with the methods used to achieve a majority vote, with the skill of UN personnel in conducting their affairs, and with the degree of continuity between the UN resolution and the traditions of approved international practice; but recognizing that particular resolutions have different degrees of moral authority does not invalidate the assertion of common usage that such resolutions have a moral authority.

Robert Jackson understands contemporary foreign policies to be subject to both the procedural norms of customary diplomacy as well as the charter of the UN, the Helsinki Final Act, various regional charters, and other treaties, conventions, declarations, and resolutions. He sees a global covenant evolving from European statecraft since 1648 that provides a "fundamental normative reality of international ethics."[9] Jackson knows all of these norms are violated, but the violation of norms does not mean their nonexistence. Furthermore, the increasing dominance of procedures of democracy, human rights, and market capitalism around the globe testify to an emerging recognition of normative agreement among sovereign nation-states.

Moral Confusion in International Politics

Modern nationalism has suppressed supranational ethics in the twentieth century, and the ability of the nation to exert compulsion upon individuals has increased. The nation has available vast means of persuasion due to technological developments. The prestige of the nation has increased in a time when loyalty to a nation may require the destruction of several thousand lives by one individual in the name of national loyalty. The weight of the national prestige and the decline of universal ethics combine to force people to bow to the orders of the nation.

Thinkers have sought to reconcile the tension between national interest and supranational ethics by equating national mores with values that should prevail over the world. Claims of morality were used to disguise the rivalry for power between the United States and the Soviet Union, and there was a tendency to see the Cold War in terms approximating the religious wars of the Crusades. The equation of universal ethics with national goals inserted an element of fanaticism into the competition.

The morality of the particular group, far from limiting the struggle for power on the international scene, gives that struggle a ferocious-ness and intensity not known to other ages. . . . Thus carrying their idols before them, the nationalistic masses of our time meet in the international arena, each group convinced that it executes the man-date of history, that it does for humanity what it seems to do for itself, and that it fulfills a sacred mission ordained by Providence however defined.

Little do they know that they meet under an empty sky from which the gods have departed.[10]

Equating supranational ethics with national interest is not only politi-cally disastrous; it is also morally indefensible. The Greek tragedians and biblical prophets stand against the pride that equates a particular national-ism and the will of Providence. The blasphemy of identifying the will of God with national political interests is clearly illustrated by ministers who serve the same God yet bless warriors on opposite sides of the battle line. Morgenthau's polemics were consistently directed against such expressions of idolatry.

Morgenthau makes plain in his book *In Defense of the National Interest* that one of the major problems of U.S. foreign policy has been the creation of an artificial dichotomy between national interest and moral principles. The substitution of moral principles for national interest is both an intel-lectual error and a perversion of morals. The national interest has an inher-ent dignity. Only by each nation maintaining order and preserving its national community can even minimal values be realized within each nation. Politics presumes the existence of power and interests, and to sep-arate a nation from the pursuit of its interests is to violate the art of poli-tics. Morgenthau writes, "The choice is not between moral principles and the national interest, devoid of moral dignity, but between one set of moral principles divorced from political reality, and another set of moral princi-ples derived from political reality."[11]

As a philosopher of international politics, Morgenthau is concerned that the method of policy formulation be as rational as possible. He believes that the confusion of morality and the pursuit of national interest in the minds of American policy makers have weakened American foreign policy. He admitted, after his tirades against American moralism, that in spite of moralistic speeches, the United States has usually tended to act, as all nations do, in power-political terms.

Morgenthau believes all human action is corrupt. He refuses to reconcile ethics and political action and avoids three traditional ways of obscuring their differences: the doctrine that the end justifies the means, the justifica-tion of action by intention, and utilitarianism. He writes, "The tendency to justify otherwise immoral actions by the ends they serve is universal. It is merely most conspicuous in politics."[12] His central attack on the doctrine that the end justifies the means is based on subjectivity of the relationship itself. The relationship of ends and means is totally relative to the particular social vantage point of the observer, he argues. One person's means may be another person's ends. The question of which political group is to be sacrificed can never be decided objectively on the basis of this doctrine. No ethical distinction between various types of political action can be drawn on the basis of this doctrine, since all actions are judged in relationship to the intended goal. The very concept of end implies a termination of political action and reaction that never occurs. This end-justifies-the-means doctrine was present in its most brutal form recently in the communistic societies that have permitted great personal suffering for the absolute good of the arrival of Communism. Since this doctrine has no objective criterion of decision, it tends to reduce ethical judgment to the intention of the actor.

The criterion of good intention for the judgment of action is especially irrelevant to the field of international politics. The very social relevance of political action is obscured by judgment on the basis of good intention. The good-intentioned, politically naive actor may do more harm than the ill-intentioned professional politician; judging their actions on the basis of good intention ignores the significance of their actions. Morgenthau quotes Abraham Lincoln repeatedly to stress the importance of results when judging political action. "I do the very best I know how, the very best I can, and I mean to keep doing so until the end. If the end brings me out all right, what is said against me won't amount to anything. If the end brings me out wrong, ten angels swearing I was right would make no difference."[13]

The dominant school of ethics in the United States, Morgenthau thinks, is utilitarianism, which teaches that acts are right inasmuch as they promote human happiness. This school does not ask the ethical question at all, Morgenthau maintains, but only tries to calculate rationally what action will result in the greatest happiness. He dismisses this school rather lightly by pointing out that modern humanity cannot indefinitely remain oblivious to the eternal ethical problems.

Despite his critique of the utilitarian position, it is difficult to distinguish Morgenthau's position from pragmatism, the American version of utilitarianism. In foreign policy he is a pragmatist quite close to Niebuhr; in another realm (he isolates for purposes of analysis political man, religious man, moral man, and so on) he thinks morality consists of principles found in nature. He is caught in a fundamental dualism with knowledge of a realm of moral principles that are inapplicable to foreign policy, the realm of his interest. He welcomes the means of power politics but feels guilty about so doing.

The View of Humanity and International Relations

Morgenthau's philosophy of international politics is based on his view of humanity. When he was a child and young adult, his view of how people treat the other was shaped by the European anti-Semitism of the twentieth century, and he suffered personal humiliation as a Jew. All political theory, according to Morgenthau, is grounded in assumptions about human nature. The abolition of war, the primary problem of civilization, is made infinitely complex because the numerous causes of war have their roots in the conditions of the human soul.[14] He has repeatedly asserted that the moral problems of international politics are but a peculiar instance of the moral problems of every person's encounter with other people.

As power is a basic element in Morgenthau's political theory, so it is in his doctrine of humanity. In response to a question asking for a statement of this doctrine, he replied: "The lust for power is an intrinsic element of human nature. It is one of the basic innate tendencies of man. It tends to create societies. In various societies the lust for power may be viewed differently, or it may be differently channeled, but it is always present."[15]

The lust for power arises, for Morgenthau, out of the same source as the need for love: loneliness. Of all the creatures, only humanity is capable of loneliness. Humanity has a "need of not being alone,"[16] but in the end one cannot escape being alone. People as biological, rational, and spiritual beings find in their existential loneliness an insufficiency. This insufficiency drives them in search of love and power. Though a stable relationship of love implies a degree of power or the relationship would be nothing more than a "succession of precarious exaltations,"[17] love is basically the more satisfying and first-sought relationship. "Love is reunion through spontaneous mutuality; power seeks to create a union through unilateral imposition."[18] In the final analysis, the power relationship is a frustrated love relationship; power seekers would rather be united in love. Morgenthau sees in the great political masters a demonic seeking for power that resembles the frantic compulsion of misguided lovers who, substituting sex for love, seek to find satisfaction by multiplying their sexual conquests.[19] The unity these people seek in love can never be obtained, and so they blunder through life toward their own destruction. Morgenthau acknowledges his debt to Tillich's insight that love and power are, at their source, united.

Morgenthau is deeply aware of the tragedy and sin of the human situation and does not hesitate to use the terms in his most sophisticated political writing. His view of humanity is represented by the following statement: "Suspended between his spiritual destiny which he cannot fulfill and his animal nature in which he cannot remain, he is forever condemned to experience the contrast between the longings of his mind and his actual condition as his personal, eminently human tragedy."[20]

The fate of humanity has placed people in a world in which evil forces (not just the negation of good or the lack of education) ruin and destroy their best plans and highest dreams. Social problems are only rarely solved, but people must continue the battle, realizing that even their best efforts can produce more evil, Morgenthau insists. As evil is inevitable in politics, ethics in politics is the endeavor to choose the least evil action among several alternatives. The final tragedy is death, which every person faces alone. He believes that "our age has lost faith in individual immorality in another age" and that people's response to death determines to a large degree how they choose to live life.[21]

The lust for power in the soul of humanity creates the drive for power in international politics. Each person's quest for certainty in the midst of uncertainty characterizes the dogmatism of political claims. The egoism of self taints all political actions, yet moral yearnings force people to reject naked human egoism as normative. Morgenthau sums up insecurity, the basic problem of humanity, in this way:

> Man is a political animal by nature; he is a scientist by chance or choice; he is a moralist because he is a man. Man is born to seek power, yet his actual condition makes him a slave to the power of others. Man is born a slave but everywhere he wants to be a master. Out of this discord between man's desire and his actual condition arises the moral issue of power, that is, the problem of justifying and limiting the power which man has over man.[22]

The sources of the human problem are insecurity and the drive to overcome this insecurity; salvation lies in accepting one's insecurity and acting in the full knowledge of the limitations of one's action. As Morgenthau puts it, "The achievement of the wisdom by which insecurity is understood and sometimes mastered is the fulfillment of human possibilities."[23]

The Contemporary Moralism

Morgenthau regards the post–World War II drift in American foreign policy toward the position that the United States is inevitablly involved in all international conflicts as the most dangerous tendency in American statecraft. He believes that U.S. overinvolvement in world politics is due in part to a streak of moralism in American foreign policy makers. This moralism is expressed in a worldwide opposition to Communism or leftist revolutionary movements. Because it has posited Communism and leftist revolutionary movements as evils to be opposed, U.S. policy has neglected to calculate carefully the interests of the United States in particular cases. Despite State Department denials, U.S. policy has been set to oppose leftist forces wherever they challenge the status quo. A wise foreign policy would weigh carefully the threat of each revolutionary situation to U.S. security or well-being. The moralistic foreign policy is spared such intricate calculations, because assuming the evil of the political left and the U.S. obligation to oppose evil, the U.S. reaction to particular Communist or leftist threats to the peace is reflexive rather the reflective. Both of the two extremes in U.S. strategy, isolationism and globalism, reflect a moralistic approach to foreign policy. Morgenthau writes:

> The isolationist's moralism is naturally negative, abstentionist, and domestically oriented; it seeks to protect the virtue of the United States from contamination by the power politics of evil nations. Wilsonian globalism endeavored to bring the virtue of American democracy to the rest of the world. Contemporary globalism tries to protect the virtue of the "free world" from contamination by Communism and to create a world order in which that virtue has a chance to flourish. The anti-Communist crusade has become both the moral principle of contemporary globalism and the rationale of our global foreign policy.[24]

The twentieth century was the American century. The twenty-first century finds America as a hegemonic superpower, a reality foreseen only by Paul Tillich among the realists considered in this book. Morgenthau certainly would have continued to warn against globalism. His balance of power observations would have led him to expect new global alliances of very disparate nations to prevent dominant nations from becoming hegemonic. To American statepeople, the values of democratic market capitalism may seem universal without appearing so to other peoples. The breakdown in 2003 of the World Trade Organization meeting in Cancun is symptomatic of international resistance to hegemony.

Reinhold Niebuhr and Hans J. Morgenthau

Niebuhr and Morgenthau were the leading figures in the realist school, but other significant thinkers took up their central concerns. Morgenthau's classic work *Politics among Nations* became the central text in the debates over the theory of international politics. Niebuhr's work *Moral Man and Immoral Society* continued as the classic statement of Protestant social theory in the realist vein. The two thinkers were very close to each other. On one occasion, when Niebuhr was pushed to delineate the differences between his position and Morgenthau's, he replied: "I wouldn't say that the views of Morgenthau and myself are 'somewhat different.' We basically have common ideas with certain peripheral differences."[25]

The most significant difference between the two thinkers is in the area of the relationship of ethics to politics. Morgenthau's view of political reality remained more tragic than Niebuhr's. Niebuhr, who had held to a tragic view of history at an earlier time, came to regard history as more nearly ironical than tragic. It contained possibilities of gain as well as loss, and its configurations were continually producing surprises to both pessimists and optimists. These differences inclined Morgenthau to use ethics as a principle of criticism of politics. Ethical standards revealed that politics could not be the proper place for the good Christian. Niebuhr, on the other hand, used ethics both as a source of criticism and as a motivation for action. Politics was just the place for the good Christian, who was a responsible sinner.

Niebuhr criticized Morgenthau for his overly consistent pessimistic interpretation of life. He also was not as secure as Morgenthau in regarding the national interest as the bearer of value. Niebuhr would admit that empirically nations usually did attempt to pursue their own interests, but he countered that normative thinking could not be surrendered to this practice. The essence of the morality of international politics was in finding ways to permit the reconciliation and adjudication of the various national claims, not in sanctioning the individual nation's pursuit of its interest. He told Morgenthau, "Nations as well as individuals stand under the law: 'Whosoever seeketh to gain his life shall lose it.'" [26]

The comparison of Morgenthau and Niebuhr reveals a gradual move in both thinkers toward a more moderate realism.[27] This development led Niebuhr to question the use of *national interest* as a term carrying its own moral dignity, and events of history led both men to criticize U.S. policy in Southeast Asia in moral as well as political terms.

Niebuhr and Morgenthau surprised many of their admirers by their attacks on the Johnson administration's war in Vietnam.[28] Were not these thinkers, along with George Kennan and others, the proponents of containment, Cold War politics, and the use of power to counter aggression? The subtleties of their positions were ignored by many who, seeking simple answers, wanted global answers to particular crises, who did not understand how nuclear détente changed international politics, who sought a crusade where the realists wanted calculating, flexible, responsive use of the U.S. capacity to meet particular crises. Both Niebuhr and Morgenthau declared the war unjust and participated politically to end it.

Also, many realists, or at least those like Hubert H. Humphrey influenced by these men, continued to support the war policies long after all justifiable excuses for supporting the American venture had been discredited. Within the moral leadership of the church, those influenced by Niebuhr, like John C. Bennett, perhaps the most outspoken against the war, were opposed by Paul Ramsey, who justified the major ingredients of U.S.

policy under the rubric of just war theory. On the major issue of foreign policy of the late 1960s and early 1970s, then, the realists divided. The divisions were deep and reflected not only their different situations in life but differences in their ethical thinking and also in their judgments as to empirical reality.

The fissures among the realist thinkers were reflections, of course, of deeper divisions within the society. The realist critics of the war found themselves often paired on speaking platforms or in demonstrations with long-standing critics of the U.S. government policy who were glad for their support but regarded them as opponents. Defenders of the Administration, for example, Paul Ramsey, sometimes expressed amazement that the followers of Niebuhr, whom he had counted on to be more moderate in the criticism of the wielders of power, were so morally outraged by the U.S. role in the struggle in Vietnam.

The effect of the Vietnam crisis on the realists who opposed the war was to open their eyes wider than before to the dangers of militarism in the United States and to fresher appreciation of the fragility of democracy in the United States. They saw how easily national purposes and rhetoric were corrupted and how willing the establishment—academic, governmental, and ecclesiastical—was to be corrupted. The conflict psychologically turned them from being defenders of the broad outlines of U.S. policy to critics in exile from those who were making decisions in Washington, D.C. By providing an example of foreign policy that so flagrantly violated moral standards, the Vietnam War brought a new force into their moral critique of the United States. Rather than emphasizing the moral ambiguity of foreign policy, they proclaimed the moral horror of this particular policy. Realism as a practical philosophy was not intended by either Niebuhr or Morgenthau to contribute to the reification of certain concepts of international politics. Both thinkers rejected as quite inappropriate to the 1960s and 70s the earlier rhetoric and policies of the Cold War. The shift is best represented in Morgenthau's book *A New Foreign Policy for the United States.*[29] It was expressed in *Truth and Power: Essays of a Decade 1960–1970* and in their mutual support of Eugene McCarthy's quest of the presidency in 1968.

Niebuhr: The Kingdom of God

The Kingdom of God was clearly the master thought of the social gospel movement of Niebuhr's youth. It is also a major theme of the new theologies of hope and revolution. It is not the major motif of Reinhold Niebuhr's theology, but it is present.[30] Scholars aware of the heavier use of the Kingdom in both the social gospel and liberation ethics than in Niebuhr have treated his theory of ethics as if it were independent of the Kingdom.

Niebuhr's ethic was more in the prescriptive mood than the indicative. That is, he emphasized duty, the commandment of love, and principles of justice rather than relying primarily on a sense of the Kingdom shaping the development of history. He took account of as many of the empirical conditions as he could be informed upon, but he would not regard the shape of the Kingdom as empirically present in history. He also avoided overuse of the Kingdom concept because it had been so tarnished by sentimental Christians who either expected the Kingdom's catastrophic supernatural arrival and became socially irresponsible or who expected evolution to produce an Americanized version of the Kingdom.

However, despite the above qualifications, the Kingdom functions in his thought in an important way. His best discussion of the Kingdom is found in the last two chapters of *The Nature and Destiny of Man*. Here he clearly states, "We must seek to fashion our common life to conform more nearly to the brotherhood of the Kingdom of God."[31] Such an assertion, if not contradicted in the remainder of his thought, is a clear indication of the continuity of the social gospel in this thought.

Finally, for Niebuhr, though, the relationship of Kingdom and history is one of paradox. He explains, "History moves toward the realization of the Kingdom but yet the judgment of God is upon every new realization." History continues in its incompleteness, always needing those who will act resolutely to help complete it, but also requiring that they be able to comprehend why their actions will not complete it. The Kingdom of God was a guard for Niebuhr against utopianism and, he thought, a protection against the cynicism that resulted from utopian failures.

Perhaps because he personally was not tempted by defeatism, he could emphasize the transcendence of the Kingdom rather than its historical realization. But as in all profoundly Christian theologies, the symbols are all present and the differences among the social theologies become matters of emphasis.

As a transcendent hope, the Kingdom of God can be a guard against utopianism. It has another and more important function, though. It exemplifies the social relationships of the Christian virtues. Knowledgeable Christians adopt values, habits, and perspectives for their lives, personally and socially, and they bind themselves to these convictions. They are the rules of conscience or the laws of life by which they live. In primitive Christianity they were the elements of the way Christians lived. To be in the Kingdom of God is to adopt the ultimate lordship of Christ and to be bound in solidarity to Christ. The Kingdom or rule of God is therefore simply to live in the way of Christ. There are, of course, many perspectives regarding the actual rules of the Kingdom, but these are found within a recognizable history and range of interpretations. All of these insights as to the meaning of the Christian way or citizenship in the Kingdom of God imply a hope for eschatological realization and historical approximation. The hopes for historical realization in prophetic realism are not as extravagant as those of secular realism, Marxist determinism, social gospel optimism, or theology of hope utopianism, but they are sufficient for the struggle and for human history. Three of Niebuhr's expressions of hope conclude these reflections:

> The new world must be built by resolute men who "when hope is dead will hope for faith"; who will neither seek premature escape from the guilt of history, nor yet call the evil, which taints all their achievements, good.[32]

> Life in history must be recognized as filled with indeterminate possibilities. There is no individual or interior spiritual situation, no cultural or scientific task, and no social or political problem in which men do not face new possibilities of the good and the obligation to realize them.[33]

> There is no limit to either sanctification in individual life, or social perfection in collective life, or to the discovery of truth in cultural life; except of course the one limit, that there will be some corruption as well as deficiency of virtue and truth on the new level of achievement.[34]

A word in closing brings up a personal experience. While entering a suburban Detroit church that is a successor to Niebuhr's Bethel Church to study Bethel's records, I heard, almost antiphonally, coming from several rooms where Alcoholics Anonymous groups were meeting, the words of their motto, Niebuhr's prayer: "God, give us grace to accept with serenity the things that cannot be changed, courage to change the things that should be changed, and the wisdom to distinguish the one from the other." The prayer seems totally appropriate as a prayer for foreign policy in our troubled time.[35]

Notes

1. Paul Tillich, *Against the Third Reich* (ed. Ronald H. Stone and Matthew Lon Weaver; Louisville: Westminster John Knox, 1998).

2. Christopher Frei, *Hans J. Morgenthau: An Intellectual Biography* (Baton Rouge: Louisiana State University Press, 2001). Frei's work is the indispensable source for understanding the German intellectual roots of Morgenthau.

3. Hans J. Morgenthau, *Dilemmas of Politics* (Chicago: University of Chicago Press, 1958), 51. The discussion of the philosophy of Morgenthau is reprinted with changes from *Religion in Life* (Autumn 1965), copyright ©1965 by Abingdon Press.

4. Hans J. Morgenthau, *Politics among Nations* (New York: Alfred A. Knopf, 1958), 237.

5. Ibid., 251.

6. Morgenthau, *Dilemmas of Politics*, 374.

7. Hans J. Morgenthau, "Reaction to the Van Doren Reaction." *New York Times Magazine*, November 22, 1959, 17.

8. Morgenthau, *Dilemmas of Politics*, 3.

9. Robert Jackson, *The Global Covenant* (Oxford: Oxford University Press, 2000), 14.

10. Morgenthau, *Politics among Nations*, 259.

11. Hans J. Morgenthau, *In Defense of the National Interest* (New York: Alfred A. Knopf, 1951), 33.

12. Hans J. Morgenthau, *Scientific Man vs. Power Politics* (Chicago: University of Chicago Press, 1946), 181.

13. Ibid., 186.

14. Morgenthau, *Scientific Man*, 95.

15. Hans J. Morgenthau, lecture to International Fellows Program, Columbia University, February 23, 1962.

16. Hans J. Morgenthau, "Love and Power," *Commentary*, March 1962, 247–51.

17. Ibid.

18. Ibid.

19. Ibid.

20. Morgenthau, *Scientific Man*, 211.

21. Hans J. Morgenthau, "Death in the Nuclear Age," *Commentary*, September 1961, 234.

22. Morgenthau, *Scientific Man*, 168.

23. Ibid., 223.

24. Hans J. Morgenthau, "Globalism, Johnson's Moral Crusade," *The New Republic*, June 3, 1965, 19.

25. Reinhold Niebuhr, Hans J. Morgenthau, and Richard Hudson, "The Ethics of War and Peace in the Nuclear Age," *War/Peace*, February 1967, 3.

26. Harry R. Davis and Robert C. Good, eds., *Reinhold Niebuhr on Politics* (New York: Charles Scribner's Sons, 1960), 333.

27. This treatment is brief because I have compared the two thinkers elsewhere. See Ronald H. Stone, *Reinhold Niebuhr: Prophet to Politician* (Nashville: Abingdon Press, 1972), 200–204.

28. See Hans J. Morgenthau, *Truth and Power: Essays of a Decade* (London: Pall Mall Press, 1970), 398–432; or Ronald H. Stone, *Reinhold Niebuhr*, 191–95, 244.

29. Hans J. Morgenthau, *A New Foreign Policy for the United States* (New York: Frederick A. Praeger, 1969).

30. Reinhold Niebuhr, *The Nature and Destiny of Man* (vol. 2; New York: Charles Scribner's Sons, 1943), 308.

31. Ibid., 286.

32. Ibid., 285–86.

33. Ibid., 207.

34. Ibid., 156.

35. Niebuhr's daughter's book reflects well the original context of the prayer and its meaning for foreign policy. See Elizabeth Sifton, *The Serenity Prayer* (New York: W. W. Norton, 2003).

᭐ 4 ᭑

A Perspective on International Politics

PHILOSOPHERS AND POLITICAL SCIENTISTS have attempted to construct general theories to explain the relations between nation-states. At the present time, the attempts to provide an adequate general theory to explain the political behavior of nation-states have failed. Many empirical studies have provided data on which general theorizing could proceed. Institutional analysis has taught much about how the tools of foreign policy are used. Many excellent histories of foreign policy and of international politics supply conceptual overall views of the relevant past that could be used for the construction of general hypotheses of explanation. Case studies have given the would-be theorist episodes examined in depth on which one could generalize. All of these studies, though, have not provided the discipline of international politics with paradigms or models of understanding that could produce a prevailing consensus among scholars in the field. Theorists have the building blocks of general theory, but they have not been able to put them together. Economics, which has major divisions within its ranks of scholars, is a relatively ordered discipline in contrast to the confusion that prevails among the students of international politics.

Typologies of International Relations Theory

Recognizing the undeveloped nature of the study of international politics, several theorists have sought ways to present typologies of the various explanations given for the conduct of international politics. A brief survey of the typologies of theory of Kenneth Waltz, William T. R. Fox, Stanley Hoffmann, Kenneth Thompson, John Stoessinger, Michael Doyle, and Roger D. Spegele reveals the divergence in the field but also some interesting convergence.

Kenneth Waltz[1] has posed this question to the tradition of political philosophy: What is the fundamental cause of war? He divides the responses from the Greeks to the contemporary social scientists in three categories. Some answer that the fundamental cause of war is in the tendency within human nature to engage in conflict. Others reply that the problem is in the nation-state itself; the evilness of the state produces wars. The third group finds the cause of war rooted in the anarchic structure of the international system. Waltz himself opts for a model that has room for all three answers. The character of the interstate system makes possible, as Rousseau saw, conflict between the nations. The character of the people and the quality of the states provide the particular forces that give rise to specific conflicts.

William T. R. Fox conceives of theory as the means by which various perceptions of international relations are evaluated. In his view, Christian realism would be one of many theories, and the task of the theorist is to identify and evaluate it.[2] At one level of the analysis of the "theories" of international relations, he ranks the theories on a continuum relevant to the role of human choice they consider operative in the making of foreign policy. The doctrinaire realists have relatively little place for human choice; the empirical realists give a small place to the role of choice on the part of the policy maker; the pragmatic meliorist sees policy primarily as choice among a wide range of alternative actions; and the utopian theorist posits almost unlimited power for the policy maker to choose his or her policy. Fox conceived of himself as a pragmatic meliorist, but his refusal to take the title of realist is primarily due to his wish to avoid what he regards as the extremes of those he would call doctrinaire realists. In any case, the relevant range of theoretical debate for Fox rested somewhere between pragmatic meliorism and moderate realism.

At a second level of analysis, Fox distinguishes between three types of theory. All of these types would be options within the limitations of empirical (moderate) realism or pragmatic meliorism. Some theorists would emphasize the distinctive features of each country's foreign policy. Other theorists would give special attention to the general principles by which all states seem to behave. A third school would focus on the key relations between particular states. The first group would tend to explain the invasion of Egypt by Britain, France, and Israel in 1956 by reference to the particular features of those nations, to their sense of national interest, destiny, pride, and to the sources of power available to those countries. The second would focus more on international agreements, the United Nations, and general principles of state behavior, whether interpreted realistically or idealistically. The third school would place greater stress on the relationship of Israel to the Arab world, Britain to the Suez Canal, Britain and France to the United States, the Soviet Union to the Middle East, the postcolonial world to Europe, and so on.

Stanley Hoffmann, like the theorists already mentioned, believes the field of international relations studies suffers from disorder. One function of a theory of international relations is to say what international relations is, as well as what factors are not to be included in the field. He believes theory can be classified by reference to the purpose it is intended to serve. The term *theory* can then be applied in three different ways. First, *normative* theory studies politics in terms of desired goals, for example, Kant's theory of securing the good of humankind and perpetual peace through world federation. Second, *empirical* theory seeks to understand causal relationships, analyzes political behavior, and identifies major variables in the conduct of international relations, for example, Hobson's theory of the influence of capitalism and imperialism. Finally, *policy* theory is advice on how to conduct foreign affairs, for example, Machiavelli's theory on how a prince should conduct his policy to get and keep his throne. Hoffmann rests his hopes on progress in the realm of empirical theory, but he recognizes the need for the other two types and asks mainly that the distinctions between the three be honored.[3]

Kenneth Thompson[4] has pointed to an agreement among several scholars at a conference in 1955 to employ in the conference discussion Walter Lippmann's typology for the theory of international relations. Lippmann proposed the distinctions between normative theory, general theory, and theory as the basis for action. Lippmann's categories, upon which Hoffmann's seem to depend, did not produce agreement as to exactly what should be done within each type of theory. Lippmann's claim that there are rational sequences and causal relationships that can be generalized upon serves Hoffmann's need for a general empirical theory and avoids the problem suggested by the term *empirical*. These distinctions seem to indicate different motifs of various theories, even if actual theoretical works appear to mix elements from all three types.

Another way to look at the field of international relations theories would be to divide it in four ways, as John Stoessinger has done.[5] He regards Hans Morgenthau and his followers and fellow critics as composing a group that could be roughly labeled "the power school." The term *quantifiers* could be given in a general way to a disparate group of theorists who are trying to build the theory of international relations on models imported from other fields. The systems theory of Morton Kaplan, the communications theory of Karl Deutsch, the decision-making theory of Richard Snyder, and the game theory of Jessie Bernard are representatives of this group. The case study technique is a mode of operation of many of the outstanding theorists of international relations. In much of his work, William T. R. Fox exhibits the power of the case study approach. Another school of increasing importance is composed of those who draw on psychology for their insights into international relations. Probably the best-known work of this type is Harold Lasswell's book *World Politics and Personal Insecurity*. The school of thought under consideration here as prophetic realism does not fit any of the types of international relations theory suggested. Although aspects of it may count as part of the respective theories, it would seem that it is not a theory of international relations but a perspective on the political relations between nations. It is a perspective in the sense of a practical philosophy that contains a philosophy of life, ideas about how nations relate normative theory, and a history of many policy recommendations. From a realist perspective, an adequate way to show what its commentary means is to put it in the context of the difference between an idealist and a realist approach to international relations.

Michael Doyle's recent typology of theory focuses on the political purposes of theory and categorizes theory into three types: realism, liberalism, and socialism, associated respectively with Morgenthau, Kant, and Marx. His treatment of Morgenthau as essentially similar to Machiavelli is not persuasive.[6] Doyle's own preference for complex realism with a moral component is close to my category of prophetic realism.

Roger D. Spegele[7] distinguishes between commonsense realism and his own evaluative realism, distinguishing both from positivist empiricism (neorealism) and emancipating international relations (liberation, feminism, Marxist theories). His evaluative realism, which is a philosophic defense of and addition to the commonsense realism of Morgenthau, Niebuhr, Butterfield, Carr, and others, is similar in purpose to the thesis of this book in revising classical realism. All four of the emphases of "evaluative realism" are found in the thought of Morgenthau and Niebuhr.

Idealism versus Realism

Prophetic realism is a perspective on international relations that partakes of the policy-oriented characteristics of Hoffmann, Thompson, and Stoessinger. It is interested in providing policy advice to politicians and to members of the public who influence policy. It makes use of empirical or general understandings of international relations inasmuch as they help the formulation of appropriate policy. Its perspective features a large component of normative theory. The normative aspects of what ought to be are always in tension, however, with what is. Prophetic realism as it relates to American foreign policy is the attempt to promote certain long-range foreign policy goals of peace, order, and justice while taking account from both theological and political perspectives of the forces that resist those goals.

Realists have for decades carried on a polemic against those they considered guilty of too casually trying to replace diplomacy with a grand design for world order. Plans like some of the proposals for turning the

United Nations into a world government have evoked their wrath.[8] Other plans of world safety or rapid total disarmament schemes have often seemed apolitical to the realists, who refuse to urge statesmen to surrender their responsibilities for nation-states. The schemes to displace the rather awkward system of politics with a perfect government have reappeared from Dante to Kant to the present. This tradition of idealism emerged with a vengeance after World War I and the establishment of the League of Nations. The idealists have been able to present their plans over against known failures of the interstate political system. The realists have countered with questions such as these: Are the grand designers willing to go to war to force their system on a reluctant world? Would not a world government drift toward tyranny in the absence of world community? Is it responsible to ask a statesperson to scrap institutions in the hope that an idealistic system will work better?

Against those who would replace diplomacy as the art of international politics with various grand plans, the realists have insisted on the political aspects of the major problems. Cooperation among the leadership of various religious groups does not produce brotherhood. Feeding populations does not eliminate war. The education of people does not produce aggression-free statesmen. Goodwill trips and cultural exchanges do not deeply affect the passions and emotions of the masses of nations. In short, the realists see international politics as a realm of intensive struggle and some cooperation. The prophetic realists understand these dual drives, toward national power seeking and international community building, as having their roots in the nature of humanity and its history.

The realists' quarrel is with what they regard as a too-easy moralism in the United States. Americans tend to be unsophisticated in assuming the rightness of their cause, the goodness of their motivations, and the appropriateness of claiming moral sanctions for national policy.

Though the realists disagree among themselves on many important issues, it is possible to speak of them as a school of thought. Kenneth Thompson[9] has isolated five elements common to the individuals discussed here as a school of thought: (1) They tend to avoid moral absolutes. Though the movement has part of its origins within the struggle to reform Protestant ethics, it has become deeply involved in planning and recommending policy. (2) They reject attempts to escape from the problems of power politics. International politics is the search for national security in a very frightening context. (3) They distrust theories of moral progress and utopian plans. They tend to assume that though the present system is risky, for the relevant future the mutual interplay of independent nation-states will continue to be the context for international relations. (4) They exhibit a passion for the study and interpretation of history. Stanley Hoffmann, following Raymond Aron in *Paix et Guerre entre les Nations*, calls for a historical sociology of international politics. Pages of Hans Morgenthau's book *Politics among Nations* and Reinhold Niebuhr's book *The Structure of Nations and Empires* provide examples of such reflections. (5) They agree that a rather explicit doctrine of humanity is helpful to political thought. As noted above, they do not hold themselves to one doctrine in the school. There is a predominant tendency, however, mostly due to Niebuhr's influence, to take very seriously the Augustinian understanding of humanity, expressed differently in Luther, Calvin, Hobbes, Montesquieu, and Madison, and to avoid highly optimistic pictures of the species.

Critique of Realism

Raymond Aron, a leading French theoretician, has accused the realists of mixing theory and the science of policy making (praxeology). He feels that their failure to distinguish adequately between perennial and contingent features of the international scene has led to confusion. This criticism is true in part; they do tend to judge theoretical insights by practical results, and they explain practice in terms of broad theoretical considerations. They are, in part, political essayists with a philosophical bent. Walter Lippmann, their realist journalist, published works on social philosophy, while their major ethicist, Niebuhr, wrote hundreds of journalistic articles on politics. When the realists were close to power in 1947 on the Policy Planning Staff Committee of the State Department under George Kennan, they worked explicitly on the development of a body of theory that was applicable to U.S. foreign policy. Aron is correct that they move quickly from reflections on theory to judgments on the quagmire of foreign policy. The movement, of course, is not one of deducing practice from theory; rather, it is a practical judgment utilizing theory and empirical data. Whether such movement is as ill advised as Aron seems to think remains an unresolved issue.

Stanley Hoffmann has subjected the realist school to a thorough critique.[10] The organization of his attack is rather loose, but he seems to make six general points.

1. Realist theory fails because it views the world as static and perceives the relations between nations as endlessly repeating themselves. He believes this is true because the realist understanding of power is too limited. At various points he charges that Morgenthau's understanding of power is (a) confined too closely to a limited set of variables, (b) too nearly equated with violence and evil, and (c) portrayed as an end while it should be seen as merely an instrumental concept. Hoffmann points out that the term *power* as used by Morgenthau has more ambiguity than

should be tolerated in a key concept.[11] This ambiguity or even improper use of the term *power* hardly freezes the realist theory into a static worldview. The realist theory of Morgenthau and Niebuhr, rather, seems to engage itself with questions regarding the way that power relations among states are to be understood in a new nuclear age. Both theorists worry about the impact of ideology and revolution on the conduct of foreign policy. Niebuhr's book on imperialism is a study of the ways in which the phenomenon of one nation controlling others gets changed in different empires and epochs. The charge of articulating a philosophy in which "power relations reproduce themselves in timeless monotony" would be a severe one if it were not so far removed from the realists' actual work.[12] Hoffmann's general point that more rigorous analysis of key concepts (e.g., national interest) is needed is a fundamental challenge to the realists to sharpen their distinctions.

2. Hoffmann's implication that the realists treat international politics apart from reflection on national politics and processes is not true. Hans Morgenthau's book *A New Foreign Policy for the United States*, Reinhold Niebuhr's book *The Irony of American History*, and John C. Bennett's book *Foreign Policy in Christian Perspective* all treat foreign policy as a reflection of domestic politics, fears, national history, and public ideologies. All three participate in internal national debate for the sake of influencing international relations.

3. The suggestion that sometimes the realists have assumed national interest to be too clearly defined is a reasonable critique. Hans Morgenthau's early work *In Defense of the National Interest* made this mistake. John C. Bennett's rather careful analysis of the national interest in *Foreign Policy in Christian Perspective* and Morgenthau's polemical articles criticizing administration understandings of the national interest belie the suggestion that the use of national interest is an essential weakness of realist theory.

4. Hoffmann criticizes the realists for asserting that morality in international relations is determined by national interest. The preceding chapter showed that Niebuhr would not treat national interest as the determiner of morality. Morgenthau's point is that national interest, properly understood, carries a certain moral dignity as it bears the hopes, interests, and security of a people. Most realists use the national interest as a corrective against idealists who would engage in crusades for various causes. The realists want to limit policy to what can be defended as promoting a

prudently defined national interest. Morals cannot be deduced from national interest; if some of Morgenthau's statements imply that they can be, he was mistaken. Morgenthau's more customary position, though, is to see morality as one of the factors that limits nations from pursuing their interest through power.

5. Hoffmann misunderstands realist theory when he criticizes it for overreliance on the "rationality of foreign policy." Realist theory assumes one to be as anxious and passionate in politics as one is in sexual life. Politics is not a science but an art. Still, the responsibility of the theorist is to be as rational as possible in explaining the irrationality of politics. If Hoffmann had taken more seriously the realist theory of human nature contained in Reinhold Niebuhr's book *Moral Man and Immoral Society* and Hans Morgenthau's book *Scientific Man vs. Power Politics*, he would not have raised this point of criticism. Rather than regarding the political process as rational, Niebuhr and Morgenthau often criticize other approaches to international politics as being overly rationalistic. Hans Morgenthau leveled precisely this critique at Richard Neustadt's institutional analysis approach:

> Professor Neustadt's abortive attempt to overcome the hazards of foreign policy with knowledge is the latest but probably not the last undertaking of this kind. . . . Academics in particular are forever searching for the philosopher's stone that will show them how our rational propensities can be superimposed on a rationally intractable reality. They have not succeeded and cannot succeed because they are up against the immutable nature of foreign policy which yields to intuitive hunches about someone's actions and perceptive estimates of changing historical forces but not to prediction derived from complete knowledge.[13]

Whether or not he is overly hard on Neustadt's study, his criticism is certainly not the critique of a rationalist.

6. The final point of criticism, that realist theory does not seriously attend to those activities taken by extragovernmental forces in international relations,[14] reveals Hoffmann's own desire to set international relations as a master paradigm for the other social sciences. Realists, though, having broad interests and writing extensively (perhaps too prodigiously) on most human endeavors, try to limit the study of international politics to a set of relationships that can be studied. All aspects of life—for example, the relationship of humanity to nature, religious loyalties,

ideological conflicts—are considered in the theory but usually as they affect the quest for power, peace, or security on the international scene.

Hoffmann's critique, in summary, reveals that the realists need to apply more rigorous analytical work to some of their concepts, but his attack fails to displace the realist model from its central role in understanding international relations. Much of Hoffmann's explicit attack was limited to Morgenthau's thought and probably only to some of Morgenthau's writing.

Another valuable type of critique was that undertaken by a panel of theologians who focused explicitly on Reinhold Niebuhr's understanding of Christina realism.[15] Underlying the discussion was the general feeling that a philosophy articulated in the 1930s, 40s, and 50s would have to be revised for the late 1960s and 70s. All of the panel members knew that Christian realism was flexible and could adjust to changing situations, and so they commenced a discussion of how it should evolve. John C. Bennett, the one in the panel closest to Reinhold Niebuhr by the longest association with him, indicated that the nature of nuclear war, changes in the Communist world, the need for revolutionary change in much of the world, and the peril of American counterrevolutionary tendencies were forcing adjustments away from the earlier Cold War stance of Christian realism.

All of the panelists agreed on the desperate straits of the American republic in the late 1960s. Many of them found the philosophy of Christian realism unable to propose ways to deal with revolution, technology, and the imaginative lifestyles of the counterculture. Occasionally they suggested that Christian realism had a conservative prejudice, but they knew that the charge was irrelevant to the philosophers they were discussing. It was more that the mood of Christian realism was prudent action, while the mood of the times and many of the panelists was revolutionary rhetoric. While realism asked the professors to imagine that they were calculating statesmen, some of the professors wanted to imagine they were revolutionary leaders.

Many of the theologians, especially Shaull, Cox, and Driver, exhibited uneasiness over the lack of imagination in Christian realism. They called for a revival of apocalyptic motifs and the legitimization of utopian thought. Others were very suspicious of the usefulness of apocalypticism to politics. Though the panel could not agree on a proper formula, they appeared to reach the consensus that hope deserved a larger place in Christian theology than it had recently received. Hope that is not illusion can stimulate wise action and help desperate people continue the search for possible avenues of social change.

Though uneasiness about Christian realism had prompted the reevaluation, the discussion indicated that realism had not yet been displaced in political ethics. With a few minor exceptions, the uneasiness could not be translated into alternative paradigms of understanding political reality in theological perspectives.

To this point, the evaluation of the critique of realism has suggested that, generally speaking, the realists were wiser than their critics. The criticism was often based on a misreading of the realists or on rather exotic notions of politics resting on the quicksand of the latest fads of the counterculture. Following are certain points of critique that must be made concerning the realist school as it has influenced U.S. foreign policy.

1. The realist analysis tended to separate too widely the demand of conscience and the realities of politics. There was no need for their polemics separating moral reflection from political reflection. They polemicized against the moralism of Woodrow Wilson, John Foster Dulles, and others with statements that were too broad for their targets. They argued against the influence of morality in foreign policy when their real opponent was a misconceived understanding of the relationship of morality to politics.

2. The realists helped cripple political liberalism with statements that dismissed the whole liberal tradition. In fact, they were and remained liberals in political philosophy. However, the optimism and even sentimentalism of some liberals drove them to discredit the whole movement. Reinhold Niebuhr particularly used liberalism as a synonym for optimism and sentimentality in politics.

3. The realists often failed to analyze central concepts rigorously enough. The terms *power*, *balance of power*, and *imperialism* all required more thorough analysis than they received at the hands of the leading realist philosophers.

4. The realists did not have enough information to see the divergencies within the Russian hierarchy. Georgi Arbatov's later reflections in *The System*[16] provide a needed perspective on the ideological turmoil within the Russian leadership. The realists were not able to foresee the collapse of the Soviet Union, but then neither was Arbatov or Gorbachev or Yeltsin. It was the fashion during the Cold War to suggest that the realists were too critical of the Soviet Union. Since the fall of the Soviet Union, however, Russian critics who had the wherewithal to know of problems in the USSR have been even more severe in condemning domestic practice in the USSR than the realists were.

5. The realists persuaded the churches and helped to persuade the country that world government was neither feasible nor desirable. They won their point that a tolerable world government would have to presuppose a tolerable world community. More

suggestions for the first and second steps toward the achievement of a tolerable world community would have been helpful. Polemics against the illusions of many world government advocates are not enough; strategies for reducing nationalism and encouraging the development of internationalism are needed. Then realists have a hard-won credibility; what is required is assistance in helping conceptualize how to maximize multinational programs and international cooperation.

Notes

1. Kenneth N. Waltz, *Man, the State, and War* (New York: Columbia University Press, 1965).

2. In Horace V. Harrison, ed., *The Role of Theory in International Relations* (Princeton: D. Van Nostrand, 1964), 98.

3. Stanley H. Hoffmann, ed., *Contemporary Theory in International Relations* (Englewood Cliffs, N.J.: Prentice-Hall, 1960), 8–9.

4. Kenneth W. Thompson, "Toward a Theory of International Politics," *American Political Science Review*, September 1955, 733–46.

5. John Stoessinger, in a lecture to the International Fellows Program, Columbia University, May 1, 1964.

6. Michael A. Doyle, *Ways of War and Peace* (New York: W. W. Norton, 1997), 49–92. See chapter 5, "Ontology of Peace," for a more fulsome critique.

7. Roger D. Spegele, *Political Realism in International Theory* (Cambridge: Cambridge University Press, 1996).

8. Reinhold Niebuhr, *Christian Realism and Political Problems* (New York: Charles Scribner's Sons, 1953), 15–31.

9. Kenneth W. Thompson, *Political Realism and the Crisis of World Politics* (Princeton: Princeton University Press, 1960), 8–14.

10. Hoffmann, *Contemporary Theory*, 30–37.

11. I. L. Claude has demonstrated this ambiguity. See I. L. Claude, *Power and International Relations* (New York: Random House, 1962), 25–37.

12. Hoffmann, *Contemporary Theory*, 30.

13. Hans J. Morgenthau, "Wild Bunch," *The New York Review of Books*, February 11, 1971, 40.

14. Hoffmann, *Contemporary Theory*, 35.

15. The panel consisted of John C. Bennett, Richard Shaull, Alan Geyer, Tom F. Driver, Roger L. Shinn, Harvey G. Cox, and Robert W. Lynn. Their discussion was published as "Christian Realism: Retrospect and Prospect," *Christianity and Crisis*, August 5, 1968, 175–90.

16. Georgi Arbatov, *The System* (New York: Random House, 1993).

5

Ontology of Power

THE PERSPECTIVES OF Reinhold Niebuhr, Hans Morgenthau, and Paul Tillich were developed in the conflicts of democracy with Nazism and Communism. While acknowledging their contextual limitations, what can we learn from these realists for the peacemaking tasks ahead? This chapter will synthesize their philosophies and present the synthesis as a recognizable school of thought. The argument assumes that though the twentieth-century needs of American foreign policy shaped their thought, at its deepest roots were images of prophetic realism from the Bible. Between the Bible and foreign policy, they explored many sources of thought, both Western and Eastern. Rather than dividing realist philosophers into Jewish realism and Christian realism, this study joins them as prophetic realism.

The recognition that prophetic realism is found within a long tradition of particular religious communities points to the validity of the language for those communities. There is no need to try to refute this language from narrow canons of linguistic positivism or recent social science. It has its own legitimacy represented in the nine steeples of churches I observe from my office window. It is the language of a particular community and of these public philosophers. Nor does the moral relativism of postmodernism threaten, because the language is in reference to a witness to an absolute who is judge of heaven and earth. The rejection of metanarratives represented by Jean-François Lyotard in *The Postmodern Condition* is simply another perspective of moral nihilism and irrelevance to international politics. The prophetic realists are persuaded not only of the reality of an absolute but also of the desirability of theological insights, which Lyotard finds incredulous. Convinced of the reality of both religion and politics, the prophetic realists are hardly tempted to reduce life to a text.[1] The developments of ontology within the school have provided a philosophical basis to their reflections beyond their use of prophetic biblical sources.

The Morgenthau-Niebuhr-Tillich perspective on international affairs has been important in the preparation of policy papers for several mainline church denominations. It has not been the only school of thought, and it is probably less influential in denominational and ecumenical councils than it was earlier. Liberation theologies and feminist perspectives have eroded the prophetic realist paradigms, while both the national Council of Churches and the World Council of Churches have reduced their staffs and influence in international affairs.

Because Christianity was relatively nonpolitical in its origins, it is always prone to return to its first-century origins and forget its political-historical foundations in the Hebrew Scriptures. Churches are also tempted to become utopian because of utopianism's affinity with some strands of eschatology. As some churches—Catholic, Calvinist (including the United Church of Christ), Lutheran, and Methodist among others— are organized transnationally, they tend to tilt toward international organization that may obscure national power centers.

The Morgenthau-Niebuhr-Tillich school, while clear about its peace-making and justice commitments, has presented them in the context of power struggles among nations. This has been helpful in formulating church policy in eight ways.

1. The ethics of international affairs are not determined by the practice of international affairs but are found in philosophical and confessional sources of ethical wisdom.
2. The nations are important actors, but they are not gods, and the forms of governmental organizations vary widely, including clans, tribes, nations, empires, federations, alliances, and international organizations.
3. While universal peace is not expected in history, many potential wars can be avoided; nuclear war or wars of mass human destruction must be avoided.
4. Political actors tend to corrupt political practice, but their roles are necessary and important, and the dangers of the corruption of power can be ameliorated.
5. The goals of foreign policies reflect the particular histories of the societies. In the case of the United States, the purposes of foreign policy include peace and justice as well as economic and strategic security. From the human rights wing of realism, particularly Jimmy Carter, Andrew Young, and John Bennett, the purposes also include the prudential promotion of human rights.

6. The doctrine from Paul Tillich of "kairos" has become important, from the Presbyterian Church (USA)'s first use of it in 1980
   to South African kairos theology and Central American political
   theology.
7. Nazism and Communism required the responsible use of U.S.
   power, including force, and present crises still do, particularly
   humanitarian rescue operations.
8. Finally, moving beyond their context and time, the ethics of sustainable human development strategies and the ethics of just
   peacemaking can be articulated in realist terms congruent with
   Christian ethics.

Rather than repeating what I have written earlier on Hans Morgenthau,
Paul Tillich, and Reinhold Niebuhr, I have chosen to critique the work of
Michael Doyle on realism. Doyle's major book, *Ways of War and Peace*,[2]
begins its close reading of theory with Thucydides. He mentions that he
begins his international relations class with the same author. The part on
realism is much longer than the parts on liberalism or socialism; these
three types of perspectives make up the major focus in his book. He recognizes the dominance of realist international relations theory and defends it
against many of the charges leveled at it. The conclusion of the book, entitled "Conscience and Power," is a phrase directly quoted from Reinhold
Niebuhr. The concerns for the role of morality and religious movements in
international relations are akin to Niebuhr's own probing of these issues.
So what more could realists want? They would, I think, want to resist the
too rigid, typological method of Doyle. Reinhold Niebuhr scorned his
brother H. Richard Niebuhr's placement of him in the "Christ and culture
in paradox" motif in his definitive work *Christ and Culture*.[3] Similarly, I
would protest against the label and type of fundamentalism for Machiavelli
and Morgenthau in Doyle's work. A sympathetic reading of them will not
reduce their theories simply to attribute war to the defects of human
nature.[4] Machiavelli was very conscious both of the nature of the state and
of international anarchy. Morgenthau's pithy, bold writing, like
Machiavelli's, allows him to be misinterpreted as focusing primarily on the
psychological dimensions of the elite. But his theory is too rich to characterize it as only dependent on human nature. Doyle recognizes that
Machiavelli and Morgenthau also attribute war to defects in the state and
emphasize international anarchy. Such recognition is inadequate, however,
as Doyle had before him the model of Thucydides' own "complex realism."[5]
In an academic treatise, why label one of your most respected theorists a
"fundamentalist"? The term *fundamentalism* arises from a protest of very
conservative Presbyterians to the historical-critical method in scholarship
and against modernism. This is a very strange term for scholarship to apply

to a Renaissance thinker like Machiavelli, an American modernist and exiled Jew like Morgenthau, or a liberal, existentialist theologian like Tillich.

It would be foolish to deny the importance of religious anthropology to Tillich, Morgenthau, or Niebuhr. They all regarded their anthropology as important to their political philosophy. It is equally important for clarity to note other important sources of their thought. Unresolved tensions in their perspectives would incline one to think of Doyle's terms *complex realism* or *pluralist theory* instead of *fundamentalist-realist theory*.

Before returning to the center of this thesis, permit me to digress further into a critique of the typological structure of Doyle's argument. If realism is one type and socialism another, how are we to understand Reinhold Niebuhr, who first wrote in a realist vein "The Morality of Nations"[6] while a socialist? No one can deny Niebuhr's identification as a realist, but Norman Thomas also recognized "Niebuhr being considerably to the left of me" while Niebuhr served as vice president of the American Socialist Party. The realism itself continued into the 1950s when he and Arthur Schlessinger Jr. worked together to draft the foreign policy positions of the liberal lobbying group Americans for Democratic Action. Tillich's socialism was deeper and longer lasting than Niebuhr's, and only in the kairos circle of revolutionary Berlin did it have utopian themes, as the rest of his writing was characterized by his "faithful realism." At least in the complexity of the biblically based realism of two of our thinkers, the realist approach characterized both their socialism and their liberalism as these concepts were experienced in North American politics.

Morgenthau's five references to Machiavelli in *Politics among Nations*[7] include one that is affirmative of his insight, two that are negative, and two that are neutral. The chapter "Morality, Mores, and Law as Restraints of Power" stresses the reality of these restraints on power. It rejects the theories of Machiavelli and Hobbes and finds both biblical ethics and democratic constitutionalism restraining power drives. And it also affirms the greater potency of Locke and Augustine over the views of Machiavelli and Hobbes. In *Truth and Power*,[8] an appreciation of Machiavelli's warnings to the weak of the dangers of depending on the powerful is balanced by two rejections of Machiavelli's morality and one neutral comment. The volume contains some of Morgenthau's strongest affirmations of Hebrew and Christian images of "wise and good rulers" as well as transcendent moral values. The case for Morgenthau's similarity to Machiavelli is defeated by Morgenthau's own meager references to him and rejection of his project at several points. On the other hand, all of the references to Thucydides in Morgenthau are positive. In Doyle's view, Morgenthau belongs in the category of "complex realism," of which Thucydides is the major example. Tillich ignored Machiavelli. Niebuhr's references to the "notorious realist" both use the same quote about seeking the reality of politics. Elsewhere,

Niebuhr dismisses Machiavelli as a cynic. The texts of the philosophers Morgenthau, Tillich, and Niebuhr reveal their essential agreement, some mutual dependence, and fulsome praise of the others' thought.

In a tribute to Niebuhr, Morgenthau spoke of Niebuhr's contribution to political thought in five ideas, all of which were near the center of Morgenthau's own thought. He said, "I have always considered Reinhold Niebuhr the greatest living political philosopher of America, perhaps the only creative political philosopher since Calhoun."[9] Eduard Heimann, who responded critically to Morgenthau's tribute, said, "I much admire the speech we have just heard by a man who has come to an alliance with Reinhold Niebuhr without being his pupil. Here are two movements, two ideas, moving closer and closer together until there is a kind of identification."[10]

Niebuhr did not respond to Heimann's critique, saying only, "I am not certain that anything which I might do to amend or explain the *position which Morgenthau and I have in common* could quiet the criticism of my old friend Eduard Heimann."[11]

One of the more interesting conversations between Morgenthau and Niebuhr was in *War/Peace Report* in 1967. Here the two dialogued about morality and foreign policy, expressing their essential agreement. In response to the editors' attempt to propose a division between their thought, Niebuhr responded, "I wouldn't say that the views of Morgenthau and myself are 'somewhat different.' We basically have common ideas with certain peripheral differences."[12]

Tillich, at the same conference, indicated his general agreement with Niebuhr but criticized Niebuhr's critique of ontology. The following discussion suggested less distance between the two even here. So why denote them as prophetic realists?

Prophetic Realism

M. Benjamin Mollov's dissertation traces the documentation of the Jewish origins of some of Morgenthau's thought. He shows from Morgenthau's own writing his consciousness of himself as a persecuted Jew, as a Jewish refugee from Hitler, and as a supporter of Jewish causes, as well as his particular connections with the Lubavitch Hasidic community at the end of his life. Recognizing that Morgenthau did not have a prominent Jewish mentor in the study of politics, human nature, and international relations, Mollov's work credits Niebuhr as the source of Morgenthau's biblical, or what I call prophetic, realism. Mollov quotes Morgenthau from a lecture to students at the University of Chicago: "A theologian like Reinhold Niebuhr has made the greatest contemporary contribution to the understanding of basic political problems"—a *theologian* rather than a professor of political theory.[13] Mollov refers repeatedly to Morgenthau's advice to politicians as prophetic speaking of truth to power and finds Morgenthau himself identifying with Isaiah by "speaking in the wilderness."

Mollov's view of Morgenthau and Niebuhr as prophetic realists echoes Paul Tillich's use of the terms *spirit of Judaism* and *prophetism* in his 1933 book *The Socialist Decision*.[14] He could have used *prophetic realism* to describe the position that holds to the seriousness of divine judgment, the reality of moral principles, the contingency of history, the recognition of sin, the frequency of historical catastrophes, human opportunity for avoiding political destruction, newness in history, and hope for humanity in the face of political failure and social collapse. Tillich described his own position challenging Hitler directly in the name of religion as religious realism. No one should claim the title of prophet for oneself. But there is a recognizable position here and enough continuity with Isaiah, Jeremiah, and Amos (Niebuhr's favorite prophet) to recognize the two German refugees and Niebuhr, their German-American friend, as prophetic realists. Furthermore, the term *prophetic realism* is true of most of their whole careers, whereas the categories of Doyle of liberal or socialist theory are representative only of contingent aspects of their political thought. Jewish realism and Christian realism both grounded in the prophetic heritage are very similar. The thinkers are distinguished more by their prayers than by the philosophic structure of their thought about international politics. The recent appearance of one of Niebuhr's prayers in a prayer book of Reform Judaism nuances even this posited difference to a minor one.

Max Weber connects the term *prophet* in a sociological understanding with the rise of empires, the proclamation of moral judgment, the bearing of personal charisma, the sense of a meaningful world, and particularly with international politics. "Their [the prophets'] primary concern was with foreign politics, chiefly because it constituted the theater of their god's activity."[15] Later he wrote, "Hebrew prophecy was completely oriented to a relationship with the great political powers of the time, the great kings, who as the rods of God's wrath first destroy Israel and then, as a consequence of divine intervention, permit Israelites to return from the Exile to their own land."[16] While it may be Niebuhr and Tillich who most closely resemble the type, I would include Morgenthau of the Vietnam War years as well. Further development of this theme of prophetic realism as understood by Max Weber would have to deal with the study of Weber and the appreciation of him by both Niebuhr and Morgenthau.

Another break with Machiavelli of the prophetic realists is that while they contended for their views, they did not pursue political power for themselves. George Liska finds Morgenthau's antithesis in Machiavelli. Morgenthau's liberal values meant that as a commentator he could not degenerate into realpolitik. He was interested in speaking truth, not in fawning upon the prince for power. He knew the rulers would use power, and he explained its intricacies, but its pursuit was not good in itself. Without mentioning it, Liska captures the tension in the title of Morgenthau's book of 1960–1970 essays, *Truth and Power*, and understands his distrust of power. He writes, "The distrust of power, fraught with the tendency to repudiate it under stress, comes through in Morgenthau's Niebuhrian (and Augustinian?) identification of the drive for power with sinful lust—with man's fall from grace into depravity."[17]

So in commenting on his own lack of political ambition, Morgenthau said, "By no means am I sorry about this lack of political activity in my life. It has simply been a part of my whole personality to be theoretically interested in power but not personally so."[18]

Prophetic Realist Contribution

The contribution of the prophetic realists has been to try to make the politics among nations work better. These politics represent both struggle and cooperation, reflecting the tendency among humans toward egoism and the preference for their own families and tribes. The prophetic realists have not written simply descriptively; they have written to persuade. They have wanted to persuade an empire tempted by swings toward isolationism, imperialism, moralism, Manichaenism, and materialism to conduct its affairs diplomatically and persistently in a manner of broadly conceived national interest and national restraint. In my reading, Tillich, Morgenthau, and Niebuhr do not escape from trying to reform U.S. policy; they provide a perspective on that policy. The perspective is in terms of a philosophy of history and a philosophy of humanity that can be regarded as a biblical and Augustinian expression of liberal ideals under conditions of international conflict.

Prophetic realism tends to be rather eclectic in its use of the history of ideas. While some of Niebuhr's ideas can be traced to Augustine, Kant, Marx, and James, his synthesis is his own. Tillich criticized Niebuhr for his overly sharp "no's" to many philosophers. Tillich thought his own dialectic method appreciated the philosophic ideas in his own time better than did Niebuhr's comparative method. One can find elements of Aristotle, Kant, Nietzsche, Niebuhr, and others in Morgenthau's thought. But Morgenthau's fashioning of all of these elements into his own theory of international politics is, I think, a relatively unique contribution.

Niebuhr expressed in his journal his sense of Morgenthau's accomplishment in his first American-published book:

> The consequence of the element of contingency in the realm of history and of the relativity in the observers of history makes it impossible to reduce the stuff of history to pure rationality. For this reason

history will remain a realm of contending social forces, and these forces will embody power and use power. Dr. Morgenthau shows very clearly why it is vain to hope for the gradual elimination of the moral ambiguity of politics through historic development. He contends that every moral action is more ambiguous than the abstract analysis of a moral action and that a political action is doubly ambiguous, for it involves the power impulses of a group. The general thesis is one which is not unfamiliar to readers of this journal. The book should have a wider acclaim than it will probably get.[19]

When Morgenthau listed Niebuhr's contribution, he summarized it as the rediscovery of political man.[20] He meant that to a degree the political sphere is autonomous, that the lust for power characterizes human political history and human nature, that the lust for power and Christian morality are not reconcilable, that ideology distorts political understanding, and that political history is not scientifically reducible to patterns because of its contingencies. His tribute to Niebuhr reflects his own understanding as formulated in part 1 of *Politics among Nations.*[21]

Niebuhr, Morgenthau, and Tillich all actively and consistently supported the establishment and defense of Israel. All three urged clarity in U.S. purposes, defense of Europe, and adjustments in disputes with the Soviet Union. Niebuhr and Morgenthau along with John Bennett led the realist criticism of U.S. Vietnam policy under Johnson (Tillich died in 1965). Tillich and Niebuhr both condemned the atomic bombing of Japan and argued against defending Berlin with nuclear weapons in the 1960s. Tillich's call to resist reliance on nuclear weapons was more strident than Morgenthau and Niebuhr's more developed essays on the subject that urged restraint and diplomatic efforts to ensure their nonuse.

All three were critical of John Foster Dulles's moralism and legalism, stressing the dynamic shifts in an ever-changing world political scene. All three were critically supportive of the UN, with Morgenthau being the most critical while Niebuhr served as a delegate to UNESCO for a brief time before his 1952 stroke. Utopian plans for world government as well as universal peace proposals, whether religious or secular, were debunked at different times by all three.

Ontology of Love, Power, and Justice

The seizure of the German government by Adolph Hitler in 1933 forced our thinkers to live their lifetimes in a time of war. Unity and reconciliation of peoples would remain a hope, but disunity and war or potential war were the reality. Their times fit Hobbes's description as a state of war inasmuch as he said that a rainy season does not mean continual rain but only the inclination to rain. Their reading of biblical prophets inclined them to expect war and destruction, and their ontologies reinforced an inclination toward the expectation of conflict.

Langdon Gilkey's book *On Niebuhr* makes the case that it is Niebuhr's ontology upon which his realism rests. According to Gilkey, Niebuhr accepted the modern ontology "of radical temporality, of change of fundamental forms, of contingency, relativity, transience, and autonomy in the light of creation, sin, and grace, of creativity, anxiety, self-concern, and self-deception rescued by divine judgment and mercy."[22] While rejecting the modern myths of progress of liberalism or revolution of Communism, he viewed the world biblically, with a transcendent God related to the world in grace and judgment.[23] "Niebuhr's theology represents, therefore, a correlation, if ever there was one between a modern ontology and biblical symbols, a correlation in which each side reshapes the other—and makes possible a Christian existence within the precarious terms of modern life."[24]

Niebuhr did not use the terms *ontology* and *correlation* as Gilkey did in their Tillichian meaning, but Gilkey is persuasive in his Tillichian interpretation of Niebuhr. Gilkey gives Niebuhr credit for protecting the distance between God and humanity and the freedom of humanity,[25] pointing out that Tillich's ontology is less successful in expressing the transcendence of God. Even if we use ontology to describe Niebuhr's systematic insights, he remains less mystical and more ethical in the structure of his theology than does Tillich. Gilkey's study of Niebuhr is excellent in showing how much philosophy Niebuhr used, even if it was not the ontology of Tillich. Gilkey writes, "This is a theology of catastrophe, nemesis, and renewal in history, not one of progress."[26] To a large degree, Tillich shared this prophetic reading of history; but his ontology (the desire to understand being overcoming estrangement) led him to stress the beneficial as well as the negative side of the concept of utopia and to see positive possibilities in the dialectics of history (the karios) that were greater than those seen by Niebuhr.

Likewise, Tillich's understanding of love as the drive for reunion contrasts with Niebuhr's understanding of love as a duty to seek the other's good. So in Niebuhr, justice as a form that allows for the reunion of being contrasts with justice as rules by which the good of people in society are protected. Niebuhr has a vision of the whole, but the dialectics of yes and no are stressed more than in Tillich's ontology, which pushes toward unity. Just as one is inclined to give Niebuhr the nod of approval for political discourse and confine Tillich's *Love, Power and Justice* to the philosophy classroom, however, Hans Morgenthau is seen referring to Tillich's ontology.

Morgenthau's essay "Love and Power" quotes Tillich, but he does not stay with Tillich. He notes that Tillich needs the term *justice* in his reconciliation of power and love. But Morgenthau does not want the reconciliation. Power is for Morgenthau the psychological relationship by which one imposes one's will on another. He writes, "Love is reunion through spontaneous mutuality, power seeks to create a union through unilateral imposition."[27] For Morgenthau, both love and power arise from the ultimate loneliness of the human being, who needs community. The imperial political leaders he discusses in his essay wanted love but despaired of achieving it and pursued the never-ending quest for power. Morgenthau's pessimism about what can be achieved in politics flows naturally from his Jewish background and Old Testament international politics, but it is reinforced by his rather bleak ontology. We come into the world needing others, but when these relations do not develop well, we seek power. But the quest for power is rather futile, and finally, at least in Morgenthau's 1962 essay, we die alone after peopling the heavens and the next world with imaginary companions to provide love. In the same time period, Morgenthau wrote about the fear of nuclear war denying meaning to death and about President Kennedy's inevitable need to make choices out of ignorance that very likely would have tragic outcomes. His 1962 essay in *Commentary* is extraordinarily bleak for Morgenthau, but this note of tragedy regarding the international political situation is a perpetual theme in his ontology. Like Niebuhr, he rejects the optimism of both Communism and liberalism; but his own accommodationist foreign policy is more pessimistic than Niebuhr's or Tillich's.

From conversations with both James Muilenberg and Reinhold Niebuhr, I have always thought that both of them felt Paul Tillich's book *Biblical Religion and Ultimate Reality* was directed at their respective methodologies. Reinhold Niebuhr made the difference between his and Tillich's ontology quite clear in his review of the book. Niebuhr thought that if ontology was considered as "everything that concerns being," there would not be any inevitable conflict between philosophy and the biblical ways of thinking about God. He worried that if ontology was too narrowly pursued as a "science of being," it might be overly rational in its exclusion of symbols or poetic thinking and thereby reduce the "transcendence" of both the divine and the human.[28] For Niebuhr, the drama of human life has elements of both meaning and meaningfulness, and religion ought not try to subsume the whole drama to an ontological system of meaning. He wanted to rely more on glimpses of love in human relations and the symbol of the cross than on a completely rational system. The differences between Niebuhr and Tillich were clearer after World War II in the late 1950s and 60s when Tillich reduced his political writing and began to explicate his system. Niebuhr, after the war, wrote less systematically in theology but published more on international politics (see *The Structure of Nations and Empires* [1959] and *The Democratic Experience* [1969]). Roger Shinn has recorded that this divergence was at first clearer to students who were listening to and reading the early drafts of Tillich's system than it was to Niebuhr who had not read the drafts.

Niebuhr's thought on the relationship between love and power is not ontological even if Gilkey is correct that his biblical faith conceptions imply an ontology. Love is the gracious love of God, or agape, and human expressions of it are approximations of agape; but under the conditions of sin, love is the obligation to treat the neighbor as the self or to take care of the neighbor's real needs. It is not a sharp dualism, but it is love under conditions of the divine and under conditions of human sin. Life is a struggle that under sin often takes the form of struggles over power, which is most often understood as control over others. But Niebuhr does not carefully define power. It seems to me that his use of the word *power* is understandable in the different contexts in which he uses it. In economics and politics, it inevitably is exercised within sin, and the most just resolutions of conflicts occur when power, as the capacity to influence, is roughly equally balanced among contending parties.

The Concept of Power

Three attitudes toward the concept of power appear in Niebuhr's political philosophy. Power is, in one sense, morally neutral. It is simply the vitality of human life and is almost synonymous with energy. In this sense Niebuhr uses the term *balance of power* to mean the state of equilibrium that permits the vitalities of social forces to be expressed without annulling any one of the forces.[29] Niebuhr's second attitude toward power regards it as an outgrowth of human pride and the false attempt to gain security by dominating others.[30] This use of *power* equates it with the capacity to impose one's will upon others[31] and has led Niebuhr frequently to equate power with force. The third major use of the term *power* is to treat it as a necessary expression of social organization and cohesion.[32] Given human nature, an organizing power is needed to prevent social chaos. In this sense *power* has a more positive moral connotation than in the first two uses. Depending on the particular context, Niebuhr may regard power as morally neutral, negative, or positive.

Not only its moral connotations but also the meaning of power varies in Niebuhr's writing with the context. The importance of the term *power* to his political thought, however, requires that the central meaning of the term be understood. Niebuhr characteristically states that "the contest of power . . . is the heart of political life."[33] In this sense, which is fundamental to Niebuhr's political thought, power seems to be the capacity to realize one's purposes, either through authority or force. The struggle, which characterizes politics, is for control of the institutions and forces that permit one to realize one's goals. It is not always clear in Niebuhr's writing that his definition of power includes the goal factor; often he appears to be thinking only of the control of the institutions or the forces. But the goal factor, a necessary ingredient for an adequate definition of power, is presupposed in Niebuhr's thought by his doctrine of man, which insists that every political self has certain interests that he or she is attempting to maximize.

All communities are, in Niebuhr's thought, representative of a balance of power. That is, humankind covertly lives in a state of anarchy, with each individual pursuing his or her own interests and trying to achieve a security that he or she cannot attain.[34] Social peace or the order of any community represents an achievement of order, though the peace is never final. The peace achieved is not "the peace of God" but a mere armistice.[35] The armistice is based on the balance of power; that is, some adjustment and accommodation of interest have been agreed upon by the major contending forces. The adjustment made is dependent on the relative power of the contending groups. All such adjustments are regarded as tentative, and "the principle of the balance of power is always pregnant with the possibility of anarchy."[36]

Though the balance of power does not play as significant a role in Niebuhr's thought about American foreign policy as it does in the thought of Morgenthau,[37] its role is very significant. The balance of power in the domestic sphere represents the achievement of order, which is enforced by the authority and force of the dominant group. In the international sphere, the balance of power represents an accommodation of interests of nations relative to their power that is sufficient to prevent major wars. The international sphere lacks the organization that can coerce submission and require that the interests of the system be protected. The maintenance of a tolerable degree of order in international relations therefore devolves upon the major countries. They must exercise their responsibilities for the order of the world while attempting to refrain from excessively exploiting their advantaged position.

During World War II, Niebuhr's writing on the reconstruction of the postwar world emphasized the relationship between America's responsible assumption of a position of power and the need to overcome anarchy. He declared, "The world must find a way of avoiding complete anarchy in its international life; and America must find a way of using its great power responsibly. These two needs are organically related; for the world problem cannot be solved if America does not accept its full share of responsibility in solving it."[38]

The old balance of power had been destroyed by the two world wars; the choice now was between a new balance or continued anarchy. Throughout the war Niebuhr pleaded with his reading public to accept the responsibilities that the United States' new role gave her.[39] He recognized that assuming the task of shaping a new world order would expose the country to the charge of imperialism. He counseled against both isolationism and imperialism in the postwar period, but he insisted that a new balance of power required active U.S. involvement.[40] Even while counseling the United States to accept its role as a world power, Niebuhr saw the dangers of pride. "It is intolerable to imagine an America so powerful that we are held responsible for vast historical events in every part of the globe beyond our knowledge or contriving. Nothing is more dangerous to a powerful nation than the temptation to obscure the limits of its power."[41]

In the postwar world, Niebuhr saw a bipolar balance develop that was secured by the balance of nuclear terror. His primary focus in international politics was the way this balance was influenced by events. The balance differed from previous balances in three respects: it was worldwide, it was bipolar, and it was enforced by nuclear terror. The responsibilities of the United States left it no retreat from maintaining this new type of balance; the security of the United States depended on its maintenance, but there was no final assurance that this new balance of power was stable.

Hans Morgenthau's magnum opus, *Politics among Nations: The Struggle for Power and Peace*, brings the struggle for power into the subtitle, and the theme of power continues throughout the analysis of international politics. The struggle for power, or the capacity to dominate another's mind and actions, is rooted in human nature for Morgenthau, and it is inevitable. Not all relations among nations are political, but when they are political in Morgenthau's sense, they involve power as "man's control over the minds and actions of other men."[42] Power derives from expectation of benefits, fear, and love or respect. Power is different from force, and there are distinctions between "usable and unusable power" and "legitimate and illegitimate power."[43] Much of the rest of Morgenthau's book analyzes various uses of power and strategies of balancing power and the quest for peace. The inevitability of power struggles inclines Morgenthau to dismiss plans or schemes for peace that presuppose ending the power struggle and to lean toward accommodationist and diplomatic maintenance of the balancing of power. Morgenthau's study is a profound philosophy of international politics for the guidance of U.S. foreign policy. Calling it an ontology would be a stretch, though it has some ontological tendencies that remain undeveloped. The role of God in the book seems to be restricted to that of "the judgment of God, inscrutable to the human mind."[44] The conviction that the will of God "is always on one's side"[45] of the conflict he regards as blasphemous. The hidden ontology is that of God as judge and humanity as practicing the sin of the struggle for power. The morality of Morgenthau remains mainly a critique of that which he finds inevitable. Such a morality can be regarded as a prophetic morality, especially if the hopeful conclusions to most of the prophetic books of the Bible are dismissed as editorial additions. Still, if ontology is seen in a broad sense, Morgenthau's politics might be said to have an ontological pattern. Theologian Adrian Thatcher writes, "Metaphysics does construct patterns according to which we see ourselves and our world in a particular light, but it does so in the knowledge that there is an ontological reality which gives itself to the pattern and upon which even the pattern itself depends."[46]

Of the three realists, the one with the most developed ontology was Tillich, who foresaw, even in 1954, the emergence of *one* superpower "through liberal methods and democratic forms."[47] He could not foresee a world state, for that required a spiritual unity, which the world lacked. Possibly continental federations would emerge, but he seemed less hopeful of these in 1954 than he had been during World War II. He was cautious, but in his ontology of love, power, and justice, he was driven toward "the rise of one power structure"[48]; after its dominance perhaps, that power's ways could become universal. But even then power struggles, disintegration, and revolution could tear apart the synthesis. To the question, can humankind never become as a whole a structure of power and a source of universal justice? he was forced to say the analysis leaves history and flies to the relationship of love, power, and justice to the ultimate.[49]

Perhaps after the rise of a dominant power: "the law and the justice and the uniting love which are embodied in this power will become the universal power of mankind."[50] Such a unity would call for resistance, though, and would not be permanent. Tillich's other writings on the world situation[51] were more pessimistic, because after World War II he had seen the democratic market economy emerging from the Leviathan of modern capitalism, which had to be resisted. Capitalism represented the controlling, technological will of the bourgeoisie that disrupted community, trivialized religion, and dominated the churches. Tillich was wiser than Morgenthau in these postwar writings, as he refused, unlike Morgenthau, to disentangle economics from politics. His actual political influence decreased with the breakup of the Council for a Democratic Germany, while Morgenthau's noneconomic politics increased and Niebuhr's mixed-economy political ethics gained favor. Niebuhr and Morgenthau kept giving advice to political leaders who would listen, while Tillich wrote more for the religious, cultural, and psychological leaders who would listen. The division of his homeland Germany into East and West was a shocking blow to him and he could not say much about practical politics beyond that, though he could make it clear that temporary retreat was better than first use of nuclear weapons to defend either Berlin or West Germany. His last political essay, "On 'Peace on Earth'" grounded in the prophetic tradition of Scripture and in the love and justice imperatives of Protestantism, criticized the exclusiveness and utopianism of the papal encyclical *Pacem in Terris*. Tillich, as he affirms realism twice in the essay, hopes for "partial victories over the forces of evil in a particular moment of time."[52]

Probably in the end, it is the prophetic tradition that unites the three realists at the deepest level despite the possibility of recognizing ontology in Niebuhr and even in Morgenthau. In Tillich's most passionate political writing,[53] he does not mention ontology or rush to generalize and unify. In his speeches against the Third Reich (1942–1944),[54] he identifies with the prophets of disaster. He discusses Jeremiah extensively and views the anti-nationalism of Judaism as prophetic. The necessity to speak truth and judgment rings throughout the speeches. At the end, he promises hope to Germany but only on the other side of defeat. Germany's punishment at the hand of the Allied Forces is seen as God's judgment, and the nation's hope is in the rediscovery of its Christian-Judaic-humanistic sources.

Notes

1. See Robert K. Garcia, "Apologizing to the Postmodernist," *Journal of Interdisciplinary Struggle*, 22, no. 2 (2000): 1–19.
2. Michael W. Doyle, *Ways of War and Peace* (New York: W. W. Norton, 1997).
3. H. Richard Niebuhr, *Christ and Culture* (New York: Harper & Brothers, 1951), 183.
4. Kenneth N. Waltz, *Man, the State, and War: A Theoretical Analysis* (New York: Columbia University Press, 1954), 16–41.
5. Doyle, *Ways of War and Peace*, 49–92.
6. Reinhold Niebuhr, *Moral Man and Immoral Society* (New York: Charles Scribner's Sons, 1932), 83–112.
7. Hans J. Morgenthau, *Politics among Nations: The Struggle for Power and Peace* (New York: Alfred A. Knopf, 1967).
8. Hans J. Morgenthau, *Truth and Power* (London: Pall Mall Press, 1970).
9. Hans J. Morgenthau, "The Influence of Reinhold Niebuhr in American Political Life and Thought," in Harold R. Landon, ed., *Reinhold Niebuhr: A Prophetic Voice in Our Time* (Greenwich: Seabury Press, 1962), 109.
10. Eduard Heimann, quoted in ibid., 111–12.
11. Reinhold Niebuhr, quoted in ibid., 122, emphasis mine.
12. "The Ethics of War and Peace in the Nuclear Age," *War/Peace Report* 7 (February 1967): 3.
13. M. Benjamin Mollov, *The Jewish Aspect of the Life and Work of Hans J. Morgenthau* (unpublished dissertation, Bar-Ilan University, 1995), 103.
14. Paul Tillich, *The Socialist Decision* (New York: Harper & Row, 1977), 20–26.
15. Max Weber, *The Sociology of Religion* (Boston: Beacon Press, 1963), 51.
16. Ibid., 58.
17. George Liska, "Morgenthau vs. Machiavelli," in Kenneth Thompson and Robert J. Myers, eds., *Truth and Tragedy* (New Brunswick: Transaction Books, 1977).
18. Hans Morgenthau, quoted in "Bernard Johnson's Interview with Hans J. Morgenthau," in Thompson and Myers, *Truth and Tragedy*, 386.
19. Reinhold Niebuhr, "Hans J. Morgenthau, Scientific Man versus Power Politics," in Charles C. Brown, ed., *A Reinhold Niebuhr Reader* (Philadelphia: Trinity Press International, 1992), 147.
20. Hans Morgenthau, quoted in Landon, *Reinhold Niebuhr*, 99–104.
21. Morgenthau, *Politics*, 3–22.
22. Langdon Gilkey, *On Niebuhr* (Chicago: University of Chicago Press, 2001), 248.
23. Ibid.

24. Ibid.

25. Ibid., 20.

26. Ibid., 22.

27. Hans J. Morgenthau, "Love and Power," *Commentary*, March 1962, 248.

28. Reinhold Niebuhr, "Review of Paul Tillich, *Biblical Religion and the Search for Ultimate Reality*" in Brown, *Reinhold Niebuhr Reader*, 157.

29. Reinhold Niebuhr, *Nature and Destiny of Man* (vol. 2; New York: Charles Scribner's Sons, 1943), 257–58, 265. The text from footnotes 29–41 is an edited version of Ronald H. Stone, *Reinhold Niebuhr: Prophet to Politician* (Nashville: Abingdon, 1972), 178–80.

30. Reinhold Niebuhr, *Nature and Destiny of Man* (vol. 1; New York: Charles Scribner's Sons, 1941), 192.

31. Niebuhr, *Nature*, vol. 2, 258.

32. For example, Reinhold Niebuhr, *Christianity and Power Politics* (New York: Charles Scribner's Sons, 1940), 123.

33. Reinhold Niebuhr, "Leaves from the Notebook of a War-Bound American," *The Christian Century* 56 (November 15, 1939): 1405.

34. Niebuhr, *Moral Man*, 19.

35. Reinhold Niebuhr, *Discerning the Signs of the Times* (New York: Charles Scribner's Sons, 1946), 187.

36. Niebuhr, *Nature*, vol. 2, 258.

37. Cf. Morgenthau, *Politics among Nations*, 161–218.

38. Reinhold Niebuhr, "American Power and World Responsibility," *Christianity and Crisis* 3 (April 5, 1943): 2.

39. Reinhold Niebuhr, "Power and Justice," *Christianity and Society* 8 (Winter 1942): 10.

40. Ibid.

41. Reinhold Niebuhr, "The Limits of American Power," *Christianity and Society* 18 (Autumn 1952): 5.

42. Hans J. Morgenthau, *Politics among Nations*, Brief Edition (Boston: McGraw Hill, 1985), 30.

43. Ibid., 31.

44. Ibid., 15.

45. Ibid., 13.

46. Adrian Thatcher, *The Ontology of Paul Tillich* (Oxford: Oxford University Press, 1978), 176.

47. Paul Tillich, *Love, Power, and Justice* (New York: Oxford University Press, 1954), 105.

48. Ibid., 106.

49. Ibid.

50. Ibid.

51. Paul Tillich, *Theology of Peace* (ed. Ronald H. Stone; Louisville: Westminster John Knox Press, 1990), 150–51.

52. Ibid., 181.

53. Paul Tillich, *Against the Third Reich* (Louisville: Westminster John Knox Press, 1999).

54. Ibid.

6

On Power and Purpose

THE REALISTS RELATED THEIR USE of the concept of power to the tasks at hand for their national communities.[1] They understood that liberal democracies had not used power to prevent Nazism's rise. Power had to be used against Hitler, fascists in Italy, and Japan in World War II. Their post–World War II years were filled with the use of power against the Communism of the Soviet Union. They regretted the misuse and squandering of American power in Vietnam while advocating the use of American power to support Israel. All of them resisted the overextension of U.S. power or its translation into simple terms of military force. That is to say, the meaning of central political terms within prophetic realism is influenced by their context and that context related to the securing of Europe, America, and Israel. Our contemporary explanation of prophetic realism requires an understanding of power as a hegemonic superpower.

The relationship of power and purpose is a perennial question in social ethics. Each thinker has to reformulate it for the current period and purpose. This attempt builds on the classical realists but moves to join the two more closely than Morgenthau and Niebuhr were able to relate them. Tillich's ontology unifies the terms too much for our broken historical existence.

Just as Machiavelli did in his treatise *The Prince*, the advocates of realpolitik divide purpose and power. "Neo-Machiavellians" have continued the tradition as represented in the policies and language of Richard Nixon and Henry Kissinger, in some of the advice of the Reverend Billy Graham to President Nixon, and in neoconservative power politics. These exaggerations of the gap between moral purpose and power lead to the assertion that a new understanding of the relationship of purpose to power is needed. The popular disjunction that leads American citizens to question whether there is any connection between politics and ethics must be overcome.

The Ambiguity of Politics

There is an essential moral ambiguity, though at different levels, to both domestic politics and international politics. The society requires peace, order, and justice; but the society also requires the fulfillment of the vitalities of its respective parts. The state is simultaneously the desired prize of the various parties of the society and the instrument that preserves order and justice. The Utopians have seen the peacekeeping function of the state and have neglected the vitalities of parties of the society. The Machiavellians have pointed to the struggle for control of the state in preserving order and justice. The Utopians either lose sight of the vitalities of life or dream of mastering them through a legal system. The Machiavellians, often in reaction to the illusions of the Utopians, see nothing but the struggle and the prize of the state and regard law and ethics as ideological illusions justifying and reinforcing the position of those temporarily in power.

Sir Thomas More and Machiavelli may be regarded as symbols of two different views of the state. The one regards the state as the agent of justice. The other regards justice as irrelevant and views the state as the prize to the victor. What divides them is the dualistic character of politics. An adequate solution to the problem of the relationship of purpose and power must take into account this dualism and recognize that, though More and Machiavelli are powerful symbols of political life, they each basically represent only one side of it. It is necessary to grasp that throughout history those who control the instruments of deciding and implementing justice exact disproportionate rewards for their distribution of justice. However, such a view, whether based on an Augustinian view of man or on generalizations from empirical observations, does not necessarily drive one to the conclusion that justice is totally fraudulent or should be dispensed with lightly. The modern welfare state reveals this moral ambiguity well. The state is responsible for the fulfillment of a broad range of programs to promote the well-being of the population; however, the competition for the control of the state is conducted with very little regard for the welfare of the people.

If the modern Machiavellians have not fully appreciated the dualistic character of political life, neither have they understood ethics sufficiently. One source of the origin of the contemporary political realist movement was a protest against certain tendencies of liberal Christianity. To reform the ethic of liberal Christianity, the realists found it necessary to show that the teachings of Jesus were not directly relevant to the reform of the industrial-military complex. The distinctive feature of realism was its propensity to emphasize the factors in humanity's collective life that resisted moral solutions or pressures. Such a corrective was needed; liberal American Christianity had been naive about the relevance of Jesus' ethic to politics. In the case of some spokespersons of the realist camp, however, the polemics against the too-easy moralization of politics developed into the separation of moral considerations from the struggle for power. The attempt to correct heresy in the liberal camp became heresy itself by overemphasizing its essentially correct insight that humanity's social life resists moralization.

Ethics is the critical inquiry into moral principles and the quest for wisdom concerning the good life. Ethics, then, includes the search for wisdom, temperance, justice, and courage as well as faith, hope, and love. It inevitably involves considerations of people as social animals. Strictly speaking, there is no such thing as a purely personal ethic, and realist attempts to divorce personal ethics from social ethics have been unsuccessful. They could not be successful, because personhood inevitably involves one as a social animal and, except in a mythical realm of nature, as a political animal.

Power Reconsidered

The concept of power has played a central role in recent writings on political theory. It has been the pivotal concept in realist writings. Hans Morgenthau's book *Politics among Nations* bears the subtitle *The Struggle for Power and Peace*, and most commentators see that volume focusing on the struggle for power. Inis L. Claude's work *Power and International Relations* found Morgenthau's discussion inadequate but still regarded the concept as the key to understanding international politics. Raymond Aron, who wrote in a different political environment and different sociological theoretical tradition, shared the above theorists' fascination with the inquiry into the meaning and analysis of power.

Claude devotes almost ninety pages to demonstrating that Morgenthau and others use the term *power* equivocally. Probably Morgenthau's use of the word can be deciphered in each particular context, but the furor over Morgenthau's understanding of the concept points to a real problem. Morgenthau risked lack of clarity in his concept of power by deliberately using it very broadly. He argued, "The value of any concept used in political science is determined by its ability to explain a maximum of the phenomena that are conventionally considered to belong to a certain sphere of political activity."[2] His criterion of breadth produced ambiguity. His further elaboration, "By political power we refer to the mutual relations of control among the holders of public authority and between the latter and the people at large,"[3] left the term too general for the purposes for which he wanted to use it. It also implied something that Morgenthau himself would deny, that those "mutual relations of control" are measurable without calculation of the goals, situation, and peculiar features of the actors involved.

Niebuhr's use of the term *power* varies from essay to essay and alternatively takes on three major meanings analyzed in the preceding chapter. Because of his three uses of *power*, with neutral, negative, and positive value connotations, Niebuhr's intentions are sometimes obscured.

In the most general sense, power means the capacity to do, to make, or to destroy. It is the self-realizing capacity of all that is. Paul Tillich, who has demonstrated the greatest aptitude for articulating the abstract, defines power as being overcoming nonbeing. He writes, "Power is the possibility of self-affirmation in spite of internal and external negation."[4] This definition is particularly apt when the power of a nation that is threatened from both within and without is under consideration. An understanding of power in international relations ought not to stray too far from this general understanding of the concept.

Theories of international relations often list the elements of national power even when the theorists are not clear about the meaning of power itself. Hans Morgenthau lists (1) geography, (2) natural resources, (3) industrial capacity, (4) state of military preparedness, (5) population, (6) national character, (7) morale, and (8) diplomatic skills. N. J. Spykman focuses on (1) surface of the territory, (2) nature of the frontiers, (3) population size, (4) raw materials, (5) economic and technological developments, (6) financial system, (7) ethnic homogeneity, (8) degree of social integration, (9) political stability, and (10) national morale. Guido Fischer listed essentially the same factors under the headings of political factors, psychological factors, and economic factors.[5] These and other lists resemble one another, but in themselves they do not provide adequate theory; they only point to factors to keep in mind when estimating a nation's power.

The enumeration of such factors is useful and causes problems only if it is taken too seriously. Such lists do not provide relative weights to the various factors, nor do they show how the weight of each factor varies from situation to situation. The listing of such factors is a disservice only if statespeople mistake such lists for science. F. C. German's essay "A Tentative Evaluation of World Power,"[6] which actually assigns numerical values to various factors, including area, population, gross product, military personnel, strategic air power, and planned economy, represents the absurdity of thinking that power can be measured abstractly without reference to goals or situations. His results were not too surprising; perhaps his ranking of countries according to their power represented the reigning common judgment of American political scientists. North Vietnam did not even make the list of almost twenty "powerful" countries. The problem of such thinking is that it does not adequately protect the insight that politics depends on contingency and passion. Clausewitz, who in many ways was very realistic, knew that chance is a major factor in war. Barbara Tuchmann's history of the beginning of World War I, *The Guns of August*, is a powerful antidote to the illusion that international politics can be rationalized or even that the movement of armies can be planned accurately in war.

The approximate calculation of a nation's capacity to make war in certain prescribed ways, if many variables are assumed to be known, is possible. In our present world, when the ways of war—ethnic, nuclear, terroristic, or guerilla—are unknown even to the best strategists, great humility about the calculation of power is in order. Probably the attempt to compute power, except with a full consideration of particular situations, should be abandoned and our rhetoric changed to account for the new realities.

The quest for an understanding of ethics and politics that will respect the dualistic nature of politics while avoiding the errors of Utopianism or Machiavellianism requires a reconsideration of power. Can power be conceived in relationship to purpose? Can it be conceptualized in any other way? Vietnam provided the primary example of the difficulty of speaking of power in static terms. If military force was power, the United States had overwhelming power in Vietnam but could not realize its purposes. Was it helpful to speak of the United States as a "superpower" and Vietnam as a "power vacuum" if the United States could not prevent its allies from engaging in religious persecution or even guarantee the freedom of its own press there? By all of the conventional indices of power—population, military machine, morale, efficient organization, economic base, and so on— the United States is a very powerful nation. However, many reports from Vietnam indicated that the United States was powerless to persuade it allies to reform, its enemies to surrender, or the population to adopt its cause. The conventional use of the term *power* to mean a static entity belonging to a nation forces a paradoxical description of the United States as both powerful and powerless. Paradoxical language is sometimes justified, but in this case it reflected confusion in the use of the concept of power.

The confusion that inevitably results from defining power in such static terms as force, money, position in hierarchy, and so on is eliminated by conceiving of power in relational and purposive terms. A definition of power that eliminates the confusion of the static approaches and also reconciles power with purpose is the following: power is the capacity to produce intended effects (purposes) in relation to others (field of action) under certain conditions (context or understanding of the context).[7] The power of an actor depends on goals, the domain in which his action is intended, and the context in which his action is to be executed, as well as on his ability to draw on the sources of power—be they geographic, military, organizational, traditional, economic, or ideological. Applying this understanding to Vietnam, one can see that the United States had power to fulfill certain purposes but lacked the power to fulfill others. It follows that delineating the purposes of policy was a prerequisite of any estimate of U.S. power in Vietnam. It also follows that the debate about U.S. objectives in Vietnam was more relevant to a Vietnam solution than controversies about the stopping of the bombing, the timing of negotiations, or the legitimization of the military junta that governed Saigon. The emphasis on purpose in an understanding of power indicates the relevance of moral considerations to power politics, for one who would deny that the selection of goals is free from moral considerations and ethical reflection has misunderstood the meaning of ethics.

Recently the capacity of terrorists to strike New York City and Washington has raised questions about power. Is the United States powerless to defend itself? No, a relatively adequate defense is possible if the United States values it. The terrorist power seems confined to spreading fear and is inadequate to force U.S. disengagement from the Middle East. The limitations on U.S. will in the Middle East reveal that the United States should not be regarded as a worldwide empire but rather as a hegemonic superpower that must engage in diplomacy to advance its interests. The purposes of the U.S. invasion of Iraq are still a matter of debate and traditional military power is frustrated by guerilla warfare resistance.

Christian Purpose and Power

The mainstream of Christian thought has consistently held that political power comes from God. Government as an order is instituted by God through sinful humanity to act as a limit on their sinfulness and as a source of order and justice for their lives. Love and power are regarded as ultimately united in God and eschatologically united in the fulfillment of history in the Kingdom of God. Within the broad confines of the tenets of Christian attitude toward political power, there have been endless variations on the relationship of political power to Christian purpose. Five motifs on the relationship of purpose and power stand out in bold relief from the maze of intricacies characterizing the Christian purpose. These five motifs do not represent a typology of Christian response to power, for the word *types* implies mutually exclusive systems. *Motifs* suggests distinguishable characteristics that can be used complementarily.[8]

The first motif is that of the opposition of Christian purpose and political power. Christian purposes are defined in terms of radical love and hope for renewed life. Political power is suspect because it is connected with a dying, passing world. Christians live fundamentally apolitical lives, because the Kingdom of God is not of this world. Whenever the kingdoms of this world are judged by the standards of Christianity, they are found to be profoundly lacking in harmony, justice, and charity. Tertullian exposed the contradictions between the Christian purpose and political power by emphasizing the degree to which political power depends on military force. Christian purpose is antithetical to political power, and the use of military force is rejected, because Jesus had, "in disarming Peter, unbelted every soldier." The motif of the opposition of Christian purpose and political power was predominant in the young church, and it is reawakened in each age of Western history when some theologian or sect takes with utmost seriousness the radicalness of the love ethic and emphasizes the brutal nature of political power.

At the opposite pole is the motif that harmonizes Christian purpose and political power. This harmonizing is characterized by the selection of certain movements in political life as representative of Christian purpose. It may be expressed in very traditional states; for example, the divine-right-of-kings doctrine as it was elaborated for the rise of the absolute nation-states harmonized the requirements of Christ and the need to legitimize a relatively stable but parochial manner of assuring succession to the seat of government. On the other hand, when Christian revolutionaries proclaim Christ as a revolutionary, they represent the harmonizing of Christian purpose and one type of power. The harmonizing of Christian purpose and power in traditional, liberal, or radical ideologies has the advantage of releasing the energy of absolute devotion for what are considered valid political causes, but it has the disadvantage of encouraging moral fanaticism in politics.

The previously considered motifs represent extremes within the church's thought on the relationship of power and purpose. H. Richard Niebuhr has delineated three middle positions in his typology of Christian ethics: the *synthesists*, the *dualists*, and the *conversionists*. Transposing his categories to the discussion of the relationship of purpose and power allows them to be expressed as purpose regulating power, purpose and power understood dialectically, and purpose transforming power.

The ideal of Christian purposes regulating the institutional life of humanity in a direct fashion was expressed by Thomas Aquinas at the end of a period in which the church was gradually winning control over a Europe recovering from the destruction of the Roman Empire. In theory, Christian ideals were supreme, and in fact the church was supreme in many instances. The church accepted responsibility for all of society. The church accepted the wisdom and institutions of the world while regarding its own wisdom and institution as higher. It attempted to Christianize the culture it accepted without identifying itself completely with that culture. In terms of power politics, when the church was consistent with this motif, it insisted that public policy serve its purposes.

Augustine provided a dualistic answer to the question of the relationship of purpose and power. He saw the world as characterized by two communities. Both communities seek peace, which, when fully understood, includes justice. Both communities are subject to God's purposes and derived from God's power. In this world the two are intermingled. God's purposes and power for the two cities differ. The city of earth, founded in the love of self, is given power to limit chaos and to preserve, through coercion, a type of peace. The city of God, founded in the love of God, gives people the peace of God, including salvation and true justice. Christians are citizens of the city of God and sojourners in the city of earth, and they are enjoined not to love the passing things of the city of earth. Christians may work through politics, but when they do, they must use the means of power, even though these means are in themselves corrupt. Augustine's writing includes several of the suggested motifs of purpose and power, but its most representative view is that of the state having both purpose and power from God but in a different manner from the way the church has purpose and power.

The motif of Christian purpose transforming political power was predominant in the moderates of the social gospel movement. To the degree that Walter Rauschenbusch maintained that the Kingdom of God is not to be realized by people and that structural change is required to complete salvation, he represented this motif. The moderates of the social gospel advocated a mild form of socialism while judging all means to achieve socialism against Christian principles of morality. They hoped for an immanent renewal of society through the political process. The democratic process was at hand, and they hoped to realize Christian ends by working through the process. It was fundamentally a reform movement; many of its advocates, particularly Rauschenbusch, recognized the degree to which human selfishness was stifling the fulfillment of Christian life. Social gospelers disagreed regarding how much reform was necessary for the regeneration of the social order, but they agreed that their faith was relevant to the use of power to rebuild American society.

There is wisdom in Christian ethical scholarship refusing to exclude polemically any of the major motifs of Christian ethics from consideration.[9] Each of the five motifs discussed has strengths and, in certain contexts, definite weaknesses. The relationship of Christian purpose and political power cannot be decided abstractly but depends to a significant extent on the form of the institutionalization of the political process as well as on the shape of the purpose. Christians who exclude from consideration any of the above motifs cut themselves off from a possible source of Christian wisdom. Relating the best combination of the above motifs to particular political situations depends on the habit of prudence.

Though the question considered here cannot be solved for all time, a contemporary resolution of the relationship between Christian purpose and political power is required. Within the pluralistic societies of the West, where Christians are free to advance their purposes through the political process, the most appropriate motif is that of purpose transforming power, corrected by the emphasis on the dialectic nature of the relationship of purpose and power. This motif, which has evolved on democratic ground, needs to be modified by an Augustinian realism about the frustrations of political life. It is also the motif that is consistent with an understanding of power as the fulfillment of particular purposes in relationship to other selves under specific circumstances.

Therefore, the purposes of the United States to promote democracy, human rights, and economic prosperity are only ambiguously pursued and limited in achievement. Too many forces within and without the United States resist the above values for them to be fulfilled. The international world does not even permit the United States, which favors the promotion of democracy, to do so consistently. Sometimes the enemies of our enemies are not democratic, but we must hold to them provisionally in alliance to thwart the purposes of our more threatening enemies. U.S. foreign policy over two centuries has been successful in general terms but far from pure.

National Purpose and Foreign Policy

Christian purposes are not the same as the purposes of a nation-state, though considerable overlap may exist. The argument of the preceding pages assumed that in some sense purpose or the definition of goals would be an ingredient of power. Christian goals focus on the liberation of people to develop to their fullest capacity as worshipers of God and responsible participants in society. National purposes are used by Christians to influence international processes so that humanity is liberated to develop fully. Probably nations should remain vague about their ultimate allegiances while permitting and encouraging citizens to seek adequate definitions of their ultimate loyalties. While nations do not need to include the proper worship of God in their understanding of purpose, citizens inevitably must define their ultimate convictions in religious or pseudo-religious terms.

Nations must continually seek to understand their purposes in the light of shifting circumstances and the conscious development of their peoples. The purposes of the nation will condition, to a large degree, the way the resources of the country are used to affect the future.

The realist tradition has hidden the concept of national purpose within its own concept of national interest. In their writings on the morality of international politics, realists have attempted to show how the pursuit and/or defense of the national interest is a moral policy. John C. Bennett revealed his own sensitivity about pursuing the national interest but accepted the inevitability of conceiving international politics in terms of the national interest: "Whatever we think about the moral issue involved in the behavior of nations, we must come to terms with two major concepts, the concept of national interest and the concept of national power. I shall discuss these in turn. It would perhaps be easier to teach Christian ethics in a world in which neither existed, but that is not my privilege."[10]

National interest is a concept. It may be a helpful idea or a poor idea, but an idea it certainly is. It is possible to conceive of international politics without the difficult concept of national interest. The difficulty of national interest rests in the ambiguity of the term. The concept is value laden and consists basically of what the policy-making elite decide is the national interest. The government of Great Britain agrees to the dismemberment of Czechoslovakia and months later goes to war over the invasion of Poland, and both are in the national interest as it is conceived by the policy makers at different times. The other meaning of national interest stresses the more "objective" side of the phrase. A strong economy, a favorable balance of trade, strong military defenses, secure borders, and so on are said to be in the national interest. Debate can arise as to how much oil needs to be imported or how much of the scarce mineral resources of the world needs to be controlled, but seeking and controlling resources is part of the national interest. It is this second use, particularly, in which national interest is taken to be self-evident, that confuses the discussion of international relations. National interest too easily becomes a slogan that stops the political process. Debate is cut off because the national interest is being pursued. People who debate over national policy in terms of national interest find it very hard to suggest that fundamental shifts in policy must be affected. The economic thinking of the government presses toward the conclusion that if the U.S. economy needs roughly 25 percent of the raw materials of the world to function, it is in the national interest to secure access to those raw materials. Prior questions (e.g., whether or not the purposes of Americans are served by that economy and that scramble for resources) have no way to enter into the debate on equal terms with the economic needs once the whole question of policy is perceived in terms of national interest. Sensitive people do not construct their models of life solely on their own interests. They articulate models of social existence and conduct in terms of fitting responses in a world in which many beings coexist. Their actions take on a goal orientation; they articulate their actions growing out of needs in terms of purposes that are compatible with the articulated purposes of other selves. So within national debates over international policy, they do not pursue interest, at least not in the second sense of self-evident quantifiable interests, but they pursue rather sophisticated purposes that contain their needs, their dreams, their morals, and of course, their illusions and their pride.

The above analysis suggests that American policy is not intelligible on the basis of understanding any quantifiable definition of the national interest. It further implies that the ambiguity of *national interest* renders it particularly inappropriate for a discussion of foreign policy. Purpose is a more helpful concept than interest. Purpose is rooted in the national history of a people, and the definition of *purpose* is a function of poet and philosopher as well as the lawyer turned statesman. Definitions of purpose will vary; foreign policy varies. Our foreign policy is the temporary synthesis of American self-understanding as translated through the foreign policy apparatus in its attempt to realize the goals of some Americans beyond the borders of the nation.

With the beginning of the John F. Kennedy presidency, Morgenthau, the great defender of the centrality of the national interest, came to see the need to enrich the interest discussion with purpose. He wrote *The Purpose of American Politics*, in which he argued that American policy reflected the struggle to bring political realities in harmony with the purpose of America. He understood that purpose to be the realization of "equality in freedom." As this purpose was incapable of realization, it committed the United States to "an endless process." The understanding of American purpose as "equality in freedom" is reminiscent of Niebuhr's understanding of justice. In Morgenthau's book, purpose stood alongside national interest, with both pursued by power. Historical trends since 1968 obscure the national commitments to equality while affirming the American pursuit of freedom.[11]

Another realist, Robert Kagan, also saw that values were part of national interest in 2004. He deplored the overly simple realism of the Bush administration and Condoleezza Rice's narrow focus on national interest. While refusing to grant much influence to world opinion or to the United Nations and insisting that the United States retain the right unilaterally to attend to its own defense, he saw the need for values. He noted that the Bush administration paid a price for not securing more European support for the invasion of Iraq. He regarded Europe and America as the center of support for liberal democracy. American national interest if conceived narrowly lacked legitimacy. If American power was seen to be pursuing humanitarian values and liberal democracy, he believed its international legitimacy would be perceived by European allies. He feared that European dissent from American policy would weaken even domestic support for U.S. initiatives. He regarded these democratic values as both part of U.S. national interest and necessary for the successful use of U.S. power. The need, of course, is to avoid an overly moral presentation of U.S. policy that obscures the more selfish motives of U.S. policy that are always involved in the synthesis of interest and purpose.[12]

The statesperson for our time and place is the one who knows that a grasp of purpose is relevant to the struggle for power. Though the struggle for power is strange to Christian purpose, the greatest power comes from the appropriate merging of goals and means. It is this uniting of purpose with the means available that is the strange and awesome work of one who attempts to embody Christian political leadership.[13]

Notes

1. This chapter is adapted from chapter 8, "Power and Purpose," in Ronald H. Stone, *Realism and Hope* (Washington: University Press of America, 1977), 143–58.

2. Hans J. Morgenthau, *Politics among Nations: The Struggle for Power and Peace* (New York: Alfred A. Knopf, 1967), 25.

3. Ibid., 26.

4. Paul Tillich, *Love, Power, and Justice* (New York: Oxford University Press, 1954), 40.

5. F. C. German, "A Tentative Evaluation of World Power," *The Journal of Conflict Resolution*, March 1960.

6. Ibid.

7. This definition is from Professor W. T. R. Fox of Columbia University. A former student of Professor Fox, I am unable to claim that all the subtleties of his discussion of power are recognized here, nor do I now know if this definition is an exact quotation. However, the relational-intentional emphasis of the concept is certainly Professor Fox's idea.

8. The motifs discussed in this section are a modification of the Christ and culture motifs of H. Richard Niebuhr in *Christ and Culture* (New York: Harper & Brothers, 1951).

9. See Edward L. Long Jr., *A Survey of Christian Ethics* (New York: Oxford University Press, 1967), vi.

10. John C. Bennett, *Foreign Policy in Christian Perspective* (New York: Charles Scribner's Sons, 1966), 53.

11. Roger L. Shinn pointed out this evolution of Morgenthau's thought in "The Continuing Conversation between Hans Morgenthau and Reinhold Niebuhr." A prepublished version of this essay is in the author's possession. The phrases in quotes are from unnumbered introductory pages of Hans J. Morgenthau, *The Purpose of American Politics* (New York: Random House, 1963).

12. Robert Kagan, "The Purpose of America's Power," *Pittsburgh Post-Gazette*, March 17 2004, J1, 3.

13. Some aspects of this chapter are traceable to my early publication on the subject. See Ronald H. Stone, "Purpose and Power," in *Social Action* (New York: Council for Christian Social Action, January 1968).

⚏ 7 ⚏

Prophetic Realism and Peacemaking

THE EMERGENCE OF PROPHETIC REALISM as a force in U.S. foreign policy thinking coincided with the decline of the League of Nations and the rise of Nazism. Its major policy concerns have been the defeat of Nazism, the containment of Communism, the futility of the war in Vietnam, the avoidance of a nuclear war or a war between the superpowers, and the defense of Israel. The major remaining issue of Israel complicates U.S. policy in the Middle East and leads to terrorist actions. The previous generation of realist theologians found no need to deal with terrorism in major studies. Before critiquing alternative theologies of peacemaking in the following chapter and articulating realist thought about important emerging foreign policy issues, I present in this chapter a realist theological ethic of peacemaking.

First, some definitions are in order. According to Old Testament scholar Gerhard von Rad, in its most frequent use in the Old Testament, "shalom is an emphatically social concept."[1] It has a broad range of meanings and has a certain imprecision in particular usages. It means "well-being." It points to national prosperity. As a personal greeting, it is a wish for health. Between peoples it implies an alliance, a relationship, a covenant. There is shalom between Solomon and Hiram when they make a treaty (1 Kgs 5:12). The covenant of God with Israel is a covenant of peace (Isa 54:10). In its full meaning, *shalom* is a religious term because it is a gift of God. Shalom is often one of other expected elements of eschatological fulfillment (Zech 9:10).

In the Prophets, *shalom* refers to a practical or real political peace for the nation of Israel. The false prophets prophesied such a real peace when it was not to be realized. Jeremiah and Ezekiel pleaded for Israel to see that its real prospects in the immediate future were war and destruction. *Shalom* can be translated as "salvation" and von Rad says that the translator of *shalom* is often at a loss over how to express it exactly.[2]

The New Testament, through its dependence on the Greek translation of the Hebrew Bible, brings the meaning of "well-being" of *shalom* into Greek, displacing the more passive Greek word *eirene*, or the state of being at rest. Both *shalom* and *eirene* have the meaning of peace as opposed to war. This is the fundamental meaning of peace in the realist approach to international issues. Peace does mean well-being, even salvation. It means being with God, particularly in the New Testament. It is used in greetings in both rabbinical literature and in the New Testament to wish well-being. In the New Testament usages, various layers of meaning exist, including (1) peace as a feeling of rest, (2) peace as reconciliation, (3) peace as salvation, and (4) peace as healthy relations among people.[3]

Jesus' words in Matt 5:9, "Blessed are the peacemakers, for they will be called children of God," contain the only use of *peacemaker* in the New Testament. Biblical scholar Werner Foerster writes, "The reference is to those who disinterestedly come between two contending parties and try to make peace. These God calls his sons because they are like Him."[4] Here, as in other Greek literature, we see peace used as the opposite of war. Sometimes the peacemaker is the ruler who establishes peace in the world.[5] Jesus' blessing may be eschatological, but it recommends an active role in promoting peace. It is stronger than Paul's recommendation in his list of moral teachings to the Romans in Rom 12:18: "If it is possible, so far as it depends on you, live peaceably with all."

Shalom, or *eirene*, meaning "salvation," is at the center of the Christian faith. It is more than vision: personally and in community it may be realized. Socially and politically it is not realized, but in both Old Testament and New Testament, the faithful are urged to live peaceably, to be peacemakers.

There is no credible way to imply that ancient writers knew anything at all about the possibilities of humanity ultimately destroying itself. Confronted as we are, however, with the question of whether human beings will survive, the meaning of peacemaking for our time involves the salvation of humanity as a species. Peacemaking and the promotion of peace may go on in the family, in school, in business, in church, and in government, but in most cases these are not ultimate questions of being. Theologically speaking, peacemaking today means the practical, activist work in society to prevent the destruction of the human species. Its primary focus is preventing global nuclear war. The further meaning of peacemaking is developed by inquiring into the origins of war.

The Origins of War

Human history is filled with war. No people have been free of conflict for very long. The epics of Western civilization, whether the Greek *Iliad* or the Hebrew Bible, point to the story of history and myth as one of renewed warfare. We know of peace as a longed-for time of dreaming and innocence, a time before civilization. We know of it as a promise for the future, the time of restoration of innocence, but actual history is filled with the noise of battle.

War is fascinating and frightening. Humanity is both drawn into its vortex and appalled by its horror. In such recognition the attractive power of war is seen. War participates to a significant degree in the description that Rudolph Otto applied to the holy. The experience of the holy is awesome in its attractiveness and in its dread. In Otto's book *The Idea of the Holy*, the meaning of the holy is found partially in the feelings of a fearful awe and fascination. As Christians, we tend to be so comforted by trust in grace that we forget the judgment of the ultimate. Fear is somehow foreign to us. Yet this ambiguity of the divine confronts us in the phenomenon of war. We can be fascinated by movies showing the destruction of the earth or even the Star Wars movies of the destruction of worlds beyond our nuclear-wrecked earth, yet we know that the threat of massive war will obliterate all our meanings.

Ancient sources of wisdom, whether Hindu, Hebrew, or Hellene, see war as the work of gods. People do not really decide for war; they are pawns of the spiritual forces that in their own contradictions cause humanity to fight. In our present state of Christian monotheism, which emphasizes that freedom is necessary if humanity is to fulfill its purpose of loving God, we cannot blame the gods for our wars. Yet we are wise to recognize the reality of the forces of human spiritual principalities and powers, which flow through us individually and communally and drive us toward war. In the *Iliad*, the Old Testament, and the *Bhagavad Gita*, the responsibility of the gods for war should certainly teach even the most rational among us to recognize what the ancients knew: war is a problem of our existence. It is not just a political problem; it is a problem of our spiritual-political life. It is a problem of our species and of its organization.

In a brilliant analysis of the history of the philosophy of war, Kenneth Waltz finds three major explanations for the origin of war in the history of Western thought.[6] The first explanation of war is that humanity is flawed. Whether the major cause is ignorance, pride, greed, or alienation, the problem is in human nature. The second explanation is that the nation-states are organized to pursue war. Whether war is related to economic self-interest, national pride, national insecurity, the political pressures of the masses, or the structural place of the military in the country, wars are basically due to the follies of nations in their organization and policies. Finally, there are those thinkers who place the origins of war in international anarchy. As long as there is no sovereign to enforce order, autonomous units of the international system will resort to armed conflict to resolve their inevitable tensions. Whether the tensions are the result of economic competition, exaggerated nationalism, border disputes, or ideological disputes, it is the international anarchy that permits war. Waltz's book *Man, the State, and War* provides a necessary perspective on the complexity of the causes of war. Obviously none of the factors that have been identified as primary sources of war can be excluded. Christians who fully realize that we are living in a season of "war and rumors of war" appreciate all three sources of war: international anarchy, war-structured states, and the foibles of human nature.

Using this stylized presentation of Western thought regarding the origins of war as a principle of interpretation permits us to discover the same patterns in the eighth-century B.C.E. prophet Isaiah of Jerusalem. Isaiah's prophecy is inscribed on the Isaiah Wall in front of the United Nations headquarters: "They shall beat their swords into plowshares, and their spears into pruning hooks" (Isa 2:4). The vision of peace is, of course, a vision of a transformed humanity, nation, and international order. It is not a task for the political rulers of Jerusalem to accomplish; it is an eschatological vision of hope. Underneath the eschatological vision, in the first three chapters of Isaiah, is Isaiah's critique of Judah, revealing the origins of war. The vision itself, verses 1–4 of chapter 2, contains the structure of international order replacing anarchy. "All the nations" are brought to the teaching of God's ways. An international community is founded on accepted teachings and accepted ways of life. There is also common judgment and the recognition of a common sovereign. "He shall judge between the nations, and shall arbitrate for many peoples" (Isa 2:4). After the common sovereignty and practice are accepted, disarmament follows: "They shall beat their swords into plowshares, and their spears into pruning hooks." Finally, after disarmament, or more profoundly, after the conversion of weapons into agricultural tools, the nations abandon teaching and planning for war: "Nation shall not lift up sword against nation, neither shall they learn war any more."

Here in Isaiah's vision, elements of international sovereignty, accepted teaching, agreed-upon patterns of life, and common judgment proceed disarmament and the abandonment of war. All those who stress that the origins of war lie in anarchy should be encouraged by this wisdom. Certainly the Isaiah text is a fit text, though visionary, for a United Nations that was born amid hopes of abridging international anarchy.

However, in turning to the chapters of Isaiah surrounding the vision, we find the reasons for the wars that were to destroy Jerusalem. The nation is described as a "sinful nation." It has rebelled against the Lord in specific, identifiable ways: justice has been corrupted (1:4); there is "no soundness in it" (1:6); the worship of the people has been accompanied not by justice but by violence, so the religious life is corrupted and rejected by God (1:14–15); the rulers associate with criminals (1:23); and the weak are not defended (1:23). Jerusalem is given a chance to escape war through repentance, but the nation will have to become just. The very wealth and pride of the nation are seen as evils leading to idolatry (2:7–8). The critique that promises war as punishment is against the pride of the nation and particularly against its armament program (2:15–16). Our stylized principle of interpretation confronts a difficulty in the reality of the text. It is impossible to know precisely whether the condemnation of the elders of Jerusalem for preventing justice belongs more appropriately to the corruption of the nation or to the failings of individuals, but the expression is so general that it can be included under the failure of the nation.

Isa 3:14–15 says, "The LORD enters into judgment with the elders and princes of his people: It is you who have devoured the vineyard; the spoil of the poor is in your houses. What do you mean by crushing my people, by grinding the face of the poor? says the Lord GOD of hosts." This text certainly assumes that the punishment of war falls on corrupted states that neglect justice. When a nation is unsound, full of pride and exploitation, there can be no peace. We can say either that there is no peace without justice or that peace includes justice. We are not entitled to conclude that relative justice in the nation ensures peace, because the nation still in history is a unit in anarchy, which can be led into war by broken leaders.

The text from Isaiah presupposes that the world is such that war destroys the unjust. The picture is of God actively calling the enemy army to invade from afar (Isa 5:26–30). We know of many cases in the last few years in which national injustices led to war. A theology that followed Reinhold Niebuhr would probably trace out the many historical causes that led from injustice to war while proclaiming the just God as the meaning and fulfillment of history. A theology following Alfred North Whitehead would see God, as the structure of value of the universe, producing war when humans pursue injustice in the conditions of international anarchical instability. Liberation theologians with some reference to Marxist-Leninist theories of the wars of imperialism can see how the exploitation of the poor by the wealthy leads to war. In each of the four schools of thought, whether it be the simple action of God presupposed by Hebrew Scripture or the more modern translations of that faith in terms of human freedom, national corruption brings war.

Finally, the text teaches individual human responsibility for war. Human beings as persons are corrupted, and their actions bring war. Political leaders accept bribes, and corruption reigns; they seek gifts and do not administer justice (Isa 1:23). The judges and counselors have fallen away (1:26). Individuals as well as the community have rebelled and forgotten God's purposes (1:2–3). The people are unfit to worship; their "hands are full of blood" (1:15). Isaiah's description of the evils of Jerusalem remind the reader of the realistic descriptions by Machiavelli in sixteenth-century Italy or Hobbes in seventeenth-century England. It is hard to know exactly the chief expression of human failing in Isaiah since the text is so synthetically rich and not explicitly analytical. An analysis founded on the perspective of Reinhold Niebuhr would tend to focus on the critique of pride, which is explicitly emphasized. Here the pride of the male rulers is complemented by the haughtiness of the rich women of Zion. The women are blamed not for misrule but for prideful conspicuous consumption (1:16). Pride is usually regarded as more basic to sin than greed in Niebuhr's analysis. Liberation theology would tend not to emphasize the pride as much as the consumption and could focus on the fifth chapter, which condemns the displacement of the small farmer from his land. The Whiteheadian perspective would see the ruler's corruption as breaking the harmony and violating the unity. It also would highlight the ignorance of the knowledge of reality: "The ox *knows* its owner, and the donkey its master's crib; but Israel does not *know*, my people do not understand" (1:3, emphasis mine).

The first three chapters are illuminated by Waltz's categories, but in a very powerful way, the fifth chapter of Isaiah exhibits a cause of war that needs for our day to be highlighted. It reflects all three prior motifs—the weakness of persons because of human alienation, the corruption of the state, and international disorder—but the focus is on the displacement of the peasant from the land.

In the eighth century B.C. in Judah, the plight of the majority of the rural population worsened. It was a time of expanded military and economic power for both Israel and Judah. The powers of the ruling elites increased, while the peasant landholdings decreased. The larger estates helped to produce olives, grapes, and grain for export. The exports helped finance the urban luxuries and the armies of the centralized state. As a consequence, the deprivation of the peasantry worsened; the eighth-century prophetic oracles address this issue.

The prophetic oracle in Isaiah 5 predicts two consequences. The large estates will be overthrown and the country desolated. Foreign armies will invade and ravage the land. Peacemakers need to mediate on these beautiful but devastating oracles to understand the present. They reinforce the liberation theology message that depriving the poor farmer of the land (whether it is Israeli deprivation of Palestinians, or Central American elite deprivation of peasants, or Indian landowners' deprivation of rural workers in India) leads to social failure and to war.

The oracles of Isaiah 5 portray Israel as God's vineyard, which the Lord lovingly tended. But the vineyard did not produce. God looked for justice and saw violence. The powerful expanded their fields and deprived the poor, and the result was disaster. In a study of comparative sociology's relevance to these oracles, the Old Testament scholar D. N. Premnath has focused on Isaiah 5:8–10:[7]

> Ah, you who join house to house, who add field to field, until there is room for no one but you, and you are left to live alone in the midst of the land! The LORD of hosts has sworn in my hearing: "Surely many houses shall be desolate, large and beautiful houses, without inhabitant. For ten acres of vineyard shall yield but one bath, and a homer of seed shall yield a mere ephah."

This impoverishing of the rural population, which the oracle condemns and which contains within it the promise of conflict, is real in India today. The poverty of the rural class continues and by some measures worsens. Technological globalization has not helped the rural peasants. As a result, violence bubbles in the population just below the repression. Liberals in the Western world know the truth of the problem when they preach land reform. But their practice belies their preaching. The Alliance for Progress promised land reform for Latin America at a time when even in North America the poorer agricultural population was being displaced from its land. In the 1980s land reform was promised in Central America, but its administration in the hands of the American allied elite doomed it to frustration. The problem is not just one of North American greed, though, or capitalism. State socialism has shown the same tendency to displace peasants from their land. In Stalin's Ukraine, millions starved to death under the forced collectivizing and usurping of agricultural produce for the urban population. Out of this horror, sectors of the population were ready to welcome even Hitler's liberation until they discovered the invaders to be worse than the Russian oppressors. Hebrew nobility, Indian landowners, North American capitalists, and Stalinist socialists all sow havoc as they take the land. These prophetic oracles of the eighth century B.C. provide a valuable insight into the origins of human conflict and the causes of war.[8] The oracle foretells that the large landowners too shall be displaced, their beautiful houses left empty. Finally, after listing the evils of Israel and Judah, the fifth chapter concludes with war. A terrible army is to come that cannot be resisted: "Their roaring is like a lion, like young lions they roar; they growl and seize their prey, they carry it off, and no one can rescue" (Isa 5:29).

From Waltz's twentieth-century book and the first chapters of Isaiah's eighth-century B.C. book, the multifaceted origins of war are seen. If war's scourge falls on us because of the weakness of human nature, the inadequacy of our nation-states, the anarchy of our international order, and our human greed displacing the people from the land, can we avoid it? Can we

be both realistic about the persistent tendencies toward war and affirmative of the centrality of peacemaking to the Christian faith? As a Marxist
philosopher engaged in seeking peace asked me in a meeting in Prague,
"Does Christian faith show a way through the danger of war?" For our time
the question becomes, "Can prophetic realism illuminate a path beyond an
ever-escalating worldwide war against undefined terrorism?"

Christian Ethics and Peacemaking

The collapse of the Soviet Union did not bring peace; it brought ongoing
historical problems. A utopian dream of a Pax Americana collapsed with
an attack on the American symbols of power. We are located in a particular history threatened in particular ways by the divisiveness of the political
economy of the twenty-first century. Our religious tradition calls us toward
peace with justice, but the way is impeded by perceived restraints located
in the human self, in our oppression of the poor, in our nations, and in our
international disorder. The commitments already made incline us to find
guidance within the center of Christian tradition related to public ethics.

Summaries of Christian theory abound, but the focus in this study on
peacemaking ethics leads to the Pauline statement on the theory of Christian
life: "And now faith, hope, and love abide, these three; and the greatest of
these is love" (1 Cor 13:13).

These three virtues are essential. They are not all of Christian wisdom,
but they summarize the transformative power of Christian virtue on
humanity. If we were to desire a guide to Christian life, we could do no better than Augustine did in using these three virtues as an outline and inte-
grating the four classical virtues into the theological. Here these virtues are
discussed in relationship to twenty-first-century conflicts and expanded to
include wisdom, courage, temperance, and justice.

Faith, Not Idolatry

The first issue of life still remains faith versus idolatry. The first commandment of Israel is, "I am the LORD your God, who brought you out of the
land of Egypt, out of the house of slavery; you shall have no other gods
before me" (Exod 20:2–3). With Islam, Judaism, and Christianity, the
polemic against idolatry is the first requirement of faith. In the Western
world, we are inclined to think that idolatry has been overcome. A cursory
examination of our cultures reveals their idolatrous character, however.
Idolatry is the elevation of concerns that have relative value to the role of
ultimate concern.

Experience in India in the midst of its many idols has freed me to
appreciate more deeply the Hebrew polemic against idolatry and also to see

its role in both North Atlantic countries and in the former Communist European countries. In India, idols are ubiquitous. They decorate the temples, they are beside the roads, they are in the museums, they are present at festivals and in parades. Their movements are described in the newspapers, and devotion to them has a social-political importance. The Hindu philosopher who escorted me through the Meenakshi Temple in Madurai directed his worship to the "One." His One had the characteristics of a Tillichian understanding of the ground of being. But he said that the people had no understanding. They basically worshiped the idols. The idolatry is woven into the national literature, the caste system, the subjection of women, the sanctity of cattle, the art, and the Hindu relativism. There are so many claims to ultimate reality that life, it seems, remains an illusion. One story is as good as another. Abuses of idolatry still involve sacralizing prostitution and human sacrifice and endorsing fatalism. The resultant pluralism of an idolatrous polytheism psychologically reinforces tolerance of disorder, extreme communalism, and the relative neglect of a transforming ethic. All of this can easily drive Muslims and Christians into a fanatical rejection of Indian life, which when combined with imperial power has wrought terrible human destruction. India's internal disorder may render the nation less dangerous on the international scene because its resources are underdeveloped and fragmented.

The three most dangerous societies in the world were descended from the Hebrew polemic against idolatry. Neither Islam nor the formerly Christian West and the formerly Christian Eastern Europe suffer from the sort of idolatry that dominates India. European secularization continues the anti-idolatry of the Hebrew prophets who smashed idols physically and with scorn. The secularization in the West has been inspired both by Protestant theism and enlightenment humanism. In the Communist world, the motivation has been more from a militant atheism. Both societies officially operate secularly, and Christian minorities play roles of varying importance. It is really impossible to say whether the Christian minorities play a greater role in the former Communist countries or in the mixed-economy democracies. Was the public role of the church, for example, greater in Canada or Poland? The idolatry of the Eastern European countries was state idolatry. The state, in the name of an abandoned utopian revolution, assumed the economic role as well as the governance role. The role of the priests was reduced, and the commissar assumed the roles of both the business leader and the political leader. This shifting of roles was evident to visitors from the democracies in the encounter with state propaganda everywhere. The state communicated its control on radio, television, and billboards and in newspapers, film, and art. Major industries were state administered, and even the peasants served the state agricultural plans. The industrial workers, in whose name the revolution was conducted, fared better than their counterparts in India, but their condition did not compare to that of the workers of the middle-class democracies. It was not fair to compare the Russian workers' lifestyle to the Americans' perhaps, but even in relative gains, since 1917 the American worker outstripped the Russian counterpart in economic well-being, freedom, production, and personal security. More relevant is the comparison of the workers of Finland, who until 1917 were part of the Russian Empire, to those of Russia, immediately adjoining Finland. In both Finland and Germany, local workers became middle class. The workers in Communist countries were better off than they were under the czars, but the workers' revolution had not accomplished as much as unionization, pragmatic adjustment, and political reform in the democracies. The workers' paradise never appeared, and instead a state idolatry emerged.

Islam's rejection of polytheism was even more harsh than Christianity's, which found ways to express diversity even within God. The militancy of Islam led it to overrun the middle of the inhabited earth. It impressed its order from Spain to Indonesia. Its decline allowed European conquest from the sixteenth century to the twentieth, after the failures of the Crusades of the Middle Ages. The threatened return of European dominance, whether by America or Russia, unleashed the renewed militancy of the late twentieth and early twenty-first century by an Islamist minority also struggling with the alliance of Islamic "elites" with European "elites." The creed "There is no God but Allah and Mohammed is his prophet" can return to its earlier world-conquering militancy. Islamic intolerance became directed at the atheism of Communist society as well as the mixture of Christianity and secularism of the West. Whether Islam has ruled Indian Hindus, separated from them as in 1948, or lived as a minority in the restored post-British Hindu India, its relationship with polytheism has been part of its conflictual life.

A survey of the democratic mixed-economy societies reveals two idols that claim national resources and loyalty. The one overwhelming idol is the amassing of personal wealth. This idol is most extreme in the United States, with millions of millionaires, but reducing life to financial success is not uncharacteristic of the Swiss, Germans, Dutch, and other nationalities. The drive for personal wealth is blared on television and in movies, newspapers, literature, and universities as the culture of the consuming society is propagated. Salaries paid to the industrial managers soar beyond all reason, as do salaries paid to those who advertise the products of the consuming society through sports or entertainment. Americans are bombarded by messages to consume and are taught avarice. Compared with much of the rest of the world, America looks like middle-class paradise. The 20 percent failure rate of the society, represented by those who have not achieved the income necessary to rise above the poverty line, is neglected by those driven by the idol of personal wealth.

Governments were not very successful in organizing the production of wealth in either India or Communist societies. Likewise in the United States, but here the drive for wealth has bypassed the government. There is little danger of government idolatry in the United States; it is a continual struggle to get Americans to take the government seriously. The personal drive for wealth produces a pluralistic idolatry to the neglect of the state, although the second idol does involve the state. This second idol is the pursuit of national security. After World War II, the United States was left unexpectedly in a hegemonic role in the world. As the rest of the world recovered, America needed to surrender this artificial hegemony gracefully and find its own role in the world as befitted a dynamic 6 percent of the world's population. Communism's threat to capitalism and the fear of traditional Russian totalitarianism combined with American pride to produce a pursuit of national security on the world scene.

This idolatry of national security has led us into dangers of unreasonable alliances with countries that share neither our values nor our national interests. It has led us into a military stalemate on the Korean peninsula and into military defeat in Vietnam. Arming the world, which of course reduces American power vis-à-vis the newly armed, has become an American policy. Too often the "enemies of our enemies" were not really our friends; they were just allies.

Out of fear, the leviathan of a national security organization has evolved policies contrary to American democratic principles. Now the leviathan threatens to destroy us all. It is armed beyond all national needs. The arms themselves became the flash points of danger, for example, in the Cuban missile crisis. Questions of the mobilization of forces led Europe into World War I. All of the great European empires should have been adequately deterred by others. But unsure of intentions and fearing the other gaining an advantage, Russia and Germany threw themselves into the fratricidal conflict, which destroyed their empires and initiated the decline of Europe.

The leviathan of the national security system reaches out for more of the GNP, draining the economy of its technological talents. In a fantasy of science fiction, it threatens now to arm space. As we financed the wars from Lebanon and Afghanistan to Nicaragua and Grenada, our chances for success seem less the reason for recourse to arms than the need for the leviathan to be involved in the conflicts. Can it be American pride that feeds the leviathan beyond rational American needs? If so, greed and pride stand as the human forces fueling the leviathan's threat to us all. From a biblical perspective, greed and pride are among the primary causes of war.

Trust in arms is specifically condemned in Scripture. If we ultimately trust in arms, we do not ultimately trust in God. Israel says in faith, "Some trust in chariots and some in horses, but we trust in the name of the LORD our God" (Ps 20:7 NIV). Trust in armaments leads to war: "Because you have trusted in your power and in the multitude of your warriors, therefore the tumult of war shall arise against your people, and all your fortresses shall be destroyed" (Hos 10:13–14).

Faith is trust in the ultimate graciousness of life. Erik Erikson has shown how faith is given to infants as they receive security from their parents. As a human being develops, trust is encouraged or denied as life affects the growing being. Faith is not as much achieved as it is given. The baptism of children in most Christian churches affirms God's graciousness and entrusts the parents and the community to give these children the gift of faith.

Christian faith is an ultimate faith; it is a trust in the foundations of life. The other loyalties of life can be made relative. One does not need to put faith in local idols, in the state, in the acquisition of wealth, or in the national security system. They all are the work of our hands; they all will fail. Faith is the expression of Paul: "What then are we to say about these things? If God is for us, who is against us?" (Rom 8:31). In this faith (which led him to disrupt the state, the economy, and the idols at Ephesus), Paul found the peace that is the beginning of real peacemaking. "Therefore, since we are justified by faith, we have *peace with* God through our Lord Jesus Christ" (Rom 5:1, emphasis mine).

Faith is the response of the human being, and it is recognized as the foundation of peace in Islam as well as in Judaism and Christianity. Islam knows that the whole social order is involved in peacemaking, but here too the role of faith in the person is central. As the Koran says, "Those who have faith and do not let it be debased by the least injustice are those who shall have peace. It is they who are on the right path" (6.83). In Paul's religious crisis, faith in God's grace responded to the failure of Judaism, as he understood it, to achieve liberation through the law. In Luther, faith answered what the penitential system of renaissance Roman Catholicism could not answer for him: the need for assurance of salvation. In our day, faith overcomes the "meaninglessness of life" that has channeled life's energies into the idolatries of greed, statism, or militarism.

Faith is trust and not specifically belief. But in Christian life, it is not trust in vagueness. It is trust in the one God known in power and goodness as the author of creation. Behind the evolving world of matter, energy, and life is a benevolent purpose seeking a free humanity's love. Goodness united with ultimate power is God, so although Christians fear power without goodness, the union of goodness and power is divine. The possibility of human life responding in human power to God's graciousness is believed by Christians to have been realized in Jesus Christ.

Christ was expected in power, but he came as a servant and suffered. He was a teacher of morality, a healer, a founder of a community, and he realized the purpose of the universe in a life given completely to God. People responding to him have found peace and come to understand themselves as peacemakers. The Christian Trinitarian belief proclaims that the Spirit of God in Christ nurtures human life today. The Spirit, though never contradicting the picture of Jesus as the Christ, moves freely among human beings, nurturing faith and inspiring new forms of community among people. Many people testify to the knowledge that the spirit of Christian community, transcending national and denominational barriers, is most real in peacemaking efforts.

Christian faith frees human beings to be human. People's efforts to become minor deities are pathetic, and faith frees them from this impossible compulsion. On the other hand, some people are trying to become slaves to something or to someone else, and faith frees them from this sacrifice of their humanity. In most areas of human endeavor, the fear of being a vulnerable human being drives people to pretend to be all-powerful, all-knowing, or perfectly moral. In international politics nations act to fulfill the frail egos of their insecure people by maximizing power, judging other nations by their own particular standards (not those of the nation being judged), and claiming absolute loyalties of the people. As the people surrender their human freedom to the politicians or the states, the nations become more dangerous and the people less human.

Humans are meant to be neither slaves nor gods. Yet in existing between slavery and divinity, they are tempted in their anxiety to surrender their humanity either to pretend to be the center of the universe or to fall into servitude to another finite reality. In surrendering their humanity, the pretenders to divinity become more credible to themselves and to others, thereby increasing their pride.

Faith in God allows human beings to live as vulnerable human beings. They do not need to surrender their freedom to others, and they can resist tyranny and the claims of absolution of various idols. Faith also breaks the pride of those who would claim absolute power or knowledge or morality. Faith in the absolute God makes other loyalties relative and reduces the temptation to destroy the world to protect an American understanding of free enterprise or a Russian understanding of Communism. There is no need for holy wars, because the God who is holy desires peace. Faith is an antidote to greed and pride.

Feminist critiques of Christian theology have clarified an important point. Christian teaching emphasizing self-sacrifice mistakenly encourages less than human life. People have been led to sacrifice their selves for the interests of others. Self-sacrifice is part of the Christian life, but it is the sacrifice of the old prideful self or the old idol-infested self to God in order to receive in faith a new self that can be free. By losing our old selves, we are given new selves. Women particularly have been kept the poorest of the poor. Nothing in Christian faith, rightly understood, requires a sacrifice of them other than the sacrifice of that enslaved self so that they can be free. In their becoming free, the structures of all social relations are fundamentally shaken. As the woman abandons servitude, she frees the man from the role of master. The oppressed and the oppressor both are freed; but of course, it is more difficult for the oppressor to see the more human quality of new, fairer structures of life.

Faith is exactly what the strife-torn world needs, for it encourages the oppressed to revolt for their true humanity. It allows the oppressors to help the revolt succeed for their true humanity. Faith allows justice to be arranged in ways that encourage the humanity of all to flourish. For in faith our meaning is not in wealth, consumption, position, or control but in relationships to God and humanity. Faith does its work for peacemaking in the interiors of human selves, allowing them to live freely without exploiting.

Of course, faith drives toward particular works for peacemaking. That is obvious. The world is in danger; the faithful will act. James put it clearly: "For just as the body without the spirit is dead, so faith without works is also dead" (Jas 2:26).

James did not remain abstract in his reference to works. He warned his readers against the injustice of riches. Faith that will not feed the hungry and clothe the naked is dead. His charge of "unfaithful creatures" (Jas 4:4 RSV) is directed at those whose covetousness causes wars: "What causes wars, and what causes fightings among you? Is it not your passions that are at war in your members? You desire and do not have; so you kill. And you covet and cannot obtain; so you fight and wage war" (James 4:1–2 RSV).

With millions hungry and a minority overfed, there is little chance for peace. The passions in ourselves lead to greed and to war; faith can counter those passions and create the humble person honored in James's letter. This humble person is the one who carries out the works of kindness and righteousness: the healing, the feeding, and the clothing. These works require hope of fulfillment; faith undergirds hope and leads to hope.

Hope, Not Armageddon

The references in preaching and in the remarks of former President Reagan and Secretary of Defense Weinberger to a final battle or a final nuclear holocaust called Armageddon revealed more about the speakers than about Scripture. The word *Armageddon* appears only once in the Bible. It is in the Greek of Revelation 16:16 (NIV): "Then they gathered the kings together to the place that in Hebrew is called Armageddon." We cannot tell what this Hebrew word means since there is no other reference to such a word. It may refer to the mountain of Megiddo, but more likely it refers to the Megiddo where Ahaziah died, perhaps the city of Megiddo. It is possible that it refers to Jerusalem, since the context suggests Zion. But in any case, the kings of the world were to be assembled there in this vision of judgment in John's revelation.

The next chapter removes any chronological confusion; the vision is explicitly about the destruction of the Roman Empire, which was persecuting Christians. Rome is judged, the rulers are listed, its burning is described, the collapse of commerce is detailed, and its allies are grief-stricken. Revelation, written in a time of Roman political persecution of Christians, has an explicit political theology involving God's work to overthrow Rome and save the people.

Actually, of course, Rome was converted to Christianity before it was destroyed, but at the time of the writing of Revelation, such a historical outcome would have seemed less probable than God's justice destroying Rome. Armageddon, this obscure word with its one biblical appearance, cannot bear the weight of nuclear theology. There is no biblical reason to think it has anything to do with nuclear war. To project a final war on the basis of Revelation threatens God's terrible judgment, but Revelation concludes with a vision of a new earth and a new heaven, a restored city of peace. The Lamb is the Prince of Peace for whose coming Christians pray. The book is eschatologically optimistic for Christians who would read it and understand it in the midst of Roman persecution. Failure to read it and understand it in its historical setting, like the failure to understand the book of Daniel in the Old Testament, feeds fantasies, and in the hands of people with power, these fantasies can be dangerous. The historical settings are clear enough; once the apocalyptic language is understood, the dangers are easily avoided.

The prophetic books are realistic about human suffering, and, as in Joel and Ezekiel, those who have done violence to Jerusalem suffer for it. In most of the books, the final pattern is that of Isaiah or Amos; Israel will be restored in righteousness and peace. "The mountains shall drip sweet wine, and all the hills shall flow with it. I will restore the fortunes of my people Israel, and they shall rebuild the ruined cities and inhabit them" (Amos 9:13–14).

Jeremiah prophesied the destruction of Jerusalem. He foresaw the ravishing of the small countries of the fertile crescent. He even announced the coming destruction of Babylon. Yet even in Jeremiah the oracles of peace are heard. He criticizes those who promise peace before it is to come. He has little use for cheap comfort. However, he realistically advises the Hebrews going into exile, "Seek the welfare [*shalom*] of the city where I have sent you into exile, and pray to the LORD on its behalf, for in its welfare [*shalom*] you will find your welfare [*shalom*]" (Jer 29:7). He spurns the illusions of those who promise Judah a quick return, but then he gives a word of hope: "For surely I know the plans I have for you, says the LORD, plans for your welfare [*shalom*] and not for harm, to give you a future with hope" (Jer 29:11). The historical details, of course, are not our own details. No literal or even analogous reading is intended. But a theology of realistic hope is affirmed here. Life is tough, but we are to seek peace in the city where we are destined to exist. The Lord's plan, the intention of the universe, is to give us a future with hope.

Christians daily pray, "Thy Kingdom come," which means, "May the order of justice and peace be established in historical fact" (or "on earth as it is in heaven"). The Kingdom has started, and each Christian can tell of moments of the realization of God's reign, yet Christians long for its fulfillment.

Romans 8:22–24 captures the basic Christian eschatology of realistic hope as well as any single New Testament text: "We know that the whole creation has been groaning in labor pains until now; and not only the creation, but we ourselves, who have the first fruits of the Spirit, groan inwardly while we wait for adoption, the redemption of our bodies. For in hope we were saved." The hope is not a hope that turns Christians away from the world's travail. Persecution is expected, but Christians living in hope will seek peace and refrain from returning evil with evil. Instead, they will overcome evil with good.

Christian eschatology, like Hebrew eschatology, is rooted in the historical conditions of the time of its writing; it is meant to reinforce Christian practice, and it is hopeful, not despairing. Eschatological formulations of our time are faithful to Scripture by expressing the hope of Scripture, by being rooted in the agony of our time, and by encouraging historical action. The Committee of the World Council of Churches, which held hearings on nuclear weapons in 1983, understood the relevance of eschatology. The committee counseled Christians facing the apocalyptic dimensions of nuclear warfare against responses of fatalism, facile optimism, or the abandonment of faith. Holding to the World Council of Churches' stance of hopeful activism, the committee affirmed, "We believe that the authentic Christian response to such threats is to accept our calling to be fellow-workers with Christ in the redemption of the world from evil. Our mandate is to go on praying, believing, working and hoping, no matter how daunting the task."[9]

Hope Inspires Action

Ethics assumes hope because ethics is about what we ought to do. It is reflection on future-oriented action. It assumes that action toward the future makes a difference. The future is open to a degree. The inquiry into peacemaking focuses practically on problems in American political-economic policies, relations with Islam, the "war on terrorism," and human rights. In all of these areas, the past has shaped our alternatives, but the alternatives are there, and we as humans may choose and act. Our actions cannot eliminate the ambiguities of our historical heritage, but they can eliminate particular forms of evil. In our free actions within history, we become more human. And as we become more human, we become more hopeful, even if the struggle prevents us from relinquishing a realistic evaluation of the opposition.

The American civil rights movement expressed hope in the dream of Martin Luther King Jr. of a beloved community. For a time he achieved a transforming beloved community in the Southern Christian Leadership Conference. He united the realism of the pain of the black experience with the power of hopeful black preaching. I marched with him in the 1960s, but only later would I come to know how profound a church social strategist he was. In 1963 I did not know how necessary eschatological hope was for mobilizing the forces that washed over Washington wave after wave until finally the sand castles of bigotry and legal discrimination were demolished. It is because evil is so entrenched that hope must be so full. The cadences of the "I Have a Dream" speech still roll through my mind from that hot Washington day before the Lincoln Memorial. The specifics of the dream have not been fulfilled, but a particular evil was defeated. Particular legislation was passed.

The clash with the administration over Vietnam and the deepening struggle with the FBI created the climate and opportunity for King's murder. His strategies of using the American dream, the power of black worship services, and the tactics of nonviolence acceptable to the churches were abandoned. But his dream was resurrected in Andrew Young's stances against apartheid and racism at the United Nations, in Jesse Jackson's Democratic presidential aspirations, and in the deepening of the worldwide concern for human rights stemming from the Jimmy Carter presidency. Although evil has not been eliminated, victories have been won, more are winnable, and the struggle is beautiful.

For those of us who are perpetual volunteers in the peace movement, hope is seen in our children's surviving and coming into the movement also. Particular wars that could have been fought have been avoided, wars that could have spread have been contained, and we have lived sixty years without any more atomic destruction of cities. Secular planners and nuclear eschatologists are now agreeing that nuclear war cannot be fought. We may be approaching a point of consensus that the nuclear danger must now be contained. Christian churches are being joined by Hindus, Muslims, Buddhists, and others in deepening their concern for peace. There are signs of hope.

Peacemaking efforts inspired by the threat of complete nuclear destruction are sometimes based on fear. Christians in the peace movement often decry the motivation of fear, arguing instead for inspiration grounded solely in hope. But fear is inevitable; it is a human reality that cannot be ignored. This mixed motivation is profoundly correlated with biblical eschatology, which is usually a fusion of fear and hope. The message today is to fear the evil consequences of our militarism and to hope for actions of peacemaking that will turn the forces of history away from nuclear apocalypse and toward structures of social justice. Edward Schillebeeckx links our hopes with our actions: "Christian theologians must revitalize this concept of the Kingdom of God, not seen as a kind of other-world Kingdom of God, but as a beginning to be realized in this world, here and now. There must be a positive link between our human acting in social, political, and economic affairs and the coming of the Kingdom of God."[10]

One of the significant actions of hope is that nations with the capacity to build nuclear weapons have refrained. Kazakistan and Ukraine have disarmed and removed their nuclear weapons. Brazil and Argentina have not built them. Some have built them secretly, expanding the nuclear cabal to include Israel, India, and Pakistan. The link between reactors for research and electrical energy and for nuclear weapons is largely a matter of national choice. The national restraint of Pakistan and India failed, and they entered the nuclear competition. Before India's bomb development, a Christian ethicist, Somen Das, found hope in the protests against nuclear weapons in Hyde Park, London, and in West Germany. Quoting Aleksandr Solzhenitsyn, who said, "A shout in the mountains has been known to create an avalanche," Das urged action to avert the drift toward the nuclear holocaust: "So we anticipate the future not on the basis of the present reality. In the final analysis *it is not so much a matter of anticipation but of participation*. Then nuclear war is not a matter of inevitability but the possibility of change becomes real and concrete."[11]

Our hopeful biblical eschatology leads to participation in the struggle for peace. Some have suggested God's will might include the nuclear destruction of the world. But this is impossible. The foremost commandment for human life is to "love your neighbor as yourself." There can be no nuclear destruction that does not violate this commandment. To acquiesce to nuclear fatalism is to surrender Christian ethics and to deny Jesus as a teacher of ethics. Given our hopeful eschatology, what are we to do in love?

Active, Love-Seeking Peacemaking

In Paul's summary of the Christian life as faith, hope, and love, love is the love of neighbor. This truth is clear, since in Galatians he writes, "The whole law is summed up in a single commandment, 'You shall love your neighbor as yourself'" (5:14). Paul is quoting Leviticus: "You shall not take vengeance or bear a grudge against any of your people, but you shall love your neighbor as yourself: I am the LORD" (Lev 19:18). Paul, of course, is not rejecting the tradition Jesus taught, shared in Mark 12, Luke 10, and Matthew 22, of the law being summed up in two commandments: "'You shall love the Lord your God with all your heart, and with all your soul, and with all your mind.' This is the greatest and first commandment. And a second is like it: 'You shall love your neighbor as yourself.' On these two commandments hang all the law and the prophets" (Matt 22:37–40).

The commonality of this tradition with Judaism is recognized in Mark and Luke; in these witnesses the proper understanding of the commandment is attributed first to a scribe and then to a lawyer. Paul, writing earlier than Mathew, Mark, or Luke, probably did not know of this strong tradition associating Jesus with a twofold commandment. Actually, the "love of God" in the first commandment is called faith in Paul's threefold summary of faith, hope, and love, and Paul's "love" corresponds to the love of neighbor of the second commandment.

The meaning of this love is the active pursuit of the neighbor's real well-being. It means to care and act for the other as we would care and act for ourselves. This love requirement, rooted in the faith of God's love for humanity and in the hope of God's purposes for humanity, is the foundation of Christian action. For Jesus, the meaning of love is shown in his true teaching, in his real healing, and in his actual feeding. The Samaritan demonstrated love by acting for the well-being of the hurt traveler. For Paul, the believer acts in love by clothing and feeding others. Paul's letters are full of the meaning of love as he pleads for collections of money to provide for the suffering saints of Jerusalem. "Let all that you do be done in love" (1 Cor 16:14).

A dialectical mutuality exists between this peace and justice. One cannot exist without the other. Love requires both. We can love in a world without much peace or much justice. In fact, it is in such a world that we learn to love and accept love's obligations. But love requires peace and justice in that in its active pursuing character, it reaches in hope for both peace and justice.

Justice serves love as fair relationships structure the possibility of the neighbor's well-being. Paul Tillich's understanding of justice as the social forms in which beings can fulfill themselves is correct but somewhat idealistic. Reinhold Niebuhr's understanding of justice as a tolerable balance of power in which beings do not destroy one another's vitalities is more realistic. Of course, in reality we have not achieved a tolerable degree of justice. The Christian life, in being motivated by God's love, is a struggle for a tolerable approximation of justice. Realistically the point needs to be recognized that Christianity is not radically egalitarian. Christian faith is more concerned about all contributing to well-being and everyone receiving what is actually needed than it is about absolute equality. Even when the early Christians held their property in common, they distributed it according to need and eliminated poverty in their community (Acts 2:45; 4:35). But this reservation about absolute egalitarianism does not imply that the present arrangements even begin to approximate justice. Life opportunities in the democratic nations of the NATO alliance are not distributed justly. Particularly in the United States, the gap between those born rich and those born poor is a shocking denial of justice. There is no equal opportunity for the extremes. There may be an approximate justice among the middle class, but here the opportunities of males and females and of whites and blacks violate any standard of justice. But the opportunities of the middle class are dwarfed by the opportunities of the fabulously rich, who dominate decision making in the country.

But, of course, the greatest violations of justice as fairness occur in the poor two-thirds of the world. The poor southern nations, which contain the majority of the world's population, are characterized by extreme riches and extreme poverty. Certainly the poverty of people in the south is due to exploitation by their colonial masters and by their current economic masters. Decisions made in New York, Amsterdam, Paris, and London are hardly made for the poor in the southern nations. Nor do the elites of the southern nations serve the poor. The policies of Buenos Aires, Mexico City, Delhi, Baghdad, and Tehran cannot be said to be made in the interests of the poor.

A Just Peace

Love inspires the struggle for justice and peace. Both are social expressions of the meaning of love. Yet justice and peace are far removed from historical reality.

Niebuhr followed John XXIII in naming justice as the goal and love as the motive of Christian action. In regard to the intentional arena, love seeks a just peace. The goal is ahead, but we live our lives and fashion our strategies toward that goal. The Kingdom of God is not yet realized, but because we have tasted it, we act for it and against the forces opposed to it. The present strategic need may be to prevent the present world contradictions from destroying humanity until these contradictions are overcome. So out of love Christians act toward a just peace, the realization of which they do not expect in their history; yet they act for the survival and further development of human history.

A just peace would be one in which the educational and health expenditures of the nations of the world would have supplanted expenditures of national security as national priorities. International institutions of order would be developing, and the once-dominant powers would be diminishing their competitive influence in maintaining order. The United States' reluctance to submit cases to the World Court and the International Criminal Court would have been overcome, and international institutions would be strengthening the sinews of world community.

Human rights consensus would be emerging, and totalitarian barriers to political and religious rights would have crumbled. The United States would have signed the human rights covenants, and the mixed economics would have demonstrated compassion in practice. Freed from militarism, the countries of the developing world would tend to use *satyagraha* in the Gandhian tradition and nonviolent resistance in the Christian civil rights tradition to resist tyranny and to move governments toward democracy and development.

Diplomacy and negotiations would be used more in international conflicts. Armed forces would be relied on less as the world moved toward a just peace. Gradually the need for military forces along borders would atrophy, and disarmament could follow. More and more unguarded borders like the Canadian–United States border would appear. More and more countries would no longer draw up new war plans against former perceived enemies as the old plans became redundant.

A just peace movement would not necessarily have achieved a world government, but the need for institutions of world order supplanting nuclear terror would have been recognized. The dialogue among world belief systems to find the understandings of world community would have received a priority in energy and funding. Some movement toward an appropriate equivalent of Isaiah's "lawgiver from Zion" would be recognized.

The foregoing projection is an attempt to present a picture of a possible future. It is not meant to represent a utopia or the Kingdom of God but rather a future that is possible if humanity is wise and fortunate. It is not a future we will be given; in part it is ours to make. Other pictures of a just peace are described by Edward L. Long Jr., and his own work is a projection of helpful actions for a just peace.[12] The Glen Stassen project, discussed in chapter 8, advanced the practices for a just peacemaking policy. The United Methodist bishops in their pastoral paper of 1986 listed twenty principles or guidelines for a just peace.[13] A consensus can emerge out of several efforts to think about just peace. This picture attempts to remain realistic and to account for resistance to peacemaking while motivating action. We are now at the beginning of peace thinking, but we have a long way to go before we are clear on the agreed-upon ecumenical understanding of a just peace. Michael Walzer's outstanding book *Exodus and Revolution* eschews utopianism and concludes on a note that describes the development of an ethic of realism and peacemaking.

The lessons of the remarkable actions of liberation recorded in Exodus testify to faith and organization to defeat the gods and power of Egypt—

that is, the bondage and oppression of Egypt. The lessons are "first, that wherever you live, it is probably Egypt; second, that there is a better place, a world more attractive, a promised land; and third, that 'the way to the land is through the wilderness.' There is no way to get from here to there except by joining together and marching."[14]

Even with a commitment to live toward just peacemaking and Walzer's exodus vision before us, the mythical-historical walk from Egypt to the promised land involves many casualties, much suffering, and more than a little terror.

Wisdom in Politics

The prophetic realists have all emphasized wisdom as prudence in international politics. Morgenthau, following Edmund Burke, repeatedly proclaimed it to be the chief virtue in politics. Christian thought, since the assumption of political power, has united the classical virtues with the three preceding theological virtues (faith, hope, and love). The wisdom the realists have sought has been primarily historical. They have tried to immerse themselves in the study of history, and all of them have written historically informed studies. Paul Tillich and Reinhold Niebuhr, particularly, wrote on the philosophy of history. They have been historical realists, believing that accurate understandings of historical events and historical forces are knowable. Prudence is the capacity to appropriately match insight or theory to event or practice. While theory and practice are not the same for realism, the two do meet or overlap, and the realists' writings are characterized by the attempt to find these areas of overlap. Prudence for these realists, clustered around Chicago and Morningside Heights in New York City, was fostered by their continuing conversation with one another as well as with their various sources of information. Prudence would always incline them toward caution in international politics because the stakes (the welfare of nations) were so high.

Courage

The prophetic realists were subject to strong attacks because of their criticism of U.S. nuclear policy and the war in Vietnam. Several of them were under investigation by the FBI and subject to hounding by the House Un-American Activities Committee. Courage meant speaking truth publicly as they saw it to contentious political issues.

Morgenthau suffered ostracism from the foreign policy establishment for criticism of the Vietnam War. Niebuhr was continually investigated by the government and attacked by both pacifists and militarists. John Bennett as president of Union Theological Seminary was arrested and risked alienating financial supporters of the school over the Vietnam War. Students at Union who risked arrest over civil rights issues or Vietnam War issues felt in solidarity with their professors. Similarly, the realists continued to call for policy makers to act courageously, and they respected ordinary citizen soldiers who risked everything for meritous causes.

Statecraft requires choices among difficult and sometimes evil alternatives. Courage is not the taking of unnecessary risks but a resolute willingness to decide and to assume responsibility for one's decisions. The results of decisions in the pluralistic world of complex forces of international relations are often unknown. Actions call forth reactions. The choice of a means leads not to a final end but only to the next stage. There are no ends in politics but only the unfolding complexity where statespeople must decide in the midst of history.

Temperance in Conflict

In retrospect, the causes of these prophetic realists seem to have been moderate, and they were often moderate in their recommendations for policy change. Their very reasonableness made those opposing them seem extreme.

The realists lived humbly but not ascetically. Salaries at Union Theological Seminary, even for their most famous professors, were moderate. All professors received the same base salary, and for a while the group around Niebuhr taxed themselves at the rate of 100 percent above a certain income level to support their projects in race relations and social justice. Their hospitality was generous but not extreme. Those I knew personally were very disciplined, temperate people. Paul Tillich, whom I did not know personally, was an exception in some aspects of his life to this generally temperate, disciplined lifestyle.

The realists' policy recommendations would have pushed the incomes of the country toward the middle. They favored highly progressive income taxes and quite adequate support for the poor. While politics was to be conducted prudently and moderately, their provisions for the poor were generous or liberal.

Temperance in personal life has implications for policy as well. The United States, tempted by power and wealth, needs to limit its appetites to promote the welfare of others. The strong particularly need temperance, or they crush the weak without knowing it. The severity of structural adjustments programs on the poor of the world supported the intemperance of elites where government reductions in spending came at the expense of the poor in barrios. Temperance is a virtue, and foreign policy elites need to exhibit it as much as foreign policy needs to be guided by it.

Justice

The classical virtue of justice is also a biblical virtue. As justice for Plato is the proper balance among the classes and for Aristotle the concept of each person receiving one's due, for the biblical writers it is the practice of correct behavior in the community. Micah 6:8 shows the close relationship between love and reverence: "He has told you, O mortal, what is good; and what does the LORD require of you but to do justice, and to love kindness, and to walk humbly with your God?"

Not every person or every culture will define justice in the same way, but it is a synonym for the public welfare. For citizens to practice behavior for the good of the community and for statespeople to seek the good of the world community is to cultivate the moral life and develop a more moral nation. The moral philosophers among the realists have regarded foreign policy as the pursuit of national interest.[15] This is true if the national interest is generally related to the interests of others. But in a period of superpower hegemony, the United States cannot just continue to pursue national self-interest; to be moral, it must exhibit a decent respect for the interests of others. As argued earlier, national purpose includes mutuality and the promotion of the purposes and interests of others beyond national borders.

Within the tradition described as prophetic realism, justice is not just what the strong want. Justice includes correction of the system and limitation of the privileges of the strong so that all human life can flourish. We will not see equality under the law or equality of opportunity in our history, but justice does have an egalitarian thrust. U.S. policy needs to be more tipped toward the promotion of equality and freedom of the world's peoples than it has been.

Realism takes account of the fact that hegemonic nations engender resistance by other nations. Sources of resistance to U.S. domination are emerging within Europe, China, and some nations of Islam. India has usually been impatient with the U.S. hegemony. Greater movement to include considerations of justice within policy even to the point of intentionally reducing U.S. worldwide influence may delay the formation of new alliances to thwart the United States. A balance of social forces or classes promotes justice domestically, and new balances of power internationally may serve justice internationally.

Notes

1. Gerhard von Rad, "Shalom in the Old Testament," in Gerhard Kittel, *Theological Dictionary of the New Testament* (vol. 3; Grand Rapids: Eerdmans, 1964), 406.

2. Ibid., 405.

3. Werner Foerster, "Peace in the New Testament," in Kittel, *Theological Dictionary*, 3:412.

4. Ibid., 419.

5. Ibid.

6. Kenneth N. Waltz, *Man, the State, and War: A Theoretical Analysis* (New York: Columbia University Press, 1959).

7. D. N. Premnath, "The Process of Latifundialization Mirrored in Isaiah 5:8–10," unpublished faculty research seminar paper, United Theological College, Bangalore, India, January 30, 1985, 7.

8. Ibid., 11.

9. "The Report of the Public Hearing on Nuclear Weapons and Disarmament Organized by the World Council of Churches," in *Before It's Too Late* (ed. Paul Abrecht and Ninan Koshy; Geneva: World Council of Churches, 1983), 31.

10. Edward Schillebeeckx, quoted in *Before It's Too Late*, 89.

11. Somen Das, "Anticipating the Future—Nuclear Holocaust," unpublished paper, University Scholar Seminar, Bangalore, India, April 12, 1984, 4, emphasis mine.

12. Edward L. Long Jr., "The Mandate to Seek a Just Peace,"in Ronald H. Stone and Dana Wilbanks, *The Peacemaking Struggle: Militarism and Resistance* (Lanham, Md.: University Press of America, 1985), 29–41.

13. *In Defense of Creation: The Nuclear Crisis and a Just Peace* (first draft of United Methodist bishops, 1986), 17–19.

14. Michael Walzer, *Exodus and Revolution* (New York: Basic Books, 1985), 149. Quotation from W. D. Davies, *The Territorial Dimension of Judaism* (Berkeley: University of California Press, 1982), 60.

15. See Robert Jackson, *The Global Covenant Human Conduct in a World of States* (Oxford: Oxford University Press, 2000), 21, 113.

⟪ **8** ⟫

Realist Criticism of Just Peacemaking Theory

CHRISTIAN REALISM ASSOCIATED WITH Reinhold Niebuhr, John Bennett, Kenneth Thompson, Roger Shinn, and others provided guidance for mainline Protestant approaches to international politics during the Cold War years. The critiques of realism by liberation theologians within the church and liberals or international organizational thinkers in politics weakened realism's hold on the Protestant centers of thought about international relations. Hans Morgenthau, the Jewish philosopher of politics, allied with Reinhold Niebuhr, received much critique posthumously as well. In the last half-dozen years, a reemergence of just peacemaking theory in ecumenical and denominational thinking about foreign policy also has criticized the earlier realism. Was the earlier reform-oriented realism too pessimistic about the future of international politics? In the early post–Cold War years, an optimism partially Christian and partially derived from secular philosophy began to suggest that international politics was in a more cooperative, transformative time and that paradigms of just peacemaking were needed.

Some denominations, an ecumenical group guided by Glen Stassen associated with the Society of Christian Ethics, and the National Council of Churches of Christ in the USA all articulated theories of just peacemaking in the post–Cold War years. All of these participated somewhat in the liberal, internationally oriented optimism of the post–Cold War times.

The events of September 11, 2001, and the lack of a philosophy for the United States as a hegemonic superpower raise the need for fundamental thinking about U.S. foreign policy. While the just peacemaking insights and recommendations contain needed emphases, the underlying philosophy of just peacemaking does not seem persuasive enough to guide and limit the policy of the solitary superpower. Just peacemaking remains a vision and a set of practical policies, but a more politically oriented biblical or prophetic realism is needed as the public theology to impact and reform U.S. policy for the new century. This book attempts to contribute to the dialogue by providing a prophetic realist critique of just peacemaking, reflecting on the just peacemaking critique of realism and providing a few conclusions. This chapter focuses on the ecumenical discussions of just peacemaking associated with Stassen and the Society of Christian Ethics. More of the morally concerned realist perspective was needed in some of the concurrent denominational and National Council of Church projects on peacemaking.

Today Christian realism affirms the struggles for peacemaking and justice and recognizes the ontological and theological embraces of peacemaking and justice. However, it expects less peace and justice to be realized than just peacemaker writers projected in their transformative models. The struggles for justice will continue to involve armed force and the threat of violence sometimes. The suppression of terrorism will require more justice, peacemaking policies, and the application of armed force. Sometimes peacemaking will be achieved without justice.

To the extent that the practices of peacemaking attempt to parallel the principles of just war, they fail. The principles of just war are articulated to limit the waging of war while sometimes morally affirming war. The practices of just peacemaking are not to limit peacemaking, and peacemaking requires no moral justification in itself. The ten principles of just peacemaking correspond better to the Ten Commandments than to the principles of just war.

Just Peacemaking Theory Emerges

The great significance of the concept of just peacemaking is that it provides a paradigm for religious thinking about peacemaking beyond the concepts of agonized participant, pacifism, just war theory, "obey the state" positions, or crusade attitudes toward war. It also provides for Christian church policy making a responsible framework into which other issues, such as an ethic for military intervention for humanitarian rescue, can be placed. Just peacemaking has continuity with many of our denominational quests for peace thinking, while in presenting a rather complete paradigm, it is an advance. For example, the thought of the Working Group on Just Peacemaking helped the Presbyterian Church (USA) to collect the major teachings of its own peacemaking policies and order them in a single peacemaking conceptual paper.

Just peacemaking is an emerging concept that has received an additional boost by the publication of *Just Peacemaking: Ten Practices for Abolishing War* (1998), edited by Glen Stassen. It is referenced in the policy paper resolution of the Presbyterian Church (USA) in its document "Just

Peacemaking and the Call for International Intervention for Humanitarian Rescue" (1998).[1] I appreciate this sense of an emerging concept, which was more developed in Glen Stassen's earlier book *Just Peacemaking* (1992) than it is in this collection. The new collection has an introduction entitled "Just Peacemaking as a New Ethic." Just Peacemaking's precedents in official religious language are at least as old as the debates among the theologians during the 1940s in the Federal Council of Churches Commission on a Just and Endurable Peace. The ten "practice norms" or principles of action have been documented as already existing in church social teaching in this century.

A decision was made between the final meeting of the group at the Carter Center and the book's publication to place the major discussions of international relations in the third part of the book. In response to the critique of students who read the earlier draft, issues of conflict resolution and theories of nonviolent peacemaking action were brought to the fore. So the book now moves from an introduction to New Testament–based peacemaking theology into a chapter on nonviolent action praxis; it also includes in the first four chapters independent initiatives toward peacemaking and conflict resolution and the practice of forgiveness in politics. A more detailed introduction to the Old Testament, in which the sources of injustice, pride, anarchy, and religious conflict were made clearer, would have deepened the study. Individuals and groups have a role in international peacemaking, but the weight of the structured realities of nation-states deserves roles of greater prominence.

The working group did not discuss abolishing war, and the subtitle *Ten Practices for Abolishing War* gives the study a utopian cast. Some read the Bible, particularly Isaiah 2, which contains the UN's motto about "swords into plowshares," as clearly conveying that anarchy, injustice, and pride will need to be overcome before ultimate commitments and penultimate laws can be established to abolish war and the need to study it. It is possible to agree with Stassen's exegesis of the Sermon on the Mount and its powerful message of initiating peace without believing that it and the adoption of these ten practices by several countries would abolish war. The New Testament itself anticipated the continuation of war within human history.

The ethic of just peacemaking continues five of the six principles of the Federal Council of Churches' "Six Pillars of Peace." Fortunately, it did not need to continue the fourth pillar: "The peace must proclaim the goal of autonomy for subject peoples, and it must establish international organization to assure and supervise the realization of that end." At least some colonialism is over. This still begs the question of independence for Kurds, Palestinians, Tibetans, and others, but the claims of these peoples were not elevated to one of the ten principles. Four of the other principles of the "six pillars of peace": for the United Nations, international regulation of international economy, controlling military establishments, and human rights have continued in the ten with modification. John Foster Dulles's principle of flexibility to adapt the treaty structure of the world to changing conditions is not continued, but it can be seen as subsumed under peacemaking initiatives and cooperative conflict resolution in the new principles. Interestingly, as the Just Peacemaking project was publishing its work, the National Council of Churches was engaged in rethinking and refurbishing the "Six Pillars of Peace" for the twenty-first century. This is all to say the work on just peacemaking is not all that new. Our work on just peacemaking is still in process. Though eschewing the need for assurance of success, the editors wrote in 1998, "We live at a moment when historical evidence of the promise of just peacemaking surrounds us."[2]

The chapters on nonviolent strategies of social change, independent initiatives for peacemaking, and the importance of voluntary peacemaking organizations are all advances beyond the Federal Council of Churches' "Six Pillars of Peace." Still, Michael Smith's transformative, optimistic approach to a new, stronger United Nations with its own military force will strike many as utopian. Paul Schroeder's emphasis on cooperating with the trends of the present system requires great optimism about the market system producing sufficiency, justice, and legitimacy to protect this order. His dismissal of finding the causes of war in human nature and the anarchy of the present system seems premature. The realism of Kenneth Waltz's *Man, State and War*, drawn from generations of political theorists, reinforces a realist reading of Scripture that suggests that both human nature and the lack of sufficient order in a world of conflicting religious and pseudo-religious ideologies incline us toward war. The melioristic reduction of the number of wars and the expansion of the realm of peace will call forth our full efforts. Let us follow the apostle Paul: "If it is possible, so far as it depends on you, live peaceably with all" (Rom 12:18).

Just Peacemaking Critique of Realism

Glen Stassen's own text in *Just Peacemaking* (1992) criticizes Reinhold Niebuhr only on his understanding of Jesus' ethic and tries to preserve Niebuhr's realism about the human situation. Actually, in his later life, Niebuhr learned from W. D. Davies, as Stassen did, about the Matthean construction of teachings attributed to Jesus. Niebuhr thought Davies's work could have spared him a lot of problems. Davies's work on the gospel clarified the constructed nature of the Sermon on the Mount, distancing it from the literal speech of Jesus, which Niebuhr earlier had represented as the ideal presented in ethics. Stassen is correct that Niebuhr's idealistic understanding of Jesus' ethic separates it from the world of politics and international ethics, while the love ethic is relevant to every situation. In advocating initiatives in peacemaking and reconciliation, Stassen's presentation of the Sermon on the Mount is very powerful. He also observes the way that Paul, particularly in Rom 12, develops many of Jesus' themes. Despite the facts that terms such as *peacemaking, Messiah*, and *the nations* are present in the book of Matthew, the implications that Jesus had a political message as seen by John Yoder or that Jesus taught an approach to resolving problems of international conflict seem as strained to me as the early Barth's claim that Jesus was a socialist. Of course, the gospels do not ignore political reality or the Roman Empire, but the argument that Jesus taught an ethic for international relations is not persuasive to me. Stassen is better than the earlier Niebuhr in finding concrete guidance for life in Matthew, but Niebuhr remains wiser in refusing to locate Jesus directly in international politics. It is also important to emphasize that when we are exegeting the beatitudes of either Matthew or Luke, we are exegeting those books and not any text of Jesus. Matthew is past the fall of Jerusalem, and Jesus is pre-fall. Niebuhr is probably correct that it is the love teaching of Jesus that is directly relevant to international relations and not the specific ethical guidelines of Jesus, though they too may be helpful.

The essays in *Just Peacemaking: Ten Practices for Abolishing War* (1998) feature less-restrained criticism of Niebuhr: (1) Duane Friesan, John Langan, and Stassen assert that Niebuhr taught students "to be skeptical of major changes in history" (p. 20). (2) David Steele, Steven Brion-Meises, Gary Gunderson, and Edward L. Long Jr. write, "A realist critique often characterizes international relations as similar to the 'prisoner's dilemma' in game theory" (p. 63). (3) Alan Geyer finds Niebuhr guilty of having "discounted severely the relevance of Jesus' gospel of love and forgiveness to the realities of world politics and even of international conflict" (p. 78). When Geyer quotes Niebuhr in regard to forgiving love in international politics, he finds Niebuhr to be "ambiguous and even contradictory" (p. 78). (4) Bruce Russett characterizes the realist extremist as treating "all states as potential enemies" (p. 108) and argues for recognizing a peaceful side to international relations, particularly among democracies. (5) Paul Schroeder recognizes himself as a realist in the sense of acknowledging the relative anarchy of the international system. Still, he wants to distance his position from realist assumptions that "there must always be great wars" or that "war is rooted in human nature" (p. 135). The concluding sentence of Schroeder's essay identifies his position as that of a problem solver, not a "realist" or "idealist."

A prophetic realist response follows, beginning with the final point of just peacemaking critique (5) Niebuhr certainly affirmed a pragmatic or problem-solving approach while mixing elements from idealism and realism. He would hold stubbornly to the values of a philosophy of humanity and history in discussions of international politics. (4) Realism did not discover the tendency of democracies to be peaceful among themselves; instead, it has stressed conflict models, but the realists were highly cognizant of long-term international cooperation and common interests. Still, it seems true that within its two hundred years of history, the United States has had wars or military conflicts with most of the major nations (India and Indonesia are exceptions). (3) Realists recognize forgiveness as important but do not expect it often among nations; within that framework, Geyer's quotations of Niebuhr do not seem contradictory but rather nuanced, subtle, and accurate. People do not need to subscribe to Niebuhr's portrait of Jesus from 1935 to recognize that Jesus did not give explicit advice for international politics. Geyer presents three quotes from Niebuhr, two from 1935 and one from 1952, and then observes that he finds them ambiguous or contradictory. I would not argue that Niebuhr's formulations are always consistent, particularly during a period in which he switches from being a leader of the Socialist Party to being a New Deal Democrat. The historical period in question was marked by World War II and the advent of the nuclear age. However, the quotations are typical Niebuhr material. The relationship of divine love to sinful politics is paradoxical. Politics is criticized by love and never fulfills it perfectly. Yet love and even forgiveness are great solvents to human brutality when they are found; however, they are not found very often in the prideful behavior of statespeople. Forgiveness in international politics is good, but we should not expect to find too much of it. Geyer is probably correct that the role of forgiveness in international politics is not a pacifist-realist dispute. Niebuhr's Rauschenbusch lectures of 1934, which Geyer quotes, were polemically directed at Christian liberal optimism. Perhaps Geyer retains more of that optimism than the realists, and therein rests the need for Geyer's critique. (2) It is rather silly to treat political realism as game theory of the "prisoner's dilemma" type. Realism is too historically oriented and too cognizant of the irrationalism of politics to enter significantly into the rationally modeled world of various forms of game theory. (1) On history, most readers of Niebuhr find him perceptive in seeing the shifting dynamics of America as it moved from a growing continental republic to an imperial power or the rise and fall of various empires in *The Structure of Nations and Empires*. It would be strange for prophetic realists like Niebuhr, Morgenthau, and Tillich, who combine biblical realism with debt to Nietzsche for their dynamic concepts of power, not to expect change. If the authors of the essays in *Just Peacemaking* meant that Niebuhr did not expect inevitable progressive improvement in international politics, they were correct. On balance, Niebuhr's biblical realism still seems closer to our 2000-year post-Christ history than either Schroeder's enthusiasm for peace as a result of worldwide capitalist democracy or Smith's Kantian optimism about the United Nations.

Finally, Stassen's just peacemaking theory seems overly dependent on an exegesis of the Sermon on the Mount that does not take account of the biblical witness to the persistence of violence in human history. Except for the presentations of the beginning and the end, the biblical witness is to continuing human conflict and war. Peacemaking is a vision and often a mission, but the Bible promises no abolishment of war from human history. The historical books, the prophetic books, and Jesus' own death must not be neglected in the search for biblical perspective on war and peace.

Stassen himself is passionate and powerful but irenic. He has responded to my criticisms and those of Lisa Sowle Cahill that just peacemaking theory needs more realism.[3] Two strands of his argument seem particularly relevant. First, he argues, just peacemaking theory, though a synthesis of pacifist and realist insight, is realist as it stands. He points to his own tutelage under Reinhold Niebuhr at Union and realist professors of international relations at Harvard. He argues that the peacemaking practices themselves are derived from empirical observation and are therefore realistic. He recognizes that "wars will continue to occur" and that "states are not withering away."[4] He points out that Lisa Sowle Cahill asked for the theory to deal more with sin. He argues further that Robert Jervis and Robert Keohone have shown that the international system is becoming more institutional or shifting to a complex interdependence.[5] The implications are that realist theory has changed and that much of it is compatible with institutional emphases and/or just peacemaking's institutional theoretical tendency.

Cahill was correct that more on human brokenness was needed. The pre–9/11 spirit of just peacemaking was lured into optimism because of the collapse of the Soviet system and the expanding room for humanitarian intervention and UN influence. The world was more optimistic in 1997 and 1998. A steadier focus on human sin, however named, the absurdity of the structures and personnel of many national governments, and the subterranean anarchy of an international system should have corrected the optimism of the 1990s. The period between the Cold War and the war on terrorism was the best period in international relations of my life, but it was only a phase. A peaceful world cannot be forged out of the material at hand—human or institutional.

Stassen's second argument is that classical realism, called in this book prophetic realism, is rooted in theological readings of scriptural sources. The same depth may not be present in either the institutional realists or the extreme realists discussed in Stassen's essay. Stassen has told me his further work will emphasize more Old Testament context, particularly the Isaiah themes that also appear in the New Testament. This book has tried to show that in regard to human nature and history, the Christian tradition is wise. Christian interpretation of its most important insights depends on a recognition of sin and God's grace. So arguments about the direction of international relations also have a religious dimension. Optimism about institutional complexity is more than observation, though the development of international institutions is empirically verifiable. The optimism neglects the finitude and selfishness of those who build and manage the institutions. The prophetic realists cannot neglect those characteristics, even though they may, as Reinhold Niebuhr did, serve as a delegate to the United Nations Educational, Scientific, and Cultural Organization meeting in Paris.

Just Peacemaking, Prophetic Realism, and Bush Policy

The collapse of the USSR left the United States in a hegemonic role in the world. Its navies dominate the seas, its airplanes rule the skies, and its space surveillance and weapons reign supreme in the near reaches of outer space. Its ideologies of capitalism, democracy, and Christianity are expanding, and its culture and language are the most prominent forms of communication. Its economic prowess involves it in decisive ways in many of the world's national economies. Institutions heavily influenced by the United States exert hegemonic powers in many economies. U.S. dominance assumes various forms according to the context. Unlike the evil empires of Communism and Nazism, its forms have elements of laissez-faire rather than totalitarian control. The liberal-democratic state seems supreme.

The anti-imperial, post–World War II rhetoric, the negative connotations of the word *empire*, and the recent association of *empire* with either the USSR or the Third Reich incline pro-American political philosophers to avoid the term and critics to affirm the term for the United States' international arrangements.[6]

Significant republics are not immune from imperialism; witness Athens, Rome, Venice, France, the Netherlands, and Britain as well as the United States. Alternative governmental polities also support empire or pursue hegemony. Republican institutions are neither necessary for empire nor antithetical to it.

The "father of U.S. realists," Reinhold Niebuhr, used the term *empire* in his book *The Structure of Nations and Empires* to describe American power.[7] Just peacemaking theory has not stressed the term. I used the term earlier, but the caution of an Indian theologian, Thomas Thangaraj, who grew up under the British Raj and its aftermath has discouraged me from using it. He was afraid that its acceptance by moral theologians would enforce the pride that characterizes imperial citizens. So for the moral good of the society and for political reasons, the preferred term for the United States is *solitary hegemonic superpower*.

The second Bush administration has faced a significant amount of criticism for unilateralism in foreign policy.[8] The abandonment of the Kyoto

Protocol, the withdrawal from the Anti-Ballistic Missile Treaty, the opposition to the International Criminal Court, and the willingness to invade Iraq while being opposed by significant numbers of the UN Security Council have all been sited as examples of unilateralism. On the other hand, belated seeking of UN support for "nation building" in Iraq and Afghanistan seems to signify that the Bush administration will turn to multilateralism when necessary. The failure to build a broad coalition and to diplomatically reduce opposition to the Iraq invasion is offset somewhat by the earlier UN resolution demanding compliance of Iraq with disarmament agreements. The younger Bush administration may not have enough ideological consistency to prove the charge of unilateralism to be useful.

Should not the critique of abandoning Kyoto be that in both domestic and foreign policy, the Bush administration is negligent of the seriousness of gas emissions for global warming and that it does not understand the relationship of sustainable, humane economic development to ecology? The folly in this situation is not unilateralism as much as it is ecological irresponsibility.

Opposition to the International Criminal Court neglects U.S. values for strengthening international law at the very time that such strengthening is needed to oppose criminal acts of terrorism. The absurdity is seen in the United States' urging trial by international courts of genocidal criminals from Serbia and Rwanda. A long-standing value of the United States is to strengthen international law, or at least so say the prophetic realists, both those following Isaiah and those representing just peacemaking theory.

The guilt of the United States in the invasion of Iraq is due not to unilateralism but to the failure to follow normative structures of international law and just war theory. The United States violated peace more than it violated multilateralism. The United States violated sovereignty without adequate reason, and it failed both in exhibiting prudence and in limiting the use of force. Ethical sensitivity reacts to the use of force to inflict human death. It asks, in this case, how is the taking of human life justified? The general answer is that only the protection of human life justifies the forceful death of other human beings. In international relations the just war criteria and international law have grown slowly to declare wars legitimate or illegitimate. The case has not been made that the invasion of Iraq, limited by no-fly zones, economic sanctions, an autonomous Kurdish area, and international arms inspectors, was legitimate.

Given that a humanitarian argument for the removal of Saddam Hussein could have been made because of his massacres of Kurds and Shiites, and given the U.S. domination of Iraq, the lesser evil at this time has been to capture him and to attempt to suppress opposition to an emerging Iraqi sovereignty. Further steps are required:

- the rebuilding of Iraqi police and military forces;
- cultural and educational programs for Iraq;
- internationalization under the UN of the restoration of Iraqi's sovereignty;
- civil works projects run by Iraq to rebuild the country from funds secured by future oil revenues; and
- devolution of U.S. military responsibilities as quickly as is prudent.

U.S. policy makers need to disconnect the Iraqi wars from terrorism, narrow the definition of the struggle with Al Qaeda and its allies, and explain the U.S. goals for post-Hussein Iraq in realistic terms. If the situation deteriorates, a face-saving withdrawal from Iraq, leaving the Iraqi people to struggle over their social order, may be necessary. Just peacemaking theory might apologize and ask for forgiveness. Prophetic realism would not go so far while still regarding the invasion as an immoral mistake.

Both just peacemaking and prophetic realism agree that the use of hegemonic military force by the United States is undesirable. Prophetic realism understands that peace is secured through accommodation and that diplomacy is the method for securing such peace.[9] Failures in diplomacy during the first Bush administration led to Saddam Hussein's invasion of Kuwait, the first Gulf War, Osama bin Laden's jihad, and the second Gulf War. From a prophetic realism perspective, neither the second Bush administration[10] nor just peacemaking theory explicitly recognizes enough the role of diplomacy based on the potential use of force.

Both realism and just peacemaking recognize peace as a goal of foreign policy. Realism is more inclined to recognize the role of power or the threat to use force as part of the peacemaking process. The term *peacemaker* was used of a Roman emperor before it appeared in one of Jesus' beatitudes in the book of Matthew.

Both realism and just peacemaking recognize properly applied international aid for sustainable human development as a goal of foreign policy. Just peacemaking may see this goal as more contributory toward peace than does prophetic realism, with its critique of government aid programs. The Bush administration's disconnect between announced aid goals and priority for their funding reinforces the cynicism. Both schools of thought need to stress more than they have the benefits and vast resources of the nongovernmental aid programs from the United States.[11]

Earlier I argued for the use of *national purpose* rather than *national interest* as a necessary concept for foreign policy considerations of a superpower state.[12] But whichever term is used, it seems to me and certainly to Morgenthau and Niebuhr that the concept is needed as a limiting concept and as an essential item of communication regarding foreign policy. Would not just peacemaking's program be more persuasive if it took account of the concept and of the debates around it? Should not Noriega and Hussein have been more clearly informed of the national interest considerations of the United States in the Panama Canal and in Kuwait's oil? While U.S. interests rest in the promotion of regulated mixed economic forms, in democracy, and in human rights, these values are limited also by material and security concerns of the U.S. national purpose. Neither the Bush administration's desire for domination nor the just peacemaking theorists' desire for a more secure world should push these goals toward a rhetorical crusade. It is not at all evident that the United States has sufficient power to impose democracy upon countries in the Middle East. The attempt to do so could lead to major U.S. losses.

Realists and peacemaking students both emphasize the use of soft power (education, culture, broadcasting, publishing, interpretive resources) for understanding and peacemaking. The downgrading of the institutions within the United States promoting these avenues of foreign policy has been a mistake, and the combined policies of tax cuts, military expansion, and preemptive war will for the future limit their restoration.

Prophetic realism[13] is situated between the Bush administration's realpolitik and just peacemaking's more visionary or transformative perspective on foreign policy. Until just peacemaking incorporates more attention to power, national definitions of purpose, diplomacy, and biblical realism derived from the prophets, it will remain too idealistic. Bush's imperial realpolitik is making the world worse than the one we had.

Summary

First, if the just peacemaking paradigm is to succeed, it needs to engage the classical realism of North American theology and international relations more deeply than it has. It needs to bring into its theory more than it has the fact that very significant political leadership does not want conflict resolution, nonviolent social change, democracy, or a stronger United Nations. Significant American political actors are insecure and naive about international relations and religion, and they favor the promotion of their own economic well-being and their own oligarchic-class interests. All of us who work in international relations and ethics are self-interested, somewhat provincial sinners, and we must account for this truth in our analysis.

Second, many of our allies and competitor nations are governed by people no better than we are, and their perspectives are limited by Communist, Hindu, Muslim, African, Latin American, and European prejudices. Nations are organized so as to be driven by many factors other than the concern for peace. National interests built into the governing structures of societies simply cannot be neglected when thinking about international relations. The insecurities of the elites ruling various societies are expressed not only by their personalities but by their armed forces, diplomats, corporate organization, and international relations.

Finally, even as the political scientists of the just peacemaking committee recognized, international relations are a mixture of anarchical and cooperative trends. There is not enough community in the world to build international institutions that would promote order in the world and abolish war. The world is not a Hobbesian world of war of all against all, but neither is it a world where the people of the United States, Saudi Arabia, Rwanda, Switzerland, and China support common goals toward peace.

Gazing into the ruins of the World Trade Center confirmed for me the above response to just peacemaking theory. The ruins, of course, have no single originating event, but the humiliation of Islam, the pride of the son of the greedy bin Laden family, the failure of the U.S. ambassador to warn Sadam Hussein that Kuwait was a vital interest to the Bush administration, the Clinton carelessness about foreign policy, the failure of the second Bush administration to take seriously the Middle East, and the violent tendencies of some sectarian movements of Islam all combined to topple the towers of pride.

The deep-seated origins of organized violence in the human soul require more analysis of just peacemaking theory and a more profound recognition of sin. Probably all in the Society of Christian Ethics learned from Darwin's theory of evolution, Freud's theory of civilization, Marx's theory of class, Rauschenbusch's theory of human solidarity, and Niebuhr's theory of sin, if not from the more recent writings of René Girard and Marjorie Suchocki of the deep connections of our human essence and violence.

Just peacemaking theory can supplement Christian or prophetic realism well. It seems unlikely to displace it. The practices of peacemaking are all useful, but they will not bring universal peace or the abolition of war. Realism needs reforming. The religious base of the realism called moral or Christian or prophetic needs to be emphasized. This prophetic realism derived from the Bible needs to be distinguished from realpolitik derived from Thucydides and Machiavelli. The realists' understandings of national interest and power need to be clarified and related to both values and ontology. The whole underlying moral perspective of prophetic realism needs to be explicated. The provisional division between international politics and international economy suggested by Hans Morgenthau needs to be undone and reconceptionalized. The real history of prophetic moralism, through its exponents from Amos, Augustine, Calvin, and Wesley to Niebuhr and beyond, needs a fresh narration. Finally, the deep connections between realism and peacemaking need to be explained.

The containment and limitation of human violence on the international scene for as long as international politics continues will require not only the balancing of power, diplomacy, international organization, and moral limitation but also sometimes the pursuit of peace through war. So even as our own society drifts into greater injustice, we will work for peace by building world community, providing international human economic aid, balancing power, supporting the United Nations, organizing locally for peace and justice, promoting international morality, reducing religious militancy, working for international law, struggling for ecojustice, advocating disarmament, seeking international courts, securing democratic allies, improving diplomacy, teaching our children, and saying our prayers.

Notes

1. "Just Peacemaking and the Ethics of Humanitarian Intervention," in *Selected Theological Statements of the Presbyterian Church (USA) General Assemblies (1956–1998)* (Louisville: Presbyterian Church [USA], 1998), 333.

2. Glen Stassen, ed., *Just Peacemaking: Ten Practices for Abolishing War* (Cleveland: Pilgrim Press, 1998), 22.

3. Glen H. Stassen, "The Unity, Realism, and Obligatoriness of Just Peacemaking Theory," *Journal of the Society of Christian Ethics* 23, no. 1 (Spring/Summer 2003): 171–94.

4. Ibid., 175.

5. Ibid., 181–84.

6. Dimitri Simes, "America's Imperial Dream," *Foreign Affairs*, November/December 2003, 91–102.

7. Reinhold Niebuhr, *The Structures of Nations and Empires* (New York: Charles Scribner's Sons, 1959), 15, 23.

8. A *New York Times* editorial (December 29, 2003) repeated its criticism of Bush policy unilateralism: "The White House must recognize the damage its unilateralism is inflicting on the Army and change course before the damage becomes harder to undo" (p. 20). Secretary of State Colin Powell argued in *Foreign Affairs* (January/February 2004) that the Bush policy was not unilateral but nurturing of international partnerships.

9. Hans J. Morgenthau, *Politics among Nations* (New York: Alfred A. Knopf, 1966). See the conclusion in part 10 of the fourth edition. See also Niebuhr, *Structures of Nations and Empires*, 286, 289–99.

10. For a critique of Bush's diplomatic failures, see James Rubin, "Stumbling into War," *Foreign Affairs*, September/October 2003, 46–66.

11. Carol C. Aelman, "The Privatization of Foreign Aid," *Foreign Affairs*, November/December 2003, 9–14.

12. Ronald H. Stone, "Power and Purpose," *Realism and Hope* (Lanham, Md.: University Press of America, 1976), 105–28, and above, 72–82.

13. The term *prophetic realism* is used for the thought of Reinhld Niebuhr, Hans J. Morgenthau, George Kennan, and others in the new volume *The Christian Realists*, edited by Eric Patterson (Lanham, Md.: University Press of America, 2003).

‹‹◎ 9 ◎››

Resurgent Pacifist Attack on Realism

BOTH THE TENSIONS of the Cold War and the militarism of the superpower United States encouraged pacifists to renew their attack on political realism. Actually, the pacifists should have seen the prophetic realists as allies, because the prudence of the realists disinclined them to military adventures. They wanted political containment of Soviet Communism, not nuclear war. They regarded the Vietnam War as tragically foolish. Again and again they opposed expansive military development on the part of the United States. However, Niebuhr's pre–World War II writing against Christian pacifism had earned their enmity, as had his resignation of the presidency of the pacifist Fellowship of Reconciliation society.

Niebuhr had respected Quaker and Mennonite pacifism, which frankly remained apolitical. The attacks came from a more militant Mennonite who wanted to be both political and pacifist. John Yoder initiated the critique, and Stanley Hauerwas has continued many of his arguments.

Yoder's 1953 pamphlet against Niebuhr's realism made three points: (1) sin cannot be regarded as a necessity by ethics; (2) selfish motives of self-preservation cannot be conceded to in consideration of ethics and foreign policy; and (3) moral pluralism grounded in tolerance is rejected. He then moved on to his more important theological arguments: (1) Niebuhr neglects the power of the resurrection for ethics; (2) the church is the meaning of history; (3) the church as a society is morally more developed than individual Christians; (4) there is a significant moral distance between saint and unbeliever; and (5) Niebuhr neglects the reality of the Holy Spirit. His major point, expressed in various ways, is that Niebuhr's church is not a peace church that exhibits the qualities of the Christian life that Yoder found necessary.[1] This is the central point carried forward by Stanley

Hauerwas.[2] While it is true that the Christologies of Hauerwas and Yoder differ from that of Niebuhr, there is almost no rational way to adjudicate a debate about their respective Christologies. The difference is clear enough in their ecclesiologies. Hauerwas takes up much of the idealism of Yoder's perspective on the church. Neither Hauerwas nor Yoder takes seriously Niebuhr's idea that Martin Luther's realism about the church is grounded in ministerial experience, though both Yoder and Hauerwas revel in the supposed goodness of their claims for the church. Niebuhr's view of the church, expressed in two books to which they do not refer, is grounded in the daily ministerial experience as well as in his deep experience of the German church's compromises with Hitler. Hauerwas admits his Methodist Church will not become a peace church, yet he attacks it for not becoming a peace church. Because both Yoder and Hauerwas make the perspective on the church the central issue, readers will have to decide whether Niebuhr's Lutheran ecclesiology of the church under judgment is more accurate than Hauerwas's romanticism about a peace church. Hauerwas's church is an unstable synthesis drawn indiscriminately from insights of the Roman Catholic Church and the Mennonite Church. Finally, is it not the case that Niebuhr's practical church and practical political life provided him with a more accurate perspective of both than any perspective that Hauerwas, lacking ministerial and political experience, could muster? The insistence of both Yoder and Hauerwas that the church is the center of history and that church history is the important history to know raises the questions, If they know the church history, how can they claim such moral superiority for it and its members? And is not the gospel more about forgiveness than it is about morally superior Christians?

Before entering into some criticisms of Hauerwas's career struggle with Protestant ethics of realism, we must begin at his ending. Though these comments will suggest Hauerwas is not a close reader of either John Wesley or Reinhold Niebuhr, the first question is what to do with his 2000–2001 Gifford Lectures.[3] He likes Karl Barth and is critical of William James and Reinhold Niebuhr. He analyzes Niebuhr to show that he remains a liberal pragmatist in philosophy, but students of Niebuhr have generally known that. The more troubling aspect of his critique is that he thinks Niebuhr wanted to establish his theological convictions on philosophy. Traces of this inclination appear in the theses Niebuhr wrote when he was younger. He never gave up liberalism or pragmatism, but the mature Niebuhr based his theology on the Christian tradition. The theses Hauerwas uses from 1914 to 1915 are even before Niebuhr's ministerial service from 1915 to 1928 in Detroit.

Niebuhr, like Paul Tillich, used a method of correlation. Niebuhr's was different, but he laid a basis for Christian answers by attacking alternatives and clearing the ground for a Christian response that correlated with truth about history and human nature as Niebuhr explained them. Tillich's more irenic method raised questions from existentialism that received answers from reinterpreted Christian essentialism. Neither one argued from philosophy to the Christian answers, but both used philosophy with the awareness of the need for faith to appropriate Christian answers. Hauerwas likes Barth's bolder answers of just starting with faith declarations. Barth then brings in philosophical assertions such as Albert Schweitzer's reverence for life into his Christian ethical exegesis. There is certainly room in the church for the three methods of Barth, Tillich, and Niebuhr, but the methods need to be understood before rejecting one or two of them as unsuitable to Christian faith.

At the social-philosophical level, Niebuhr presupposes violence at the root of the human situation, and he knows, as we all know practically, that in this history the state needs to use violence and the threat of violence to contain the tendencies of its citizens and to defend itself. Hauerwas, following John Yoder, I believe, finally will not recognize the way in which his ivory tower life at the University of Notre Dame and Duke University is protected by the violence of the police from the violence of South Bend and Durham. Yoder, following a relatively unique exegesis of Luke, sees Jesus urging the overthrow of the political economy of Roman-governed Palestine.[4] How this would ever be accomplished but by violence is not argued. I doubt Yoder's exegesis is crediting Jesus with a revolutionary social-economic program, but I'm certain that the governance of society depends on the violence of the state to limit violence, though Hauerwas denies this idea.

On John Wesley

Because Hauerwas's writings on the ethics of John Wesley are a mixture of Mennonite and Roman Catholic insights, it is helpful to see how he rejects the ethics of John Wesley, the father of the Methodist Church, which Hauerwas serves. On the question of pacifism, Wesley is free of illusions: he is an active peacemaker using categories of just war from natural law theory.

Hauerwas's dissertation on character published in 1975 represents his early work. He has continued trajectories of criticism from that work, so his critique of John Wesley deserves its own critique. The weakness of Hauerwas's work on Wesley's understanding of character is that it showed no evidence of having read Wesley's major work on the subject.

Wesley often referred to character. His standard works contain 344 references to the word. He refused, however, to bring it into the center of his ethics, as that position was reserved for love. Hauerwas was attempting to reformulate Protestant ethics on the resources drawn from Catholic thinking about virtue ethics.[5] Wesley's commitment to Protestant ethics and the

New Testament disinclined him from such a project, though investigations of character were a major theme of eighteenth-century philosophy and literature even in as bold a piece as Henry Fielding's book *Tom Jones*.

Hauerwas focused on Wesley's writings of perfect love and argued that character needs to be related to sanctification and that Wesley made "no attempt to clarify the kind of self that is determined to display these effects."[6] John Wesley had in fact in 1742 explicated the kind of character he was trying to meld in his societies. He built his work on Clement of Alexandria's (ca. 150–215) *Miscellanies*. He was concerned to show the principles of character to be cultivated by the young men in his society at Oxford. "The Character of a Methodist"[7] lays out principles of the authority of Scripture, language, clothing, complete religion, love of God, happiness, hopefulness, prayer, love of neighbor, purity of heart, the laws of Christ, obedience to commandments, pursuit of the good, and total service to the needs of others.

Elsewhere Wesley repeatedly spells out his belief that the lives of his followers are to be molded by preaching, visitation, correspondence, and discipline. Wesley himself was stronger than Hauerwas's study of Wesley in explicating the particular methods of self-formation used in Wesley's religious societies and in showing how the self needs to be engaged in wider social reform and philanthropy. For Wesley, no adequate Christian self can be disengaged from religious society or absent from the social reform of the self's history.

Hauerwas's Critique of Niebuhr on Society

So many individual sentences misrepresenting Reinhold Niebuhr appear in Stanley Hauerwas's writings that one is reluctantly led to the conclusion that he does not understand Niebuhr. In his essay "Ethics-Christian," he implies that Niebuhr regarded the witness of Barth and Bonhoeffer against Hitler as "socially irrelevant." That is not at all the case; he celebrated the witness of Barth and Bonhoeffer against Hitler. His critique was that neither was politically helpful before Hitler came to power and challenged the church. He did not believe that either Barth's earlier withdrawal from religious socialism or his later neutralism in the Cold War was helpful. The Barthian "no" is sometimes needed, but it is not very relevant for building structures of justice and participating day to day in the realities of politics. Both Hauerwas and his mentor, John Yoder, took an unhelpful turn in their following of Barth and his political negativism.

Hauerwas writes, "He [Niebuhr] also accepted a distinction between private and public morality whereby the ethic of Jesus was thought to be applicable only with respect to the life of the individual Christian, but not to society at large."[8] He sees Yoder's way as offering an alternative community that rejects all force and violence. Are we to assume he means the community of the University of Notre Dame, which supported them both? The hypocrisy of joining with a militaristic university yet claiming life in a peaceable community is too much. But the real argument is over what Niebuhr taught. Characteristic of Niebuhr's teaching is his belief that *nothing* separates us from the love of Christ. In history, "love must continue to be suffering love rather than triumphal love. . . . The Love which enters history as suffering love must remain suffering love in history. Since this love is the very law of history it may have its tentative triumphs even in history; for human history cannot stand in complete contradiction to itself. . . . Thus the absolute ethical and religious demands of the gospel are not irrelevant."[9] The ethic of Jesus is relevant to the struggle for justice, which will not be won in this interim history. Niebuhr knew both Luther and Schweitzer, but his ethic never dismisses the ethic of Jesus from the social realm; all of Niebuhr's students understand this. How could Hauerwas not have learned it? Was he too influenced by Yoder and by Catholic and Mennonite models of the church? The options are not church rule or church withdrawal; neither ever happened. The options are in the middle, between Augustine's two cities in various forms of engagement.

Earlier Hauerwas had caricatured Niebuhr's positions in an essay entitled "The Irony of American Christianity: Reinhold Niebuhr on Church and State."[10] He began the essay, "While Niebuhr seems never to have thought specifically about the legal relation of church and state in America. . . ." Yet the essay contains no reference to the one hundred pages of correspondence between Justice Frankfurter and Reinhold Niebuhr, much of which concerns church-state issues. Frankfurter thought Niebuhr worth consulting even if the then professor of divinity and law at Duke did not.

Hauerwas might have read "Church and State in America"; "Separation of Church and State"; editorial notes on New York divorce laws illustrating Protestant-Catholic tensions; editorial notes on the school issues among Catholics and Protestants; several pieces during 1960 about Kennedy, Catholics, and the state; an article on the Regent's prayer decision; an interview on school prayer, an article on school prayer, and "The King's Chapel and the King's Court." Hauerwas's mistake is typical of many who have not read widely in Niebuhr; it is very difficult to say that Niebuhr never thought about a subject or even that he never wrote about a subject within his areas of interest.

Hauerwas records that "one searches in vain for solid Christian theological underpinnings for Niebuhrian political realism." This is exactly what the two volumes of *The Nature and Destiny of Man* provide, and they are connected directly to his political theory in *The Children of Light and the Children of Darkness* and explicit in the doctrine of original sin. Other references refuting Hauerwas are obvious and include Niebuhr's lectures on Augustine, his essay on Augustine in *Christian Realism and Political Problems*, and his course "Theological Foundations of Christian Ethics."

Hauerwas finds it ironic that Niebuhr's politics reflect Jefferson and Madison. Hauerwas uses the word "mimicked." But it is not at all ironic; Niebuhr's political theology is indigenous to the American democratic context, which is shaped by political ideologies and settlements of the late eighteenth century, and particularly by Madison's Christian-realistic constitutionalism. Hauerwas persists in arguing that "Niebuhr believed that the scope of one's religious belief was restricted to individual conscience" and enlists John Milbank to support his view. Interestingly, he never quotes Niebuhr to support this exception to his lifetime of work to equip the church for its public ministry. Nor can he quote Niebuhr to establish the "individualistic bias" of which he accuses him.

Hauerwas polemicizes at Niebuhr for stressing the moral ambiguity of history and the sins of the church and for noting that some church teachers absorbed Stoic natural law ethics into their Christian ethics. But Hauerwas cannot show that history is without moral ambiguity, that the church or even Notre Dame or Duke is without sin, or that some church fathers did not articulate Christian ethics that reflect Stoic natural law. The accusation that Niebuhr is ahistorical strikes most readers as absurd. Maybe Hauerwas has an esoteric meaning to his "ahistorical" charge, but it does not make sense. From Niebuhr's criticism of Ford Motor Company's labor policies in the 1920s to his writing on race relations in the late 1960s, he used economic data or empirical studies and drew on a deep knowledge of history and history books to engage society in a critical way. He founded church organizations, worked in church ecumenical organizations, and taught seminarians so that the church would have a public impact. Neither of Hauerwas's charges against him—that he was ahistorical or that he taught that the church has no relevance to society—is accurate.

Ecclesiastical Politics

Hauerwas's project is one of ecclesiology and politics. It finally comes to the choice of a church in which to live. He concludes his Gifford Lecture assault on liberal Protestantism by affirming both the Mennonite Church and the Roman Catholic Church and their politics. Furthermore, he sees them witnessing to the theological project of Karl Barth. Hauerwas does not go, at least in the Gifford Lectures, so far as to claim the ecclesiology of Barth's Swiss Reformed Church. It was probably enough to be both Mennonite and Roman Catholic, reflecting his early formative years at Notre Dame with John Yoder.

John Howard Yoder and John Paul II represent the recovery of politics necessary for us. . . . John Howard Yoder and John Paul II are
particularly important for my argument. . . . Both men are representative figures of churches that have challenged the presumptions of
modernity. In particular, these churches have called into question
attempts, such as those represented by James and Niebuhr, that in
the name of rationalism and democracy relegate God to "what we
do with our privacy."[11]

While it is true that both Niebuhr and James were concerned about
"religious feelings" and psychology of religion, probably no untrained
reader could conclude that God was only a matter of "our privacy."
Alfred North Whitehead may have relegated God to "privacy" in one
unguarded moment, but it is a particularly inept judgment about
Niebuhr. The credibility of Hauerwas's work on James, Niebuhr, and
Barth rests upon his last chapter of *With the Grain of the Universe*. He
argues that his version of Christianity depends on the witnesses to his
position. He chooses as Christian witnesses: John Paul II, John Howard
Yoder, and Dorothy Day.

Dorothy Day in Hauerwas's account seems like an afterthought, as her
social concerns are absent from his hermeneutic with which he chastised
James and Niebuhr in the first two-thirds of the book. Her humble presence around Union Theological Seminary when I was a student there bears
no resemblance to the proud polemics characteristic of the males who
make up the real argument of his book. Her works of feeding the poor,
housing the homeless, witnessing to society through the press, and organizing for social justice are necessary marks of any rigorous ecclesiology today
and of life in Christian community.

The ecclesiastical censures in the respective ecclesiologies of their small
churches seem to preclude Karl Barth and John Howard Yoder from serving as model witnesses to the majority population of American churches.
The late John Paul II's stubborn misogyny regarding progress toward ordi-
nation of women in the world's largest church also rendered his church-
manship as inadequate for the churches of the American republic. His
passion for suppressing dissent in Catholic universities should also lean
heavily against Hauerwas's enthusiasm for the pope regarding American
higher education. Furthermore, the pope decided against women's right to
choose abortion or birth control. His failure in women's rights issues further weakens Hauerwas's hermeneutic of exegeting liberal Protestant
thinkers by papal norms.

The average newspaper-reading American Christian knows too much
about papal politics to be inspired to adopt it as a model. The pope is an
elected monarch serving with very weak countervailing powers within his

feudal bureaucracy. Until the Italian republics overthrew the Papal States, the pope operated as an Italian prince often in the spirit of the Medici of whom Machiavelli wrote so descriptively. John Paul II deserves humanity's praise for allying with the United States to overthrow Communism in Eastern Europe. His alliance with the CIA's William Casey in Central America as well as Poland bears little resemblance to Hauerwas's recommended pacifist politics, however.

If Hauerwas wants only to massage Barth's texts for a bold witness to a mid-twentieth-century Christian vision, no one should object. But to recommend the politics of a monarchy as a way of Christian life in an expanding democratic era really is nonsense. John Howard Yoder, on the other hand, had many helpful things to say about American politics. He was consistently a welcome voice against American militarism. His fanciful portrayal of Jesus as a political-economic radical with a proposal for reforming Palestine in *The Politics of Jesus* remains unpersuasive to most scholars; however, his own sense of political engagement, expressed in articles and books, was a welcome contribution. But to recognize Yoder's scholarship is a different matter than celebrating the ecclesiology of the Mennonite Church, which splinters and acrimoniously divides Mennonites into many denominations. Activist-servant Mennonite missionaries are a healing force in the world. The image of many Mennonites as pacifist, wealthy farmers trying to resist absorption into modernity does not seem like a model for many American Christians.

Hauerwas's own United Methodist Church's polity and social witness would have been a better witness to Christ for the American empire. Of course, Methodist witness is mixed, but at its best it supports democracy, racial reconciliation, the feeding and housing of the poor, and the struggle for economic justice and peace in a world moving in counterdirections. The Methodist Church has not been and will not be pacifist, for love has responsibility to defend, but neither will it be Mennonite communal withdrawal or proud Catholic power. In the end, United Methodist Senator Hillary Clinton is a more hopeful model/witness than any of these on whom Hauerwas grounded his critique of Protestantism.

Hauerwas on the New Testament Love Ethic

In Niebuhr's book *Human Destiny*, the love ethic is expressed in history as mutual love and justice and ultimately in the divine, as sacrificial love. In his essay "Love and Law in Protestantism and Catholicism," love as summary fulfills biblical law, but it transcends law in its universality, in its sacrificial quality, in forgiveness, and in sympathetic participation in the life of another.[12] His ethics courses dealt with the double love commandment as the essence of Jesus' own teaching.

Hauerwas was concerned to move the center of Christian ethics away from mainline Protestant–type social action toward modes normally associated with activist Mennonite practice as represented by the thought of John Yoder. Beyond Yoder, his preference for ethics seems to follow more in the pattern of reasoned ethics, or in Edward L. Long Jr.'s terms, the deliberative motif in ethics of Aquinas and Aristotle. Furthermore, his interest in biblical ethics seems to follow the stories or narratives more than the explicit ethical imperatives or commands.[13] His boast that he knew Aristotle's *Nicomachean Ethics* better than the New Testament reveals a desire to supplant the love ethic that had been so central with alternatives.[14]

Stanley Hauerwas reacted to the situational-principle debate of the 1960s by arguing against love as the primary ethical category of Christianity. That a polemic writer would overreact to Joseph Fletcher's reductionism is understandable. But no late-twentieth-century thinker could dethrone love from the pinnacle of Christian ethics, no matter how exaggerated the arguments. Hauerwas recognizes that love has a prominent place in Jesus' teaching and preaching, for example, the "great commandment" in the Gospels.[15] But he has nothing to say about its defining nature for Paul's ethic or the ethic of love in the Johannine literature. His essay "Love's Not All You Need" is bereft of the knowledge of love in the Old Testament or the recognition that the Ten Commandments themselves are further specifications of the double love commandment. He ignores the love ethics' centrality to Augustine, Calvin, Witherspoon, Brunner, and Bennett in his essay and only attacks weak representations of the love ethic of his own conjuring. One can affirm his respect for reason, the need for the category of justice, and the need for arguments and analysis beyond the imperative and summary of love, but those arguments create no need to attack the ethical teachings of Jesus as sentimental, wrong, platitudinous, and without discipline or suffering.[16] One can respect the attempt to rearrange priorities in Christian ethics in Mennonite or Aristotelian directions, but the center of the tradition as an ethic of love is too strong.

Probably some of Hauerwas's confusion was due to his not understanding that for Christian discourse the double love commandment has summarized and included the Ten Commandments. For example, the First Catechism of the Presbyterian Church (USA), designed for third and fourth graders, asks the question, "What is the main point of these commandments?" The correct response is "You shall love your God with all your heart, mind, and strength, and you shall love your neighbor as yourself."[17]

Notes

1. John H. Yoder, *Reinhold Niebuhr and Christian Pacifism* (Scottdale, Pa.: Concern, 1955), 16–19.

2. Stanley Hauerwas, *With the Grain of the Universe* (Grand Rapids: Brazos Press, 2001), 137–40.

3. Ibid.

4. John H. Yoder, *The Politics of Jesus* (Grand Rapids: Eerdmans, 1972).

5. Stanley Hauerwas, *Character and the Christian Life: A Study in Theological Ethics* (San Antonio: Trinity University Press, 1975), 2.

6. Ibid., 194.

7. Similar purposes are met by "The Character of a Methodist," "The Principles of a Methodist," "The Nature, Design, and General Rules of the United Societies," and "Rules of the Band Societies," all published in *The Works of John Wesley* (vol. 9; ed. Rupert E. Davies; Nashville, Abingdon Press, 1989), 31–79.

8. Stanley Hauerwas and D. Stephen Long, "Ethics-Christian," in *A New Handbook of Christian Theology* (ed. Donald W. Musser and Joseph L. Price; Nashville: Abingdon, 1992), 166.

9. Excerpts from Reinhold Niebuhr, *The Nature and Destiny of Man* (vol. 2; New York: Charles Scribner's Sons, 1943), 49–51.

10. Stanley Hauerwas and Mike Broadway, "The Irony of American Christianity: Reinhold Niebuhr on Church and State," *Insights: A Journal of the Faculty of Austin Seminary*, Fall 1992, 33–46. The other essays in the journal reflect more careful work, and Garcia particularly is an able refutation of Hauerwas. Garcia explicates the theological aspects of Niebuhr's thought for which Hauerwas "looks in vain."

11. Hauerwas, *With the Grain*, 217.

12. Reinhold Niebuhr, "Love and Law in Protestantism and Catholicism," in *The Essential Reinhold Niebuhr* (ed. Robert McAfee Brown; New Haven: Yale University Press, 1986), 142–59.

13. An interesting example is the role of story dominating even the love commandment. See Stanley Hauerwas, "Love's Not All You Need," in *Vision and Virtue: Essays in Christian Ethical Reflection* (Notre Dame: University of Notre Dame Press, 1981), 115. Also see Stanley Hauerwas, "Rationality and the Christian Story," in *Truthfulness and Tragedy* (Notre Dame: University of Notre Dame Press, 1977), 15–81.

14. Stanley Hauerwas, *Dispatches from the Front* (Durham: Duke University Press, 1994), 22.

15. Hauerwas, *Vision and Virtue*, 115.

16. Ibid., 113, 116, 117, 119, 126.

17. The catechism may be accessed online at http://www.pcusa.org.

༄ **10** ༄

Prophetic Realism, Human Rights, and Foreign Policy

IN CONVERSATION with an official of the Presbyterian Church (USA)'s United Nations office, I said, "Isn't human rights language the major moral language of the United Nations?" She agreed. The editing of the 2003 Human Rights Report for the Presbyterian Church's General Assembly action was compromised by political judgments. Much of the report is composed of reports from local church partners throughout the world or from the world area representatives of mission headquarters in Louisville, Kentucky. Both types of reportage are heavily politicized reflecting local interests. With politicized reporting, inadequate staff, and impossible deadlines, the report suffers and does not represent the church's best work. However, it is part of the church's moral vocabulary now and serves as background to church policy development. The United Nations Human Rights Commission also reflects the ambiguities and compromises. African nations supported the delegate from Libya as chairperson and the United States opposed him.[1] This chapter examines one case of this ambiguous role of human rights between politics and morals in the case of the U.S. Senate Foreign Relations Committee's rejection of the Reverend Dr. Ernest W. Lefever as Assistant Secretary of State for Human Rights.

The language of the United Nations about human rights is very rich, and nowhere is it fulfilled. It literally is utopian as it is both of a "good place" and "no place." Everywhere human rights are denied. The human rights story is one of the struggles of humanity yet to be resolved. Human rights are the recognition that the meaning of *human* has its guarantees in a realm beyond empirical reality. Humans strive for, sometimes demand, and sometimes fight for the conditions under which a fuller approximation of the human can be found.

Human rights are found in four categories: in the human rights covenant category of people stating their fundamental claims to humane treatment; in the philosophical category, the meaning of *human* contains certain demands or rights for human life; in the historical category, human rights are the subject matter of controversy and struggle; and in the eschatological category, rights are expressions of goals of human existence. Their realization is promised in the fulfillment of history, at the end of history, or beyond history.

The human rights issue exploded in the debates about the foreign policy of Jimmy Carter. Drawing on his Baptist tradition, Reinhold Niebuhr, and the civil rights movement, he pushed the moral demands of human rights into U.S. foreign policy. The application of the policy had consequences around the world but particularly as it intersected revolutionary struggles in South Africa and Central America. A United Church of Christ minister in the tradition of Martin Luther King Jr., Ambassador Andrew Young carried the banner until the controversy became too rancorous and he was forced out.

Neoconservatives attacked President Carter's human rights policy, attempted to discredit it, and chose to support candidate Ronald Reagan. In the early Reagan administration, the neoconservatives were pushed forward to administer the human rights aspects of U.S. foreign policy. The Senate balked at the opponent of Carter's human rights record and denied the nomination of Ernest Lefever as Assistant Secretary of State for Human Rights. In this debate the intersection of religious ideas and politics in the human rights struggle is clearly seen. Before examining this debate (which poses the issues of realism, human rights, and peacemaking), we must give attention to the origin of the concept of human rights.

Different nations represent different traditions in human rights. Though they covenant together in the Universal Declaration of Human Rights (1948)[2] or in the Helsinki Final Act (1975), they read their joint declarations from their own perspectives. This chapter focuses on an American reading of the origins of human rights. This is a radically different story of the origins of human rights from the stories of other nations. An essay on the Hindu tradition of human rights, for example, described the interpretation and development of the understanding of the great collection of Hindu law of Manu's *Dharma Sutra*. Rammohan Roy, Vivekananda, Rabindranath Tagore, and most of all Gandhi broadened the understanding of human rights.[3] These contributions are vital to understanding current Indian perspectives on human rights, but they were only indirectly relevant to the West's development of its tradition. The indirect influence is almost entirely owing to Gandhi, and his own use of Western religious concepts in his Hindu system points to an emerging synthesis that is not yet realized in human rights thinking. As Gandhi could not have been Gandhi without Jesus, so the Carter human rights policies could not have been without Martin Luther King Jr. who drew inspiration from both Gandhi and Jesus. Hence, they too depended on Gandhi. India's participation in the human rights debate has owed something to the socialist tradition and to British political thought, especially utilitarianism. Similarly, each country's participation is very complex because its traditions are uniquely its own yet in some aspects belong to the world.

Within the United States, at least three traditions compete and interrelate as they contribute to human rights consciousness. The Roman Catholic tradition[4] draws on Thomas Aquinas and papal teaching to ground human rights in natural law. Such a tradition is neglected by a second tradition of philosophers of human rights such as Ronald Dworkin[5] and A. I. Melden,[6] who engage Jeremy Bentham and John Locke respectively as conversational partners. The third tradition, the one of primary interest for this case, is the Protestant tradition. In this case it was the tradition grounded primarily in a Protestant reading of Scripture and the political history of the Western world that was at issue.

Universal Standards in the Ninth Century B.C.E.

The demand for equal treatment arises early in human consciousness. It can be seen in our children. But the natural inequalities among people and contingencies give rise to further inequalities, which the powerful enforce and the weaker gradually internalize. To treat others as one desires to be treated is the foundation of morality. Each one counts as one and only one. To root this natural sense of morality in universal standards and to require it as the will of a just God is more complicated.

The ancient Hebrews, whose lives were shaped by politics and revelation, were led through covenantal experience, resistance to landed oligarchs, and relative freedom to develop a sense of justice. In an explosion of radical monotheism, Amos would express this sense of justice or righteousness in terms that judged the inhuman conduct of all nations. This radically free agricultural laborer, living in a village on the desert side of Jerusalem, understood that all nations are under God's universal judgment. From Amos comes a trajectory of universal standards anchored in God's will. The force of this proclamation would be bent, suppressed, and ignored in the rest of Israel's history and in the life of the church, but it would reappear whenever the sense of radical monotheism, the corruption of the present, the possibility of a more just future, and the reality of God's having a will for human life intersected.

Amos did not speak of human rights, but his criticism of inhuman conduct outlines what he regarded as God's protection of human life. Damascus was condemned for destroying Gilead, Gaza was condemned for exiling a people and delivering them to another land, Tyre was condemned for surrendering a people to Edom and for not remembering *"the covenant of kinship"* (Amos 1:9, emphasis mine.) Edom was punished for not showing pity and for being ruthless, the Ammonites for attacking pregnant women, and Moab for desecrating the remains of the royal dead. Judah was to be punished for not keeping the law of the Lord. Where the covenant of the Lord was known, it was wrong not to keep it. In the other countries, a more general "covenant of kinship" was referred to or specific violations were named. Then even the Lord's host nation of Israel was condemned to punishment for selling people for profit, oppressing the poor, not comforting the suffering, sexually mistreating women, and misusing wine in the sanctuary.

Amos clearly sees God rejecting war atrocities, the selling of people, sexual exploitation, oppression of the poor, and violations of human compassion. This very rigorous standard seen in the oracles of Amos 1 and 2 could not go unchallenged. The criticism was too much, and especially when Amos in Bethel specifically prophesied the downfall of the corrupt kingdom, he was opposed by the authorities, particularly the high priest Amaziah. A high religious authority can always be found to protect political authorities from the criticism of prophetic religious teaching. Amaziah ordered Amos to stop his preaching since Bethel was the king's chapel and the king's royal residence. Amos could only reply that he was not a professional prophet but merely an agricultural laborer and that God's justice meant that Israel's atrocities doomed her. She would be destroyed in war.

Certainly the sense that one of the prerequisites of peace is the ending of the violation of human dignity is as old as Amos's ninth-century B.C.E. prophecy. The promises for Israel's restoration are the achievement of economic security and the capacity to build cities and inhabit them, to plant crops and enjoy the fruit, and to dwell in their homeland safely.

I refer to Amos here in order to note the theological grounding of universal standards, the political-religious suppression of the critics of violations of humanity, the threat to the state posed by humanitarian criticism, and the political arena of the struggle for human dignity. In Amos we can see that the source of our life forbids the rulers of the world to practice injustice, that the achievement of justice eludes us, and that the attempt to promote justice across international borders is full of peril. The roots of human rights go back to the religious transcendence of kingly rule in Israel and to the development of a critical ethic on the grounds of radical monotheism.

In Amos, a standard of justice rooted in the will of the *one* God for the one humanity was used to criticize other nations. That very standard led Amos into trouble when he took it into the royal palace of his neighboring state, Israel. The conflict is very suggestive of the debate over human rights policy for contemporary foreign policy.[7]

Other Sources

Before we move into an analysis of the current human rights debate, we need to recognize the complexity of the sources of human rights claims. Max L. Stackhouse has traced this history of human rights in his major study *Creeds, Society, and Human Rights: A Study in Three Cultures.*[8]

The roots of human rights in the Hebrew conception of a just God were nourished by the prophets and the social-religious bonding of the "covenants." Through the life of the Jewish people and the organization of the synagogue, the tradition was expressed in the humanizing teaching of Jesus and in Paul's recognition of a universal law of conscience. As the early church evolved from the synagogue, it incorporated Greek concerns for the protection of the human. Stoic doctrines of equality merged with Christian conceptions of faith, hope, and love to form a vision of human life. If one follows Stackhouse's recognition of the Council of Constance in 1415 C.E. as the birth of modernity, then we have a period of 1,005 years from the sacking of Rome in 410, during which the church sought religious freedom for itself and the protection of the rights of the Christian person from oppression. However, it was that same Council that condemned Jan Hus to the martyrdom of fire. Moreover, the church's defensiveness against the real enemies of both Islam and Christian emperors drove it into its own forms of repression. The West emerged from the medieval period with two realms of authority—church and state—and an expanding realm of economic energy. In the space provided by the freedom of the church would emerge the voluntary associations of the liberal-reformed world, which have contributed to modern forms of human rights. The thought of the High Middle Ages also contributed Thomas Aquinas's natural law theory, which could serve as the basis for Catholic thinking on human rights in the modern period. In the East, John Chrysostom and Basil defended the rights of the poor and opposed the luxury of the rulers. Basil's argument for the recognition of essential human equality was grounded in the image of God in humanity.[9] In this Orthodox history were laid the grounds for contemporary Orthodox commitments to human rights.

The Renaissance and the Reformation contributed to the liberation of the European mind in different ways and to individualism in European life. Humanity sprung into autonomous forms of life that took expression in the struggle for diverse forms of religious-intellectual expression. The Calvinist, Lutherans, and Anabaptists all expressed slightly different versions of humanity, which Europe finally had to tolerate. Covenantal political theory and the emergence of social contract theory both deepened the commitment to human rights, including individual rights of social bonding.

The Modern Situation

In modern history the expression of human rights has been to limit the state. Limits were first asserted to protect the rights of Englishmen (as in the Petition of Right, 1628, and the Bill of Rights, 1689). These ideas are reflected in the later more universal-sounding French Declaration of the Rights of Man and the American Bill of Rights.

The ground for the post–World War II Universal Declaration of Human Rights in 1948 was prepared by writings on the international concern for human rights (Francisco de Vitoria, 1480–1546), the perception of international law as resting on grounds of a universal law of humanity, the practice of "humanitarian intervention," and the development of protection for groups by treaty.[10]

This work on developing a body of proclamations on human rights continues in the work of the United Nations and its specialized agencies as well as through regional organizations. The work suffers because it lacks either the clear theological rationale reflected by declarations of the World Council of Churches or pronouncements of the Vatican or the power suggested by governmental declarations. Agreement on clear philosophical principles seems to be as elusive as the attempt to achieve theological unity would be divisive.

The pronouncements of these international bodies, then, have little authority. They represent majority vote positions on issues of human concern. Individual countries adopt their respective positions for diverse philosophical and political reasons. They have the authority of diverse conciliar statements on social-ethical issues without the councils being responsible for policy or implementation.

Within U.S. foreign policy concerns, the ambiguities that Alexander Hamilton pointed out about the Bill of Rights appear. He thought that it was more naturally appropriate to have a bill of rights in a treatise on ethics than in a constitution of a government. The human rights issue forms a point at which the power concerns of people and the ethical expressions of people find a meeting place. This chapter traces part of that ambiguous meeting in recent U.S. concerns about human rights and foreign policy. If we had a world government, Hamilton notwithstanding, a bill of rights would be very necessary. To have a declaration of rights before the government is established is to leave human rights with the force of a moral statement arrived at by compromise.

The United States' contribution to the human rights struggle has been hindered by two factors central to the meaning of the country. Slavery was overcome only after being recognized by the constitution and building wealth in the country. The fruits of slavery continued even after the Civil

War in the failure of the United States to treat its black minority justly. The very human rights policy of the government is fruit of the struggle against the racial blight of the nation. The African-American struggle contributed to the emergence of U.S. human rights policy. The great wrong of policies of genocide against the first Americans has not yet produced equal contributions to the policies of the United States. The movement of First Nations in Canada may foreshadow important developments in the United States. Prejudices and discrimination continue and prevent human rights policies from advancing.

In addition to slavery, the United States had in its beginnings a significant expression of human autonomy. The old heteronomous structures of Europe were overthrown. The myths of the radically self-determining person flourished. The social bonding of the Puritans was gradually abandoned, and the Yankee emerged. Once this autonomous individual came to believe in the myths of Social Darwinism, a socially irresponsible, technically powerful individual was let loose in the world. Whether this type evolves into the conquering hedonist-utilitarian or the escapist hedonist-expressionist, the realities of a social bond that structures human rights were dissolved. So many Americans believe they have freedom in a mass-produced consumer economy and resent all social bonding as eclipsing freedom.[11]

The strengthening of the biblical and democratic concepts of social responsibility in American culture is a necessary part of the struggle for human rights. Without social understanding and social reality, the idea of human rights sounds like moralism. Then the temptation to use it as a moralistic weapon arises. Used as a weapon, the concept of human rights is neither felt in the way one lives in the world nor meaningfully articulated.

The development of the human rights strategy in the early Reagan administration revealed this confusion. Human rights were seen on the one hand as extraneous ideals foreign to politics and on the other as symbols to be used in the Cold War.

The Nomination of an Assistant Secretary of State for Human Rights

The minutes of the Senate Foreign Relations Committee hearings on the nomination of Ernest Lefever provide an excellent case study in the difficulties of applying religious social ethics to foreign policy issues. The senators, the nominee, and the witnesses reveal both their ethics of being and their ethics of doing. The character of the nominee is probed, examined, criticized, and praised. His decisions and writings are analyzed both for their ethical sensitivity and for their political content. The ambiguity of life and its expression in ethics and foreign policy is dramatically portrayed.

Lefever's claim to stand in the tradition of Reinhold Niebuhr introduced the meaning of Niebuhr's perspective in the Senate debate. Sometimes the relevance of Niebuhr's thought and what he meant or did not mean seemed to be as much the subject of inquiry as the interpretation of Ernest Lefever's thought. However, both those who favored and those who opposed Lefever's nomination claimed Niebuhr as one of their mentors in thinking about ethics and foreign policy. The testimony of Michael Novak, the chief of the delegation to the United Nations Human Rights Commission, also emphasized the influence of Niebuhr on both his own thought and that of the nominee he supported. Lefever's record of criticism of the human rights perspectives of Jimmy Carter, Andrew Young, and Martin Luther King Jr., all of whom had acknowledged their debt to Reinhold Niebuhr, only reveals the complexity of the questions concerning the position of realism on foreign policy and human rights.

Niebuhr on Human Rights

Reinhold Niebuhr's writings on human rights often appear under the themes of social justice and international relations or in particular comments on problems in foreign policy.[12] In summary, he taught that the origins of human rights rest on humanity's freedom, because humanity was created in the image of God. The human struggle has been, in part, to realize in its political life the capacities of freedom rooted in the essential quality of humanity. These expressions of human freedom, which are difficult to contain in political communities, enrich the community in the long run.[13] So a tension exists in all societies between the forces that order society and the expression of human freedom, which transcends all particular political order. In this perspective the struggle for the freedoms enshrined in Western history in the Magna Carta, the Bill of Rights, the Declaration of the Rights of Man, and the Declaration of Human Rights represents a continuing quest for the conditions that will allow for the freedom of human nature. Particular expressions of norms for protecting human rights are contingent, even political declarations that reflect more or less accurately the need for human nature to be protected in its quest for expression of its freedom. The perspective could be thought of as a relative natural law expression. The law of human nature is to express its freedom; the human perceptions of that freedom are contingent on the perceptions of those fighting for human freedom. So Thomas Jefferson could assert that the God who gave us life gave us freedom while not being cognizant of the implication of that freedom for all members of the human species. Or Alexander Hamilton could, with most males until recently, declare that we have sacred rights written in human nature by divinity itself while being blind to the need for the female expression of freedom.

For Niebuhr, the realization of tolerable conditions of justice meant a social arrangement that would allow members of society to express their vitalities without infringing on the rights of others. Therefore, justice depended on the social institutions of a particular society more than it did on abstract pronouncements.

His social philosophy combined passion for social justice and a recognition of the forces that resisted social justice. This dual recognition is what caused him to resist idealistic posturing while still struggling for justice. He regarded this combination as part of the mixture of the English revolution of the 1640s and found in it one of the best expressions of Christian social action.

There was, for instance, Ireton's shrewd observation that he preferred "the rights of Englishmen to the rights of man," meaning that a mutually acknowledged right and responsibility was a more reliable guarantee of justice than abstractly conceived "inalienable rights." The superiority of a common law tradition, of an unwritten constitution, and of a history in which "liberty broadens down from precedent to precedent" is expressed in this preference.[14]

The sense of the contingency of human rights in the Western world encouraged doubt about the protection of human rights in societies that lacked a religious sense of the worth of human selfhood. Individualism in the West had been extravagant in many expressions, but still the appreciation of the worth of the individual pointed toward certain factors as necessary for the protection of human rights. Guarantees of freedom of expression and institutional guarantees of a free judicial system with a veto over policies and rulers were perceived as minimally necessary to protect human rights.[15] These institutional guarantees had to be buttressed by a sense of the broader community, the intellectual competence of the electorate, and a balance of power in the economic realm. Niebuhr was aware of the struggle within different Communist states and authoritarian states to realize some of these factors, but he was not at all sanguine about their realization.

Human rights were continually challenged in countries heir to Western democratic traditions and on the world scene as a whole. Human rights remain more of an ideal than a reality. American society still denies African Americans rights and hinders the development of their capacities. There are only approximations of human rights, but still they are to be contended for and institutionalized in law, practice, and economic opportunity.

The promise of justice was a major factor in the competition between the Soviet Union and the United States. Niebuhr saw the competition going on for decades, and a first priority was managing the competition in a way to prevent nuclear war. He welcomed the competition ideologically, and while regarding both laissez-faire capitalism and Marxism as badly

flawed myths, he thought the Marxist myth would have more rapid acceptance in the recently decolonized world. His critique of the Marxist myth
and of Soviet practice was part of this ideological warfare, and he hoped
that in the long run the achievements of the Western nations in realizing
an approximation of justice would assist the new nations in refusing to succumb to the blandishments of the Soviet Empire.

Niebuhr was extravagant in his expectations for Kennedy's Alliance for
Progress, but he certainly thought it was important for the United States to
set aside some of the liberal reservations about intervention for the sake of
encouraging land reform and education in Latin America. He also personally participated in the withdrawal of accounts from U.S. banks that supported the consortium efforts to increase South Africa's credit after the
Sharpeville massacre. He confided to me on one of our walks how it was
slightly embarrassing to meet one of the vice presidents of Chemical Bank
on Riverside Drive, after he in supporting the bank campaign organized by
Union Seminary students had withdrawn his account, as had his journal,
Christianity and Crisis. Niebuhr also implied that he believed the bank official agreed with the action personally and morally, though institutionally
he supported his bank's policy. The achievement of justice was both a good
to be struggled for in its own terms and an issue in Cold War competition.
Authority in the modern world rested on this expectation of justice, and
innovative ways to promote it were to be encouraged.

Of course, Niebuhr resisted abstract democratic idealism as well, particularly when it was mixed with self-inflating calculations of political
interest. His major critiques of self-righteousness in 1967 and 1968 were
directed at the shallow rhetoric of defending democracy and self-determi-
nation in Vietnam.[16]

In summary, Niebuhr regarded social justice as a major issue in the
competition of the two empires in the Cold War. It was a goal he had struggled for throughout his own life, it was grounded in the awareness of
humanity as a creation of God, and it could be misused; consequently, a
nation had to be aware of the dangers of moral and spiritual pride. Social
justice would not be perfectly realized in history, and both prudence and
passion were necessary in the effort to approximate its realization.

The Carter Human Rights Attempt

Michael Novak and Ernest Lefever, from their respective "think tanks,"
both criticized the Carter administration's approach to human rights.
Their major criticism was that the Carter policy neglected to attack sufficiently the violation of human rights in the "totalitarian" societies and
that it was too hard on U.S. allies who were practicing "authoritarian"
government.

Novak summarized the development of the human rights policy, noting how both Senator Jackson and Senator Moynihan had argued that human rights were an instrument that should be used critically against the Soviet Union. Carter was portrayed as neglecting the advantage the human rights issue gave the United States over the Soviet Union and as falsifying "the meaning of human rights." The Carter administration turned this human rights policy inside out. It did not make human rights a policy of truth. It did not make human rights a policy of political advantage. Thus, the Carter administration made an attempt to be "evenhanded" and to balance every accusation against an opponent of the United States with an accusation against a friend.[17]

Lefever stressed the importance of the distinction between "authoritarian" and "totalitarian" regimes again and again in his testimony before the Senate Foreign Relations Committee, and it was also a central theme in his essay "The Trivialization of Human Rights."[18] Lefever revealed no reservations about criticizing human rights violations and atrocities in the Soviet Union, Cuba, Cambodia, Vietnam, and North Korea. But the rhetoric of Patricia Derian, the first full-time Assistant Secretary of State for Human Rights and Humanitarian Affairs, was described as "moralistic rhetoric alien to traditional diplomatic discourse." President Carter's stance was seen as natural given his perspective as a "born-again Baptist and a latter-day Wilsonian."[19]

The critique of the Carter administration involved charges that it underestimated the danger of totalitarianism, overestimated American influence, mixed domestic and foreign policy concerns, ignored dangers of reform-intended intervention, overestimated the role of human rights in foreign policy, and was overly selective in its choice of human rights issues.

Lefever's blunt way of writing has led to his being misunderstood. His widely quoted suggestion that the United States had no responsibility to promote human rights was not meant as his last word on the subject. "In a formal and legal sense, the U.S. Government has no responsibility—and certainly no authority—to promote human rights in other sovereign states. . . . But this is hardly the whole story."[20] He certainly argued that our domestic example of honoring human rights is an important example to the world. Also, defending allies who were threatened by totalitarian influences was the second major contribution the United States could make to the promotion of human rights. Lefever saw Seoul, Taipei, and Pretoria as capitals where the practice of human rights was less than perfect but which should be defended in the name of peace and human rights. In his conclusion, he urged the president to "tone down his rhetoric," which was grounded in "a kind of vague, romantic optimism with an excessive confidence in the power of reason and goodwill."[21]

Lefever's target in Carter's rhetoric was particularly the president's commencement speech at Notre Dame in 1977. It is true that Lefever's remarks about the state of the world were more somber than President Carter's, but this particular speech from Carter has many phrases that reflect the same Reinhold Niebuhr whom Lefever quoted in criticizing the administration.

> I believe we can have a foreign policy that is democratic, that is based on our fundamental values and that uses power and influence for humane purposes. Being confident of our own future, we are now free of that inordinate fear of Communism which once led us to embrace any dictator who joined us in our fear. For too many years we have been willing to adopt the flawed principles and tactics of our adversaries, sometimes abandoning our values for theirs. We fought fire with fire, never thinking that fire is better fought with water. . . . This does not mean that we can conduct our foreign policy by rigid moral maxims. We live in a world that is imperfect and will always be imperfect, a world that is complex and will always be complex. I understand fully the limits of moral suasion. I have no illusion that changes will come easily or soon. But I also believe that it is a mistake to undervalue the power of words and of the ideas that words embody.[22]

Carter was concerned to found the human rights issues as "a broad-based approach."[23] In his speeches he portrayed it not as a weapon aimed at the Soviet Union and its allies but as a reflection of the experience and ideals of the American people. He used the term *national interest*, but that term for him included the promotion of the ideals of the people. In his judgment the human rights issue was part of the ideological competition with the Soviet Union, but it was more than that. He argued that it necessarily had to be applied to allies and foes alike for it to maintain its credibility.

> We are determined in the United States to use our economic, social, political and military strength so we can never be successfully challenged by any competitive philosophy, and we are very eager to combine with our allies and friends to make sure this is clearly undisputed by all. We have an eagerness to compete in an ideological way around the world, because we know that our commitment to human freedom, human rights and democratic principles, and our compassion toward the less fortunate than we will prevail. This is a commitment we want to share with you.[24]

Carter promised more than he could deliver in a foreign policy emphasizing human rights, but he conceded that human rights issues should not block progress on other issues such as the control of nuclear weapons. He recognized the Cold War, but he tried to downplay it, to create an attitude of détente. A major difference with Lefever is this refusal to make the clearcut distinction between totalitarian and authoritarian nations concerning human rights policy. From a moral perspective, inattention to violations of human rights in Cambodia was a failure, and Lefever correctly criticized this blindness. Carter and Derian were certainly more forthright in criticizing allied human rights violations in the developing world. Andrew Young carried the human rights banner vis-à-vis Africa in a way that contradicted Lefever's judgments, but Lefever's judgments regarding South Africa were one of the items that resulted in senatorial critique in the hearing.

Carter was a complex person, and his views on the relationship of morality to politics were deeper than his critics recognized. E. Brooks Holifield observed in Carter a rather Calvinist intraworldly asceticism in his evangelical Baptist tradition, an open American religiousity, pluralistic toleration, and a considerable amount of Christian realism.[25] And, indeed, Carter often remarked on his debt to Niebuhr. This debt to Niebuhr survives the detractions of those skeptical of the connection and is adequately defended in the arguments of June Bingham[26] and William Lee Miller.[27] Carter not only read and quoted Niebuhr; he understood politics as an expression of Christian social activism. He differed from Niebuhr in not forcefully criticizing the problems or even illusions of moral activism. It is just this critique of activism that characterized much of Lefever's writing and contributed to his defeat in the Senate Foreign Relations Committee. In a book of Niebuhr's essays, which Lefever edited, Lefever left a clue to his own style: "In fact one can perhaps best gain an understanding of Niebuhr's views on political morality by studying the criticism he makes of those persons who, in his view, misunderstand our moral responsibility as citizens and as a nation because they fail to understand the realities of politics."[28]

Ernest W. Lefever and Human Rights

It is much more difficult to ascertain Lefever's position on human rights than it is to understand either his mentor, Reinhold Niebuhr, or the object of his criticism, Jimmy Carter. Lefever's ambivalence on the application of human rights can perhaps be seen in three different periods: his critique of the Carter administration, his nomination to wear the human rights mantle, and finally his return to critiquing the U.S. emphasis on human rights in foreign policy.

In 1977 Lefever downplayed the human rights policy as seen in the Carter administration. Making human rights the chief, or even a major, foreign policy determinant carried dangers: "Giving human rights a central place subordinates, blurs, or distorts all other relevant considerations."[29] In the winter of 1978, Lefever seemed to contradict this statement in the lead sentence of his famous essay in *Policy Review*: "Human rights are what politics is all about."[30] However, the argument of the essay was essentially the same as that of the 1977 article. Human rights was fundamentally a matter of protecting U.S. allies and witnessing to the world a high standard of achievement in fulfilling human rights domestically. Several sentences in his 1978 essay deny the propriety of trying to enforce human rights through U.S. foreign policy.

> Our President and all other heads of state have authority to act only in their own states, within the territory of their legal jurisdiction. . . .
>
> In sum, U.S. aid can properly be given to encourage a friend or ally to pursue constructive external policies, but not to promote internal reforms opposed by the assisted government. . . .
>
> In a formal and legal sense, the U.S. Government has no responsibility—and certainly no authority—to promote human rights in other sovereign states. . . . But this is hardly the whole story.[31]

He went on to emphasize the major contributions the United States could make to human rights by its example and the defense of peoples threatened by "totalitarian aggression or subversion."

On July 14, 1979, Lefever testified before the Subcommittee on International Organizations of the House Foreign Affairs Committee: "In my view, the United States should remove from the statute books all clauses that establish a human rights standard or condition that must be met by another sovereign government before our government transacts normal business with it, unless specifically waived by the President."[32]

In the second stage of his involvement with human rights, as President Reagan's nominee for the Assistant Secretary of Human Rights position, Lefever indicated that he regarded his former statement urging the removal of human rights standards from the law as a "goof." He tenaciously held to his commitment to participate in a review of such legislation under the new administration, but his earlier statement was regarded as too sweeping.

The hearings were long, and the testimonies from witnesses pro and con were numerous. Significant issues of public policy and morality were debated. In the end the committee refused to recommend Lefever by a vote of 13 to 4. Different factors influenced various senators, but in associating their views with those of Senator Percy and Senator Pell, those who gave their reasons for voting against him concurred that his public record on human rights in foreign policy was inadequate. His developed views would be an unfortunate symbol to the world. The American people still supported human rights, and no signal that would encourage any harsh measures elsewhere should be given. His remarks about South Africa and Korea meant that his concern for human rights in those countries was not credible. His refusal to give an opinion on the Genocide Convention prevented him from appearing credible.[33]

Other important factors included a sense that he sublimated human rights concerns too easily to Cold War considerations. He seemed not to understand the reasons a secretary for human rights needed to push the human rights issues forcefully even if U.S. foreign policy had to consider other factors also. Moreover, Senator Percy argued forcefully that the United States was stronger as a defender of democracy if it "spoke out for human rights across the board."[34] Many of the senators spoke of their willingness to support Lefever for other positions in government, but they opposed his public position on human rights for the U.S. government.

After the smoke of the battle over nomination had cleared, Lefever returned to developing the Ethics and Public Policy Center and to lecturing on human rights. His speech in Guam started like his *Policy Review* essay, but now politics was not *all* about human rights: "Human rights and security are what politics is all about."[35]

The close linking of human rights to the Cold War dominated Lefever's presentation. An additional note was the rejection of the "so-called economic and social rights, such as the right to a job or health care."[36] These were to be regarded as objectives because only a totalitarian government could guarantee them. "The price of gaining these 'rights' is the sacrifice of freedom."[37] Societies like the United Kingdom or Canada, which do guarantee health care, would be offended by that assumption. Rights, of course, are in part objectives, and some societies achieve them better than others; what some societies recognize as realities, others only perceive as goals. The post-hearing lecture reaffirmed the Lefever the committee feared, and muted the Lefever who affirmed a more activist stance for human rights:

> The impulse to impose our standards or practice on other societies supported by policies of reward and punishment, leads inevitably to a kind of reform intervention. We Americans have no moral mandate to transform other societies, and we rightly resent such efforts on the part of totalitarians. There is more than a touch of arrogance in any efforts to alter the domestic behavior of allies or even of adversaries.[38]

Lefever, as a person of conscience and conviction, marches to his own drummer, a different drummer from the one the Senate Committee heard. His own position may not have been understood by the committee, for he did say on many occasions that the United States should use all appropriate means to defend or extend freedom. He argued for using one moral standard for totalitarian, authoritarian, and democratic states. While recognizing that we could not even fulfill our own ideals, he urged a striving for Reinhold Niebuhr's concept of "the relevance of an impossible ideal" to move the struggle for human rights further. The campaigns for him and against him both reached points not very interesting for this study.[39] The hearings and the reactions to them exhibited much spiritual and moral pride as well as human fear.

The UN Human Rights Commission

Within two weeks of President Reagan's inauguration, Michael Novak was seated as the U.S. representative to the Human Rights Commission. There had not been much time for briefing or background study. The positions expressed by Michael Novak and Richard Schifter, the alternative representative, were worked out on the spot in consultation with Washington. They found there that most of the participants did not agree on the meaning of human rights, used language differently, and differed in values. Novak characterized the discussions as being full of lies, exhibiting absurdity, and featuring much double-talk.[40] The implication of Novak's remarks, as well as the specific statement from his colleague, was that the lack of agreement about human rights "makes the Human Rights Commission one from which no great positive contribution to the cause of human rights can be expected."[41]

The speeches of Schifter and Novak read like speeches of those who trust in their position but know they will lose the vote. The collection of their speeches and the relevant resolutions reveal that they did indeed lose the votes.[42]

The U.S. delegation needed more flexibility. The United States was not alone at the session; other Western nations that share our traditions were there too. A narrow definition of human rights that rejects attempts to relate human rights to economic development and disarmament is doomed to defeat. Human rights has its meaning in broad conceptions of conditions that will allow humanity to reach toward greater fulfillment. It cannot be confined to Western-style political institutions and to an apology for allies of the United States. It was a narrow conception of human rights and a too-close connection of human rights with Cold War politics that the senators rejected in Ernest Lefever. U.S. foreign policy will defend our interests, and we are not so weak that we have to insist that our imagination is limited to our own achievements in human rights. In the human rights debate, we can afford to express our idealism. We can express

our hopes for human rights in terms that elude our grasp and their immediate resolution. A narrow defense of our national interests appears cynical
before the world. It must be mixed with idealism. The idealism of our own
civil rights movement was mixed with realism in winning the civil rights
victories in this country.

In our human rights spokespeople, we need an expression of idealism
that can agree with the hunger of the developing nations and with the idealism of many in our own country regarding the imperatives for international development and arms reduction. Christian realism at its best mixes
the insights of the idealists with the wisdom of the realists and does not
insist that the only way to human rights is through our experience. In an
earlier comment on my perspective on the tradition of Christian realism,
Novak suggested it erred on the side of idealism. Perhaps he was right, but
certainly in our struggle for the human rights emphasis in our foreign
policy, our spokespeople need to be reminded of the dangers of a realism
that is too narrow. Let us express in our human rights positions a passion
for reform even if in our full foreign policy that passion is compromised by
our defense of our interests. We must run the risk of hypocrisy (since
hypocrisy is the concession in which virtue acknowledges sin) rather than
lose the human rights struggle.

The most comprehensive study to relate theological ethics to human
rights found the Reagan administration diminishing the accents of human
rights in U.S. foreign policy.[43] Foreign policy regarding human rights was
conducted as if Lefever had been nominated. It was this passionate commitment to pursuing the Cold War that blinded Michael Novak and others
to the cruelty of the administration's policy. However, while the administration tilted toward South Africa, the American population became more
activist in attacking apartheid in print and in the streets. While the administration continued to cover up human rights atrocities in Central
America, polls showed that the people refused to support war in Central
America to defend or restore inhumane regimes. Human rights became
practically connected with peacemaking. The human rights legislation
Lefever opposed became the chief legal restraint on the administration in
pursuing war.

The Reagan administration followed its own rhetoric: it used human
rights to criticize Communist enemies but was incapable of guiding its policies toward anti-Communist allies by human rights standards. Right-wing
religious forces repeated Amaziah's mistake of thinking that human rights
concerns are not to be heard in the administration's precincts. Consequently,
refusing to end support for oppression or to criticize injustice in anti-
Communist forces, a great nation lurched along, violating the sensitivities of
much of the world and violating minimal standards of justice.

Currently

The American ambivalence concerning human rights, illustrated in this chapter by the struggle over the nomination of Dr. Ernest Lefever, continues today. Not only has the United States failed to ratify several human rights conventions, but its ambivalence has become especially pronounced in the present emergency situation.

This combination of ambivalence and an emergency situation threatens to subvert both the United Nations system and the rule of law in the United States. The United Nations system and the Human Rights Charter were products of the allies who defeated Nazism. They were designed to prevent the atrocities that arose with Adolf Hitler. Hitler's rise to power was expedited by the expectation of article 48 of the Wiemar constitution, which provided for "emergency authority" including the suspension of civil rights. Hitler had outlined this use of emergency power in the last chapter of *Mein Kampf*.[44] "Louis Henkin has referred to the U.N. Charter as 'Hitler's epitaph.'"[45] The human rights system as well as the charter are direct results of the war to stop the barbarity of Hitler's atrocities and war of aggression. The current U.S. administration's references to reducing the United Nations to irrelevance and its dismissal of the resistance of France, Germany, and Russia as "Old Europe" reveal the new directions of the United States seen in the May 30, 2002, Department of Defense document as "Joint Vision 2020," proclaiming U.S. policy to be "full spectrum dominance." This plan calls for the "National Command authorities" to direct U.S. forces unilaterally or multilaterally to "defeat and control any situation" regarding the global nature of U.S. interests.[46] Of course, U.S. interests include the vast web of human rights treaties and interests developed since World War II; but these are threatened by the U.S. assertiveness in the face of terrorist acts and the new philosophy of foreign policy.

Prudent realism and liberal institutionalism are being temporarily swamped by a world-dominating view grounded in American protestant triumphalism, the largest military budget ever (estimated at $500 billion including the war in Iraq), and an "emergency" that overrides human rights and civil rights. The move toward "preemptory unilateralism," only slightly qualified by grudging acquiescence to UN authority in the Security Council, does not bode well for U.S. interests in international cooperation or for the UN. Moreover, as David Little pointed out, the United States has failed in its international obligations under the International Covenant on Civil and Political Rights to report which human rights it has set aside for the emergency and its reasons for so acting.[47]

On the domestic front, human rights issues emerged at least weekly in 2003 in the U.S. press.[48]

1. Large numbers of aliens are being held because someone regards them as "a danger to national security." They have not been charged, but some are being held for violation of immigration laws and some have been deported.
2. The U.S.A. Patriot Act of 2001 threatened traditional constitutional rights by implying guilt by association for anyone having connections with a terrorist group.
3. Rules regarding surveillance of political groups were relaxed for the New York Police Department by a federal judge in Manhattan on February 12, 2003. It represented a victory for the attorney general's lenient guidelines for investigation.
4. Rights of assembly were restricted as authorities were given permission to deny peace demonstrators access to the near environs of the United Nations.

Cases are winding their way through the U.S. legal processes with the likelihood of some of them reaching the U.S. Supreme Court. The military commission's powers have been sharply reduced from President Bush's early declarations due to public criticism.

The United States' acquiescence to other nations' torture of suspects thought to be connected to terrorism and the treatment of detainees without charge or trial at Guantanamo Bay remain as significant violations of humanitarian principles and law. In 2004 the systematic torture of prisoners in Afganistan was exposed.

The Presbyterian Church (USA)'s annual update report on human rights adopted at the 215th General Assembly (2003) raised complaints about human rights in the United States under the following subjects:

1. immigration and Naturalization procedures under new powers to expedite removal;
2. unaccompanied immigrant children imprisoned;
3. juveniles being referred to the adult court system;
4. capital punishment;
5. economic rights;
6. poverty (Temporary Assistance for Needy Families authorization);
7. access to political information (cost factors); and
8. religious rights (threats to Muslims).

The threats to human rights raised by the Bush administration in this emergency remain to be worked out issue by issue through all three branches of federal government and local governments. Churches intervene at all levels. My local congregation secured the release of an Ethiopian detained by local police at a bus station. Moderate to progressive churches oppose publicly the war in Iraq and particularly so a war without UN sanction. More fundamentalist and evangelical churches seem not to publicly object to the war. On human rights, the differences could be narrowed as the conservative Iowa senator Charles Grassley showed by opposing military surveillance. Many who approved of pursuing Al Qaeda in Afghanistan and who object to a war in Iraq have consistently pled for the maximum possible protection of human rights during this emergency. The aerial bombardment and invasion of Iraq eclipsed all of the above-mentioned violations of human rights and the rules of war. Contemporary weapons as employed by the United States, by their nature and planned use, far exceed what can be regarded as acceptable collateral damage.[49]

Human rights are easily subject to abuse in foreign policy. Both the idealist and the cynic misuse them. Only a policy that recognizes their foundations in human nature itself, notes that historically they are realized only fragmentarily through struggle, and possesses a hope for their ever-expanded fulfillment can negotiate between idealistic moralism and political amoralism.

The United States was fortunate in World War II and the Cold War that its enemies of Nazi Germany and Communist Russia had so little moral prestige. The United States could appear as a fusion of liberator and hegemon in its victories. Usually U.S. foreign policy has mixed the struggle for economic advantage, national security, and moral values. Its policy has been to use Michael Doyle's categories, a mixture of realism and liberation.[50] The stronger part of the realism has been a moral realism, and philosophers Reinhold Niebuhr and Hans Morgenthau have contributed prophetic realism to the mixture. Presently, three schools contend for a place in American thinking: liberal institutionalism, realism, and neo-imperialism. Condoleezza Rice is representative of the realist moving to President Bush's moralistic[51] neo-imperialism with doctrines of dominance and preemptive war. An option of prophetic realism in the Niebuhr-Morganthau school would have served her Presbyterian roots well, but she has opted to explain President Bush's neo-imperialism instead. Progress in understanding human rights will need to await a new administration.

Notes

1. "U.S. to Demand Vote on Libya's Leadership of Rights Panel," *New York Times*, January 20, 2003, A4.

2. The Universal Declaration of Human Rights itself refers to inalienable rights, barbarous acts, freedom of speech and belief, freedom from fear and want, the rule of law, and the development of good relations among nations. Its words are very American, and its tradition is secular liberalism, but American liberalism is rooted in the deeper religious traditions from which the writers drew their specific values, particularly of covenant.

3. Kana Mitra, "Human Rights in Hinduism," in *Human Rights in Religious Traditions* (ed. Arlene Swidler; New York: Pilgrim Press, 1982), 77–84.

4. Pontifical Commission, "Justice et Pax," *The Church and Human Rights* (Vatican City, 1975).

5. Ronald Dworkin, *Taking Rights Seriously* (Cambridge: Harvard University Press, 1978).

6. A. I. Melden, *Rights and Persons* (Berkeley: University of California Press, 1977).

7. Human rights language is also foreshadowed in the Ten Commandments and other codes of the Hebrews, as Walter J. Harrelson demonstrates in *The Ten Commandments and Human Rights* (Philadephia: Fortress Press, 1980).

8. Max L. Stackhouse, *Creeds, Society, and Human Rights: A Study in Three Cultures* (Grand Rapids: Eerdmans, 1984).

9. Stanley S. Harakas, "Human Rights: An Eastern Orthodox Perspective," in Swidler, *Human Rights*, 17–18.

10. Egon Schwelb, "Human Rights," *International Encyclopedia of the Social Sciences* (New York: Macmillan, 1968), 540–45.

11. See Robert N. Bellah et al., *Habits of the Heart* (Berkeley: University of California Press, 1985), for a profound development of the social cost of the loss of social meaning.

12. Reinhold Niebuhr, preface to Maurice C. Cranston, *What Are Human Rights?* (New York: Basic Books, 1963), v–viii.

13. Reinhold Niebuhr, "Freedom," in *Faith and Politics* (ed. Ronald H. Stone; New York: George Braziller, 1968), 81.

14. Reinhold Niebuhr, "Liberty and Equality," in *Faith and Politics*, 195.

15. Reinhold Niebuhr and Paul E. Sigmund, *The Democratic Experience: Past and Prospects* (New York: Frederick A. Praeger, 1969), 81–82.

16. Reinhold Niebuhr, "The Social Myths in the Cold War" and "A Question of Priorities," in *Faith and Politics*, 223–44, 261–68.

17. Michael Novak, "Human Rights," paper presented at Human Rights Conference, Kalamazoo College, Michigan, April 26, 1978, 6–7.

18. Ernest W. Lefever, "The Trivialization of Human Rights," *Policy Review*, Winter 1978, 11–26.

19. Ibid., 13.

20. Ibid., 23.

21. Ibid., 26.

22. President Jimmy Carter, University of Notre Dame, May 22, 1977, as quoted in the *New York Times*, May 23, 1977, 12.

23. President Jimmy Carter, news conference, Washington, D.C., June 13, 1977, as quoted in the *Los Angeles Times*, June 14, 1977, 25.

24. President Jimmy Carter, speech delivered in Newcastle-upon-Tyne, United Kingdom, May 6, 1977, as quoted in the *Los Angeles Times*, May 7, 1977, 18.

25. E. Brooks Holifield, "The Three Strands of Jimmy Carter's Religion," *The New Republic* 174 (June 5, 1976): 15–17.

26. June Bingham, "Carter, Castro and Reinhold Niebuhr," *The Christian Century* 94 (September 14, 1977): 775–76.

27. William Lee Miller, *Yankee from Georgia: The Emergence of Jimmy Carter* (New York: Times Books, 1978), 201–47.

28. Ernest W. Lefever, "Niebuhr and the World Crisis," in *The World Crisis and American Responsibility* (New York: Association Press, 1958), 4.

29. Ernest W. Lefever, "The Rights Standard," *New York Times*, January 24, 1977.

30. Lefever, "Trivialization of Human Rights," 11.

31. Ibid., 17, 18, 23.

32. Hearings before the Committee on Foreign Relations, United States Senate (May 18–19, June 4–5, 1981), 76.

33. Ibid., 506.

34. Ibid., 505.

35. Ernest W. Lefever, "Human Rights and National Security: An American Perspective," transcript of speech delivered in Agana, Guam, September 25–27, 1981, 1. Lefever has generously provided several of his papers on human rights to the author.

36. Ibid., 2.

37. Ibid.

38. Ibid., 8.

39. The lowest argument I've seen was on a sheet Ernest Lefever sent me prepared by the staff of the American Council for Coordinated Action. It described the propaganda campaign against Lefever as a "'Reichstag Fire' kind of propaganda campaign." It portrayed Lefever as a victim of those seeking to promote worldwide socialism. The objectives of his opponents were assumed, including the intent to "protect Marxist regions from charges of human rights violations."

40. *A Conversation with Michael Novak and Richard Schifter* (Washington, D.C.: American Enterprise Institute for Public Policy Research, 1981), 24–25.

41. Richard Schifter, quoted in ibid., 7.

42. Michael Novak and Richard Schifter, *Rethinking Human Rights* (Washington, D.C.: Foundation for Democratic Education, 1981).

43. Stackhouse, *Creeds, Society, and Human Rights*, ix.

44. David Little, "Terrorism Public Emergency and International Order: The U.S. Example," unpublished paper for Violence, Religion, and Terrorism Working Group meeting in San Francisco on January 31, 2003, 6.

45. Ibid., 8.

46. From Gary Paton, "Full Spectrum Dominance and Joint Vision 2020," document of Violence, Religion, and Terrorism Working Group, 1. David Little's paper also references this new strategic vision as announced on September 17, 2002, in "The National Strategy of the United States." See David Little, "Terrorism, Public Emergency, and International Order," *Church and Society* (May /June 2004): 66–91.

47. Ibid., 33.

48. The first three categories are from David Little's paper.

49. Part of this chapter was delivered as a paper at the annual meeting of the Society of Christian Ethics, Washington, D.C., January 16, 1982. Michael Novak, the U.S. representative to the Human Rights Commission, responded, and a dialogue followed. With further editing it was published in Ronald H. Stone, *Christian Realism and Peacemaking* (Nashville: Abingdon Press, 1988), pp. 66–98. It was redrafted in 2003 for the Human Rights Conference (February 20–23) in Prague, and further edited for this book.

50. Michael Doyle, *Ways of War and Peace: Realism, Liberalism, and Socialism* (New York: W. W. Norton, 1997).

51. See Nicholas Lemann, "Without a Doubt," *The New Yorker*, October 14 and 21, 2002, 164–79.

11

U.S. Foreign Policy in the Middle East

DESPITE OSAMA BIN LADEN'S HOPES to transform his personal problems into a civilizational war between Islam and the West, the struggle is really with Al Qaeda. The war was not even with all of Afghanistan but only with his allies and protectors, the Taliban. Fortunately, the Taliban's lack of international legitimacy and the ongoing civil war with the Northern Alliance made the focus on the Taliban and Al Qaeda clear enough. U.S. rhetoric obscured the legitimacy of the war in Afghanistan under international law, the United Nations, and just war theory. The president and Congress announced a war on terrorism, trying to impose a false dualism of good and evil, either/or, for us or against us on a much more ambiguous situation.

Though Al Qaeda was originally an Arab organization, it has become a transnational actor. It is postmodern in that it is not a nation-state but interacts with nation-states. It violates international standards by attacking embassies and civilians as well as U.S. military forces. Created to fight the Soviet empire in Afghanistan, it has evolved to fight the American hegemony. The United States also has become something of a transnational reality; it has evolved into a worldwide force in economics, culture, and military power. Neither the economics nor the culture is particularly state based, but the military force is centered on the state. The U.S. capacity to use the United Nations for its foreign policy and to gather allies for its wars also reveals the transnational role of the superpower. So the struggle with Al Qaeda is unique in that it features two transnational forces fighting against each other, with one claiming religious sanction for its efforts and the other claiming moral righteousness for its war.

If terrorism is understood to be an act of violence directed against non-combatants to influence politics through the promotion of fear, then many state actions as well as non-state actions may be regarded as terrorist acts. Even policies seeking peace through "deterrence," dependent on threatening civilian populations, are a form of terrorism.

Policies of enforcing slavery through public punishment have been a form of terrorism. The removal of populations from their homelands through the killing of civilians, whether Native Americans or Bosnians, has been a form of terrorism too. The bombing of cities to intimidate governments to surrender has been yet another form. The bombing of abortion clinics, selective assassination of medical workers, and lynchings have all been part of the American experience of terrorism. In the Middle East, state policies of Israel to combat Palestinians have been terrorist acts, as have the Palestinian attacks on Israeli citizens. Terrorism itself has a history as long as recorded history and has been reinforced even in religious stories of the origins of humanity. A war against terrorism is a war against many of a nation's own policies of deterrence, attacking civilians in war, and support for terrorist allies. A war against Al Qaeda, an identifiable organization that violates international law, is another matter.

U.S. policy under President Clinton, at least after the bombing of the African embassies, was to kill bin Laden and his associates. This goal was actively pursued through missile attacks on bin Laden's camps and through undercover operations. Following 9/11, it expanded into open war in Afghanistan and operations throughout the world. The world reacted with horror to the attack on the World Trade Center, and the United Nations provided legitimacy for the U.S. effort to defeat Al Qaeda. The United States failed to defeat the terrorist organization, but it disrupted its operations in Afghanistan and elsewhere.

Many foreign policy operatives in the new Bush administration desired a war to overthrow Saddam Hussein and to remove the irritant of the Baathist regime in Iraq. The "war against terrorism" provided something of a cover for a preventive war against Iraq. Saddam Hussein had terrorized the population of Iraq with policies of political murders; near genocidal suppression of the southern peoples, particularly in the marshes of the Tigris-Euphrates delta; and murderous gas attacks on the Kurds. There is no doubt about the terror in the Iraqi population. Furthermore, sanctions and bombings had not subdued the regime of Saddam Hussein even though he was defeated in the first Gulf War. The American administration failed to gain clear support for its war in the United Nations; therefore, it tried to make a case against the regime for its development of atomic, biological, and chemical weapons in defiance of UN policy and Iraq's agreement following the Gulf War. Furthermore, it attempted to connect Iraq to terrorism, citing the probability of Iraq's support for terrorism with its weapons program. Iraq denied the continuation of its weapons programs after the Gulf War. UN inspections did not prove Iraq false, but U.S. claims of nuclear weapons development were based on forged documents, and British claims of forty-five-minute deployment possibility of chemical weapons were never substantiated. The United States' possible interests in empire, the strengthening of Israel by destroying its most powerful enemy, the destruction of a regime that purportedly threatened the president's father, and the control of oil were subjects of public but not official governmental rationale for going to war.

Whereas the case of belligerent native allies, UN legitimacy, and NATO occupation of Kabul had produced initial stability in parts of Afghanistan, the situation in Iraq was different. Though Kurds assisted the United States in the north, they were not a national alternative to the Baathist party. The well-planned "blitzkrieg" of the U.S. military was not accompanied by realistic planning for the occupation, withdrawal, and future of Iraq. The occupation received meager support from the international community. The Baathist supporters, recoiling from defeat, were more rapid to counterattack than the Taliban and Al Qaeda in Afghanistan. The generalizable, undocumentable goodwill of the world for the United States faded in the aftermath of 9/11 and the invasion of Afghanistan in pursuit of Al Qaeda. European allies were increasingly even if only temporarily alienated from U.S. leadership. Ironically, Al Qaeda, which was opposed by Saddam Hussein's secular regime, gathered strength in Iraq after the invasion. Terrorism by several forces grew in Iraq as mosques, UN installations, gas lines, electrical grids, and police stations were attacked. By the beginning of the election season in the United States on Labor Day 2003, the United States was scrambling to multinationalize and to return to Iraq responsibility for its own defense. The presence of a force of 150,000 U.S. troops, supported by 21,000 British troops and minor contributions from NATO and others, strengthened Western presence in the Middle East. However, developments by Hamas in Palestine and jihadists and Baathists in Iraq thwarted Bush administration hopes for control and stabilization in the new order. Al Qaeda, which was insignificant in Saddam's Iraq, is growing in power and influence by resisting the U.S. occupation.

The intervention in Iraq led to the strengthening of Al Qaeda and involved the United States in fighting on two fronts at the same time with only Iran between the occupation of Afghanistan and Iraq. Iran's program of weapons of mass destruction had not been limited as Iraq's was after the Gulf War of 1990–1991, and relations with the United States deteriorated. The financial costs of stabilizing Iraq and Afghanistan after initial military victories, combined with a 15 percent tax cut geared toward wealthy Americans, raised ominous signs for the American economy. The United States was in danger of financial overextension for the benefits or prestige of empire, which had driven so many previous empires to ruin.

The war in Iraq was not justified by defense against terrorism directed against the United States. An argument might have been made on grounds of humanitarian intervention against the state terror of Hussein's Baathist party actions against the people of Iraq. Such a war would have required development of a case that could win wide support in the United Nations. The unlikelihood of that development left the United States with UN inspections, sanctions, and no-fly zones. Such an outcome was undesirable, but with the United States purchasing much of Iraq's oil under the United Nations program, there were still other levers with which to push Iraq policy if a real danger were perceived. It was not a war of last resort, nor did the United States or Britain articulate just causes for the war to persuade other major nations to support it.

The "war against terrorism" in its worldwide dimensions is misguided. Policies to combat Al Qaeda could have succeeded with the support of peoples and states from the Muslim world. In the case of Iraq, imperial ambitions consistent with U.S. policy development seem to have driven the war.

The National Security Strategy, the National Strategy for Combating Terrorism, the National Strategy for Homeland Security, Vision 2020, the Patriot's Act, and other documents reflect the Bush administration policy. Combined with the "war against terrorism," they promise to defeat terrorists, deny support and space to terrorists, diminish the conditions that encourage an environment where terrorism can grow, and defend U.S. citizens and interests domestically and internationally. These four goals, in themselves, are unobjectionable; but when seen in the light of the invasion of Iraq, the goal of U.S. military full-spectrum dominance of potential conflicts, a military budget greater than the combined budgets of the next six largest military budgets, and the emerging analysis of the American empire, they appear dangerous.

It would seem that the Bush administration was jolted into a "war against terrorism" before it had agreed on a vision for the U.S. foreign policy. The policy before 9/11 seemed to be moving away from the internationalist policies of the preceding administration toward a unilateral policy of disconnecting from arms controls, ecological concerns, international criminal justice, and development of international law. The response to 9/11 substituted the broader policy of envisioning an appropriate role for the United States in a changing world with one of a declared commitment to counter terrorism universally. This degree of commitment gave the administration a purpose, which the president, with a slip of the tongue, called a "crusade." However, the hard work of creating a foreign policy that promotes greater justice, peace, international law toward order, human development on behalf of the world's poor, and worldwide ecological sustainability remains. Such goals are a distillation of the major goals of churches in the ecumenical movement. They represent religious communities' support for moral goals. They are goals beyond the particularities of the mythical heritage of religious traditions. As religion blends into morality, these goals, which can be recognized as humanitarian goals, receive religious support. But their acceptance as goals for American foreign policy requires only moral argumentation, not ritualistic acts or revelation or interpretations of sacred Scripture.

A vision of a just world moving toward harmony does not contradict the suppression of a movement that encourages terrorist acts. The capture of the terrorist membership of Al Qaeda is a national requirement. The disarming of enemies committed to killing U.S. citizens will require the killing of many of our enemies. The very meaning of national statehood requires such actions, usually more similar to large police actions than international war. In addition to police actions against transnational groups, the power of international law must be strengthened. International law and strengthened international police forces and peacemaking forces, in the future, may be our best insurance against groups that would attack international peace. The struggle against the rage that induces people toward terrorist acts requires support for policies of just, sustainable human development and peacemaking. These elements of vision will need to be transparently evident in U.S. policies to make real progress against the widespread use of terrorist acts while the members Al Qaeda are suppressed, disarmed, and imprisoned.

The same three elements of suppression, law, and vision[1] will be needed in the religious conflict over land in Palestine. The particularities of religious claims in extreme forms will have to be resisted so that religious support for compromise, tolerable justice, and peace can be appropriated. Religion contributes to the conflicts; religious support for moral solutions is part of the solution. This too will require change in U.S. policy thinking. The religious dimensions of international conflicts must be recognized, but religious resources for their solutions must be developed much more aggressively than they have been up to this time.

This argument reinforces the current tendency to recognize the importance of religion to statecraft. The secularism of American universities, the severe interpretations of the separation of church and state, and the cynical interpretations of realism have all obscured the role of vital religion in international politics. Robert D. Kaplan's recent book *Warrior Politics: Why Leadership Demands a Pagan Ethos*[2] argues that the history of international politics shows that pagan or immoral leadership would be best for the American empire. Nowhere does he show how pagan or admittedly or exposed immoral leadership could be elected in the United States. Nor does his study include as of any significance Augustine, Thomas Aquinas, Martin Luther, John Calvin, William Gladstone, Woodrow Wilson,

John Foster Dulles, Hans Morgenthau, or Reinhold Niebuhr. He does not understand that Christianity has a realistic social ethic. Christian ethics at its center is neither only personal ethics nor irrelevant idealism. Douglas Johnston's study *Faith-Based Diplomacy: Trumping Realpolitik*[3] makes the case for the importance of religion and the understanding of religion in many current conflicts. His concluding chapter is very helpful in recommending how religion can contribute to understanding and reducing conflicts. Unfortunately, he and his contributors to the volume attack realism and do not understand how a religious realism can be both peacemaking and realistic at the same time. While the search for peace will require the derivation of peacemaking resources from all of the world's religions, here I want to argue for the understanding of prophetic realism in terms of its Hebrew origins and Western development.

An ancient text accepted as normative by Judaism, Christianity, and Islam is a distant source for the way forward. Amos indicted the nations of the ninth century B.C.E. for their violations of justice and human rights. Aram, Philistia, Edom, Ammon, Moab, Judah, Israel, and others were all to be punished for their evils of destroying nations, ignoring international covenants, forgetting pity, attacking women, destroying graves, rejecting law, mistreating the poor, misusing religion, and killing the prophets. The act of violating religion by ignoring its moral restraints particularly led Amos to criticize empty ritual and false religion. From his critique of immoral religion, he wrote: "Take away from me the noise of your songs; I will not listen to the melody of your harps. But let justice roll down like waters, and righteousness like an everflowing stream" (5:23–24).

Amos brought together the boldest claims for monotheism, the foundation of all three Middle Eastern religions, with the clearest realism concerning national sins and the sharpest demand for justice. In the end of his book, restoration, healthy agriculture, and perpetual peace are promised. This union of radical monotheism with rigorous justice, realism about international affairs, and a vision is prophetic realism. Amos did not advise an empire. He moved, as far as we know, only from a desert village outside Jerusalem to Samaria. His relations with the established political order and religious establishment were precarious, but his prophecy seems to be the earliest union of monotheism and ethics by a specialist in international relations and religion. Prophetic realism seeks not to rule but only to inform and possibly persuade. Its weapon is the pen, not the sword. It approves only of prudential use of violence and not of terrorism. It cannot affirm the absolutes of jihad or other forms of holy war, nor can it affirm absolute pacifism. It allies with just peacemaking strategies while it rejects the optimism of some of its proponents and insists more strongly on the prevalence of human conflicts in the international sphere. It develops its sense of prudence from history. Prudence and a sense of limits set it against the imperial ambitions of the neoconservative policy makers around President Bush.

The world is too complicated to make it over in the American image. Political science, which cannot warn of the collapse of the Soviet Union or the emergence of religious terrorism, is too limited to advise a world emperor. The substitution of economic theory and mathematical models for history and linguistic skills may further impoverish American international relations studies. Appreciation of factors of power and the reality of certain U.S. national interests points to the diplomatic foibles of the first Bush administration, which failed to assure Saddam Hussein of the U.S. interest in Kuwait's oil. From that failure came the events that led both toward Osama bin Laden and 9/11 and toward the Second Gulf War with Saddam Hussein.

While nations pursue the vision of moral policies discussed above, they cannot neglect the realities of power and interest. Joining power to moral purpose, the accommodations of one state to another, and transnational actors to one another is the work of diplomacy. Since diplomacy today involves war (when necessary and just), international law and organization, and vision, another metaphor is appropriate. The bicentennial of the Lewis and Clark expedition reminds Americans of the skill and courage these men needed to push a keelboat up the Missouri against the current, without a map, in the presence of unknown inhabitants who had a right to the river; similarly, diplomats today need skill and courage to make foreign policy decisions that hold to the vision and values of prophetic realism.

A Church Response

The Presbyterian Church (USA), a mainline Protestant church, has never been a pacifist church, though it contains many pacifists within its membership. In fact, a draft board in New England rejected a student's request for Conscientious Objector status during the Vietnam War, saying, "The Presbyterian Church is a war church." Nevertheless, the church evolved with a programmatic and financial priority for peacemaking, and recently it has affirmed its principals of just peacemaking while utilizing just war thinking also. In 2004 the General Assembly of the Church used a rather lengthy background analysis of just war teaching to support its policy declaring the invasion of Iraq to be "immoral, unwise and illegal."[4] The charge of illegality was grounded on several articles of the UN Charter, to which the U.S. is a signatory. "Unwise" reflected the delegates' own sympathies as they voted. "Immoral," however, was rooted in just war teaching applied to the particular war.

The church policy paper, entitled *Iraq: Our Responsibility and the Future*, regarded the invasion as part of a policy of preemptive military action that stands against the criterion of just war that war is an action of last resort. Preemption comes from radically different presuppositions concerning the use of force than those of just war thinking. It is hard to say when the criterion of last resort would have been reached in the case of Iraq. But certainly there was more time, as the United States was in no imminent danger from Iraq.

The paper argued that the criterion of just cause was not met by the war. Reasons given for the war by spokespeople of the administration have not stood the examination of evidence, because no Iraqi collaborative support for the terrorist acts of 9/11 has been uncovered. It is most likely that the weapons of mass destruction programs had been discontinued as Iraq said and the United States and Great Britain denied. But more important, there is no basis legally or morally for going to war to install democracy in a country whose traditions are alien to democracy or for resorting to war because another country is arming itself.

The principle of just war thinking that war must be conducted under the legitimate authority is changing. The post–Cold War climate has leaned toward the post–World War II consensus that the United Nations was the body that could legitimately sanction the use of armed force. The administration wanted to assert the right to its own authority and build a coalition to support it. The United States obviously has the power to act unilaterally, but it would have the right to do so only in extreme emergencies when there was no time for UN consultation, and even then it would be subject to UN review. The Iraq invasion did not receive the support of the society of nations or of its organ, the UN, so the legitimacy of U.S. authority for its actions remains unproven.

Just war thinking teaches that a nation should not go to war without the likelihood of success. Success narrowly regarded might just be the triumph of the armed forces, but the church used a broader understanding of the requirement to mean that success includes the securing or defending of a better society through armed conflict and its aftermath.

While the church paper noted that efforts to spare civilians were undertaken in Iraq, the unreliability of intelligence, failed munitions, and street fighting meant that civilians were attacked and killed. The question of the means of war and their justification also faults the United States for the torture of prisoners. Unarmed prisoners have rights; in the case of the Iraq invasion, these rights were violated. To the extent that torture was a necessary part of the prosecution of the war, it falls under the ban of the use of unjust means of warfare. The probability that unjust means of coercion were approved at high levels of the U.S. command raises the issue of the United States' systematic reliance on unjust means to prosecute the war.

The reasoning in the church policy paper on Iraq and just war pointed to the requirement of truth telling as a presupposition of just war thinking. If the president and the secretary of state distort the evidence that is used as a basis for arguing for a just cause, the whole process is tainted. If the Central Intelligence Agency fails to warn decision makers about the unreliability of its sources of information used to support war making decisions, the public's right to know and debate are denied. Fundamental moral axioms requiring officials to refrain from lying and bearing false public witness must be honored for the whole process of reasoning about war to take place. If the representatives of the people are fed lies and distortions about decisions to go to war, reasoning fails, and the resort to war becomes simply an act of will of those governing the country. The church paper found the invasion of Iraq to fail the tests of just war criteria.

Reappraisal of Israel

The realists discussed in this book were all pro-Zionist. Hans Morgenthau was a Jew active in the free Soviet Jewry movement and a lifetime activist in Jewish causes after immigrating to the United States. After a history of pro-Jewish action before and during World War II, Tillich and Niebuhr, in mid-1942, founded the Christian Council of Palestine on pro-Zionist principles. Niebuhr testified before the Anglo-American Committee of Inquiry on January 14, 1946, arguing for a Jewish state and for the permission of greater Jewish immigration to Palestine. Just as biblical prophets spoke for the defense of Israel, all of these thinkers wrote and argued for the defense of Israel.

Israel is a modern nation recognized by the international community, and so its existence is legally guaranteed. Its alliance with the United States furthermore assures temporal existence in the present. The recent U.S. invasion of Iraq smashed the only military power in the region that was an imaginable threat to Israel. The Jewish presence in the neoconservative thinkers who conceived the invasion of Iraq also is a short-term guarantee of Israel's security. The neoconservative influence has eclipsed the classical or prophetic realism of the subjects of this book.

Niebuhr's occasional writings and editorials on Israel's wars treated them as struggles for survival. They were that, as very many Israeli losses would have backed them into the sea. But the victorious outcomes from 1948 to 1967 allowed Israel to expand its claims and control of Palestinians and the land of Palestine. Israel, a Jewish state, is surrounded on three sides by Arab-speaking Muslims who regard Israel as the unwanted interloper. Islam feels no guilt for European anti-Semitism and no responsibility to provide a home for the refugees fleeing anti-Semitism. The disorganization of the occupied Palestinians thwarts meaningful compromise with militant

Israel. So the issues simmer and feed the desperation of neighboring Islamic states and agitate even distant non-Arabic Muslims.

The Crusaders' kingdoms of the eleventh and twelfth centuries flourished briefly but declined for 150 years until their final demise and Europe's abandonment of the Crusaders' cause in the Arabic world. Will Israel's fate be different? Nuclear weapons are a trump card for Israel's deterrence of its Arab neighbors. But will nuclear weapon threats from Arab and Persian countries counter Israel's deterrence? This region is a repository for diplomatic blunders and catastrophic miscalculations, and one cannot be sanguine about nuclear-armed Middle East states.

To reach beyond the history of the Crusades to the times of the biblical prophets is to realize that Israel was never strong enough to remain nationally autonomous for long. Forces from Assyria, Babylon, Persia, or Egypt were always wrecking Israel. Israel is in danger as long as Islamic hatred persists. The Bible expresses the destruction of Israel theologically as the judgment of God. Political science sees the same destruction as residing in disproportionate power in the conquering countries.

Prophetic realism would have served the U.S. interests better during World War II by urging Jewish refugee immigration to the United States. America would have been more morally righteous and more powerful in political terms if it had invited Hitler's victims to migrate here. Perhaps in the long run of a hundred years of policy making, Jewish immigration finally will be encouraged. The United States would benefit immensely by providing such a welcome; in the meantime, the nation is not helped by overextending U.S. military aid and power to the cauldron of Arab-Jewish conflict.

Prophetic realism leads to the protection of a modest Israel state now but discourages the continued occupation of all of Palestine. American Jewish interests are better served by investing in the United States than by investing in occupying the West Bank.

The biblical prophets often warned of the doom of Israel and Judah. It is not the responsibility of any American to doom Israel today, but certainly the nation's future is at risk; the factor of nuclear weapons threatens cataclysmic slaughter in the future if present trends continue. The wise U.S. policy will urge, persuade, and to a degree coerce Israel toward retreating from its occupation, reduce military aid to Israel, seek settlement for genuine Palestinian grievances, and guarantee Israel's security. A genuine and mutual two-state solution might provide security for both Israelis and Palestinians overcoming the frequent warfare. Still, sufficient peace may not be attainable, Islamic power may be too great, and a retreat from Palestine to America may in the long run be necessary for the Jews. If so, the inheritors of the prophetic realist tradition will be called upon to surrender Zionism while defending and welcoming Jews.

Even for those who campaigned to free Soviet Jews and who have always regarded the armed defense of Israel as a moral option, the occupation of the West Bank has proven untenable and unacceptable. The price to U.S. national interests has been too great. Binding one nation to the fate of a weak ally is never wise.

Capitulating to the interests of an endangered ally out of reasons of guilt or sympathy is neither moral nor political wisdom. In some respects the realist commitment to Israel is commendable; the Jews needed a place to defend themselves, and the early promise of Israeli democracy and socialism was attractive. However, the resentment stirred by the occupation is negative for both Israel and its American backer. The jingoist, expansionist rhetoric for Israel to claim all of the West Bank or to fulfill the biblical suggestions of empire from the river of Egypt to the Euphrates is threatening to neighboring states and promise decades of conflict. The biblical interpretations of Israel are ambiguous, and there is some biblical sanction for the nation to have a variety of borders or to exist without statehood or to be extinguished as a nation-state altogether. The best of U.S. policies would promote a small, defensible Israel bound to a small Palestinian state by economics and a tortured history while both learn of patience and forgiveness. Hopefully this defense of Israel can persist, but if not, the solution that was not championed after World War II of a refuge in America must be developed in the long run.

The imperative now is to persuade Israel to accept its security and to persuade Palestine that modest adjustments of borders and the loss of total control over Jerusalem were the price of war. Historical traditions reflected power realities of the past and adjustments are made for present realities of power. A two-state solution somewhere between the Oslo agreements and the Geneva accords is possible, but religious fanaticism on both sides must be outweighed by the need for peace, which is also the U.S. national interest there.

Pressure to push the United States to see its real national interest as peace in Palestine will come from churches, labor unions, human rights groups, other nongovernmental organizations, and the United Nations. Years of protest against the occupation of the West Bank will increasingly develop into strategies of economic disengagement and pressure to reduce U.S. aid to Israel. It will be very hard for Jewish supporters of Israel to understand the pressure, for an evenhanded, national interest–driven policy still promises Israel security while seeking Palestinian security also. Fundamentalist and evangelical supporters of Christian Zionism may never get it. We cannot expect groups now engaged in terrorist acts to adjust promptly. An evenhanded U.S. foreign policy backed by U.S. economic and military power can help even the most extreme to adjust to reality or become irrelevant.

Notes

1. The clearest expression of this threefold approach appears in Richard Falk, *The Great Terror War* (New York: Olive Branch Press, 2003), xxvii.

2. Robert D. Kaplan, *Warrior Politics: Why Leadership Demands a Pagan Ethos* (New York: Vintage Books, 2002).

3. Douglas Johnson, *Faith-Based Diplomacy: Trumping Realpolitik* (Oxford: Oxford University Press, 2003).

4. *Iraq: Our Responsibility and the Future*, 216th General Assembly of the Presbyterian Church USA, 2004, Item 12–05, pp. 7–11.

《◎ **12** ◎》

The Peacemaking Struggle and Resistance

THROUGH THE TEACHING AND ACTION OF JESUS CHRIST, the Maker of heaven and earth has claimed us as peacemakers. God's saving love is adequate to give humanity power to struggle for the fullness of a just peace in which all interacting dynamically would nurture one another. From our creation we are blessed, but the restoration of that blessedness to our war-torn world requires more serious engagement than we have undertaken.

We are by our nature peacemakers, but in our fallenness we are bent strongly toward making war and making ready for war. Out of our yes to the beautiful creation God has given us for peace, we must now say no to the forces that make for war. Our yes to God is in gratitude for God's saving love; our no to war is said to the forces that deny the reality of that love and its commandments.

The increasing commitment to peacemaking in the Christian churches is antithetical to the deepening militarism of the world. Militarism is a worldwide phenomenon that is subject to many different definitions. It can be seen in three dynamic movements that characterize the present:

1. the nuclear arms race, the proliferation of nuclear weapons capacity, and the development of other arms of mass destruction;
2. the trade in conventional weapons and the spread of military approaches to social problems;
3. and the spread of technologies and training for the repression of internal opposition.[1]

These tendencies reinforce a process of the "militarization" of society, but my focus is on militarism as it has moved beyond policies of defense or the struggles against injustice or the gaining of independence under the limits of a means of "last resort."[2] Militarism represents the current extreme developments of military power and the too-easy reliance on military power in situations of difficult international relations. The churches have made bold calls for disarmament and policies of reconciliation through exchanges and negotiations. They have supported the work of international organizations as a move to reduce international anarchy. However, in crisis after crisis, the resort to force has thwarted negotiations. The United States has encouraged cynicism about international organizations, though it previously helped develop them. The churches have called for peacemaking emphases throughout their existence. The struggle within the church is to find means or patterns of Christian practice that are adequate to the call for peacemaking in the increasingly militarized world.

This chapter builds on the peacemaking call of the churches in their ecumenical work. It particularly grows out of the Presbyterian tradition. Christian peacemaking concerns are very broad. They include the vital preaching of the Word, the proper ministry of the sacraments, the upbuilding of Christian community, and the development of peoples through the service ministry of the church. The equipping of Christians to engage in the public policy formation of their countries and to engage in the politics of peacemaking is central to the vocation of peacemaking, and the work of Christians with others in voluntary organizations to struggle for peace is crucial to the task. Peacemaking is naturally an ecumenical task, and the restoration of peace to a divided church is important to the work of peacemaking. In addition to all of the above, more and more Christians are uniting in taking actions, some legal and some illegal, to protest their government's militaristic policies.

Various actions of selective withdrawal from aspects of cooperation with the military system may be described as resistance to militarism. Such decisions are not made without struggle. Likewise, people who are committed to cooperation with government as a necessary aspect of society find civil disobedience and tax resistance difficult modes of action. Resistance has many meanings. Here it is used in a broad sense to include actions against militarism as defined above. Resistance often involves struggles with conscience and with courage. Its modes may include demonstrations, civil disobedience, tax resistance, vocational withdrawal from the military or war-related occupations, and work within one's vocation to oppose militarism. Not all Christians will agree about the appropriateness of many of these actions. Moral ambiguity, which often surrounds human actions, is particularly real in questions of this nature. I hope this chapter will help Christians answer the question, what does obedience to God call us to do in this situation? If the direction of U.S. governmental policies is to rely more and more on the threat of world domination and on the actual use of armed forces, what are we Christians to do?

Reformed theology (and practice) is historically activist. It assumes that the Christian life is involved in both personal and social transformation. It has a high respect for the state and says yes to the state as a provider of order, the protector of the people, the source of justice for the poor, and the enabler of the weak. It also says no to the state when the state surrenders to the inevitable temptations of absolutism, imperialism, or militarism. Because the state practice is so necessary to life and because the temptations are so prevalent, Reformed persons should expect at various times in their lives to support and to resist the state. The question emerging for many Christians is, should we resist the state? The answer will depend both on our reading of the situation and on our affirmation of our theological-ethical heritage.

The Present Situation

1. Resistance to Military Neo-Imperialism

Americans normally accept that the United States has enjoyed a role of leadership in the world since World War II. They expect reasonable leadership from their powerful country. So they vote, contribute to political parties, and participate minimally in local and national politics. They recognize that the social-economic opportunities and meaning in America are found in many arenas besides government and its international politics. Power is more accessible to most citizens through nongovernmental organizations or corporations than through government. They ordinarily trust that they can leave moral-political decisions to the routine processes of politics.

Those normal processes of American politics produced support in the Cold War for the Marshall Plan, NATO, the Korean War, and significant military budgets. The first Iraq war produced significant citizen opposition to the point of resistance. Resistance here is understood as public demonstrations and activities disruptive of governmental policies (civil disobedience, tax resistance, boycotts, strikes, and so on).

The second war in Iraq engendered worldwide demonstrations against American policy and massive domestic protests in the streets. The war against Al Qaeda and the overthrow of the Taliban in Afghanistan were accepted without massive protest by the American people. So in the early years of the third millennium, resistance against the world hegemony of the United States emerged.

While there was widespread disgust with Iraqi dictator Saddam Hussein, suspicion that there might be dangerous connections between Iraq and terrorism, and worry about the unfinished disarmament of Iraq, still the war seemed premature and probably unnecessary to much of the world and to a significant number of U.S. citizens. Neither the inspectors nor the Security Council of the UN completed their work, which was dismissed by the United States.

2. Full-Spectrum Dominance

The election of George W. Bush in 2000 prepared the way for a group of neoconservative defense strategists to move into roles of significant power in the United States. These thinkers struggled with others in the administration for dominance. The events of September 11, 2001, allowed them to merge their interests with more traditional conservatives and American nationalists to help shape the president's response. Whereas Presidents Carter, Reagan, and Clinton had only intervened in Afghanistan and Iraq, the neoconservatives, in the aftermath of September 11, conquered them. The George W. Bush administration expressed its goals for Iraq as liberation from the Saddam Hussein regime and discovery and destruction of weapons of mass destruction for terrorist support. Bob Woodward, reporting on discussions within the administration, indicated that many of Bush's advisors had hoped to invade Iraq even before the terrorist attacks of 9/11 and had been forced to strike at Afghanistan first.

The bolder willingness to take the United States into war was announced on May 30, 2002, in the Department of Defense paper signed by Chairman of Joint Chiefs of Staff General Henry H. Shelton. The document entitled "Joint Vision 2020" is a plan or vision for how the United States will fight wars for two decades. It calls for "full-spectrum dominance," which means that the United States will be prepared to "win" any wars across the world, coordinating its actions when possible with other nations and multilateral agencies. It suggests that the United States shall be prepared to act unilaterally or multilaterally to control any situation. The United States must be able to achieve dominance in any realm—space, sea, air, or land—and to rapidly project power anywhere.

The elder Bush had built an alliance to attack Iraq and arranged for other nations to pay the bill; by refusing to conquer the country, he limited his war. The attempt on his life and the later frustrations with Saddam Hussein challenged his son George W. Bush to complete what his father had refused to undertake. In 2003 there were very few limits, and George W. Bush unleashed a war deeply resented by a billion Muslims and much of the world. Americans, unenthusiastic about becoming an empire, could use the failure of the war to meet the justifiable war criteria of legitimate authority, last resort, real harm to be corrected, and proportionality as a reason for protests and acts of resistance.

Beneath the issue of a particular war is the question of whether a cultural and economic hegemonic power should also become political director through the use of military power. War against Al Qaeda is a just cause;

war in Iraq may not be; world domination definitely is not. Massive world-wide protests echoed not only outrage over a particular war but also fear of U.S. dominance. Internal resistance to imperial politics is needed to pre-serve and restore democracy and to return U.S. power to developing a national life that the world will want to emulate instead of draining the homeland of power for full-spectrum dominance of the world. Beyond mass protests and the encouragement of anti-U.S. terrorism, the seeking of full-spectrum dominance will engender countervailing alliances.

Neither nation-states nor empires last forever, but the struggle to domi-nate for security's sake may bleed a country of its resources and its people. Security as a value is very high. But a nation conceived as a republic can eas-ily lose its soul in striving to become an empire. In that loss may even rest its premature demise as a nation. America has cast its lot with freedom, but it does not bear the responsibility to fight all over the world to ensure its free-dom or to impose its freedom. It simply is not the case that every cruel dic-tator threatens America. Even the invasion of one country by another does not mean that the United States needs to be involved. We can be responsible Good Samaritans without having to become Roman centurions.

3. The Comprehensive Test Ban Treaty

The Kennedy administration succeeded in banning tests of nuclear weapons in the atmosphere, in outer space, above ground, and under water in 1963. Successors to Kennedy through Carter advocated the adoption of a comprehensive test ban treaty (CTBT) that would also ban nuclear tests underground. By March 2003, 166 nations had signed the CTBT, but the U.S. Senate failed to ratify the treaty in 1999 by a vote of 51 to 48. Since that failure, both Pakistan and India (also non-ratifiers) have tested nuclear weapons. Madeleine Albright as secretary of state had warned in 1999 of such developments if the United States would not ratify the treaty. Professor Jeanne Kirkpatrick argued on the same day for testing to develop the U.S. arsenal partially as a deterrent against other weapons of mass destruction.[3] U.S. leadership in the weapons of mass destruction debate has returned full circle with a war in Iraq, with one of its many goals being the destruction of weapons of mass destruction, some biological agents of which we sold to Iraq previously. Resistance against the government's fail-ure to limit such weapons by treaty seems to be a moral option.

The immediate agenda is to persuade through diplomatic means the United States, Russia, China, Pakistan, and India to ratify the Comprehensive Nuclear Weapons Test Ban Treaty and to persuade the United States and Russia to drastically reduce their arsenals. The religious communities have not been leading in this agenda. Some thirty-six years ago, I lobbied the conservative Republican Iowa Senator Bourke Hickenlooper on both race relations and the Treaty Against Testing in the Atmosphere. I remember watching him pound his desk and say he never would have voted for the partial test ban if it hadn't been for those "damn Methodist preachers in Iowa." Where are those preachers now? Half a century ago, Paul Tillich was among the prophets warning of the threat of nuclear weapons.

Of course, it is possible that our efforts to abolish nuclear weapons will fail and that it is our destiny to destroy ourselves through the tensions within our own humanity. If so, meaning is not lost—for ultimate meaning, as perceived in our religious traditions, is not *in* our history but *beyond* our history.

If we are aware of the self-destructive tendencies in ourselves and in our societies, we are called to resist these suicidal instincts. Life and history have meanings that are worthy to be defended. We must undertake the resistance against suicidal instincts on all levels: in politics, in economics, in the healing professions, in our communications industry, and in religious life through the finding of serenity and new ways of devotion to the Creator who undergirds our lives and transcends our parochial loyalties.

Finally, this resistance to the false gods of nuclearism must be undertaken, as Paul Tillich said fifty years ago, "in acts which unite the religious, moral, and political concern, and which are performed in imaginative wisdom and courage."[4]

4. National Missile Defense

Despite the failure to establish the technological possibility of a national missile defense after the expenditure of billions of dollars, the George W. Bush administration reached the decision to establish a portion of it. This decision required the abandonment of the Anti-Ballistic Missile Treaty with Russia. That treaty permitted two sets of anti-ballistic missiles (ABMs); both Russia and the United States developed only one, which the United States abandoned as obsolete. This was the first abrogation of an attempt to limit major weapons systems since the end of World War II. President Bush defended the unproven ABM system and the abrogation of the treaty as necessary to develop means of defense against "rogue states."[5] It is probable that the focus on ABM defense during the first months of the Bush administration obscured the need for attention to anti-terrorist defense.

5. Biological and Chemical Weapons

The Geneva Protocol of 1925 reacted to the use of mustard gas weapons in World War I by outlawing their use. In 1972, following U.S. leadership, 144 governments signed the stronger Convention on the Prohibition of Development, Production, and Stockpiling of Bacteriological and Toxin Weapons and on Their Destruction. It went into force in 1975, and about a dozen countries either were seeking the weapons or had attained them.

Most major countries have the capability of producing them, and terrorist groups have used them (as in the Tokyo subway attack in 1995). In December 2001 the George W. Bush administration blocked further development of the Bacteriological and Toxin Weapons Agreement (BTW). The United States did not want any enforcement or monitoring legislation to be added to the Convention.

Chemical weapons, particularly mustard gas, made the greatest impression on the world after the Germans introduced mustard gas at Ypres in 1917. Iraq's use of mustard gas against Iran in the 1980s and nerve gas against the Kurds received the world's censure and was part of the reasoning for the removal of the Saddam Hussein regime. Russia had admitted violating the Protocol, and the United States' introduction of Agent Orange in Vietnam was either an avoidance or violation of the treaty. Agent Orange, conceived of as a defoliant for the jungle, also had nefarious affects on people, animals, and birds.[6]

6. Small Arms and Light Weapons
The world is flooded with small arms and light weapons. Kofi Annan estimates that 500 million are available—one weapon for every dozen people on earth. The United States has been "instrumental in blocking the creation or development of any instrumentation with the capacity to monitor or control the flow."[7] The United States has been opposed to a ban on sales to non-state actors, wanting instead to use the U.S. norms of responsible and irresponsible end users. The United States has not wanted its policies on weapons sales and possessions to be influenced by other nations. It also did not want to "toughen up" the 1999 treaty or offend the U.S. gun lobby. Much profit can be made in international gun sales, and the United States leads the world in exporting $14.5 billion worth of arms and military equipment, which is more than all the rest of the world exported in 2004.[8] These policies reflect the results of an administration elected with the assistance of the National Rifle Association and gun lobby. Resistance to the sales of small arms may not be a preferred tool of opposition since elections, legislation, and international conventions are at issue.

Theological Sources of Resistance

1. The Biblical Heritage
The Bible has shaped our conscience in regard to the questions we are considering. Through its use in devotions, sermons, study, and prayers, it has formed many of our attitudes. However, to throw biblical light on the question of noncooperation with the state, we must take the question to the Bible itself. Not all relevant passages can be considered here, but as G. Ernest Wrights (former professor at Harvard Divinity School) responded

to a question about civil disobedience in the Old Testament, "The most significant figures of Scripture all seem to resist established legal authority in some manner."⁹

One of the best tales of resistance is of the Hebrew midwives' resistance to Pharaoh in Exod 1:15–22. Pharaoh's attempt to limit the growth of the Hebrew people by putting their males babies to death was thwarted by the chicanery of the Hebrew midwives Shiphrah and Puah. They defied the command of their sovereign and lied to him so that the children might live. In Exod 2 Moses himself is saved through more defiance of the sovereign; this time the resistance to authority involves Pharaoh's own daughter and household. Moses, of course, saved through an act of defiance, is later used by God to defy the state openly and to lead his people to freedom. The author of the letter to the Hebrews connects Moses' salvation from death and his leadership of resistance against the Egyptians directly to faith.

A case of resistance leading to revolution is found in 1 Kgs 12. Solomon's son Rehoboam was urged to lower the taxes that Solomon had imposed for his court and building projects. Rehoboam refused and instead threatened to increase the tax load. According to the text, the Lord then brought about a "turn of affairs" (12:15) that resulted in Jeroboam's leading the tribes away from allegiance to Rehoboam and founding Israel in Bethel. Jeroboam's own place of worship at Bethel as an alternative to Jerusalem also received prophetic criticism, but the division of the kingdom held, with only Benjamin remaining allied with Judah and the house of David.

Micaiah represents the figure of the prophet who says no to the king. Throughout the Old Testament, the prophet representing God's Word challenges royal authority and is punished for speaking God's Word. Micaiah in 1 Kgs 22 warns Jehoshaphat of Judah and Ahab of Israel that their campaign against the Arameans will be a disaster. It is not a clear case of religious spokesman against royal authority, for it is also an intra-religious struggle. All of the other prophets promise success. For his negative prophecy, Micaiah goes to prison. In defiance of Micaiah's prophetic "no," Ahab and Jehoshaphat go to battle and face defeat. Their defiance costs Ahab his life; the Bible records that "the dogs licked up his blood" (22:38).

Esther's bold breaking of the law began the reversal of fortunes that saved her people from pogrom under Persian rule. Her statement of purpose to save her people represents the best spirit of action against law to save life: "I will go to the king, though it is against the law; and if I perish, I perish" (Esth 4:16).

John Calvin grounded his understanding of religious resistance to governmental decrees in reflections upon the book of Daniel. The young Hebrews, under the Persians and the Medes, simply refused to follow the orders of the emperor in matters of worship. Shadrach, Meshach, and Abednego refused Nebuchadnezzar's command to worship and honor the royal idol. Similarly, Daniel refused to stop praying to his Lord, defying a royal edict. These men were rescued from punishment by God's actions. This noncompliance when ordered to violate one's faith has been a model for much Christian resistance to religious persecution. Often the willingness to endure persecution for faith has also, as in Daniel, been an argument for honoring the faith that has strengthened adherents in the face of persecution.

A theme of God requiring resistance to the government recurs throughout the Old Testament. It is, of course, only one theme. A more prominent theme is that of covenant obligation binding the Hebrews together as a mutually supportive people. The covenant is made before God; after the Hebrews accept kinship, the ruler is obligated to God. At the foundation of Protestant political thought is the idea of the people covenanting together, and then the people covenanting with a sovereign who is obligated before God to respect the people's covenant. The idea of resistance to the sovereign never disappears. The forms of resistance mentioned in the Old Testament reappear in the New Testament: resistance to save children, resistance to taxes, violation of a law to save a people, and religious resistance to idolatry.

The question of the challenge of the Messiah's authority to political authority haunts the New Testament. From the birth narratives of Jesus to his execution as "King of the Jews," political authorities from Herod to Pilate are threatened by Him. His ministry is in the context of Jewish sects agonizing over their relationship to Rome. The Gospels reveal the context of their writers, who struggled with the antagonism of synagogue and church after the Roman destruction of Jerusalem. Paul, writing before the destruction of Jerusalem and before the Neronian persecution, understands the ethics of subordination to the state in one way. The author of Revelation, writing much later, sees Rome's destruction and the victory of the cosmological Messiah over the persecutors of his people.

The New Testament is more eschatologically oriented than the much larger Old Testament. Consequently, in political thinking stemming from the Reformed branch of the church, the Old Testament has received more use. But the insistence that the Old Testament is more political does not mean that the New Testament is free of political involvement and implications. Much of this less-political character of the New Testament is simply due to the fact that Rome occupied the land. Jews normally were not citizens, were not subject to military service, and had little political clout. The state in the New Testament is provisional; it lasts for a while to maintain order. It is not absolute, though Revelation reveals its absolute pretensions.

The central actors of the New Testament all defy the authorities sufficiently to be imprisoned or executed. The New Testament, though focusing on the inner person and focusing on eschatology, is set in a political storm. The ringing statement of Peter, "We must obey God rather than any human authority" (Acts 5:29), is from one who struggled with the political meaning of his beloved Jesus. Peter would not only question Jesus; he would, under pressure, deny him after defending him with a sword. Peter would not only defy the authorities to preach Christ resurrected; he would with God's help escape from prison twice.

2. Church History

The New Testament concludes with the struggle between the cosmological Christ and the corrupted Roman state. This struggle has shaped Christianity so that even today wild interpretations of Revelation that neglect the historical context of the book still confuse Christian political ethics. In this book only those who have refused the demands of the state are regarded as Christ's.

In response to an inquiry about civil disobedience in the early church, the late Roland Bainton of Yale Divinity School said, "From Nero to Constantine, any adherence to Christianity was civil disobedience, even though punished only intermittently."[10]

The Christians of the early church, until it was legalized under Constantine, prayed for the emperor, paid taxes, and lived lives of exemplary citizenship, but they urged their followers to resist demands for worship of or ultimate allegiance to the state's deities. Christian resistance to the imperial cult led to persecution and to martyrdom's occupation of a central place in the life of the church. Although they generally refused military service, after 170 C.E. there is evidence of Christians serving Rome in the army. Interestingly, early Christian resistance is one of the two major reasons for Christian absence from the military in those early centuries. Christian conscience forbade in many cases the honoring of the deities and the worship of the emperor required by military service. That restraint on Christians' service in the armed forces was removed with the Christianizing of the empire; the ethic of love, however, still restrained many from taking up the sword. The early church said yes to the order of the Roman Empire but no to the religious practices that legitimated the empire and expressed its claim to absolutism.

The "no" to empire became much more muted after the empire began to be allied with the church. Monasteries and ascetics still separated from the state, but the church embraced it. In the East, where the empire was strong enough to survive to the fifteenth century, the rulers tended to dominate the church. In the West, where the empire dissolved, the church tried to rally forces of order and to restore civilization. In the emergent church-feudal blended society, the church under strong leaders sometimes said no to the princes for the freedom of the church, but the "no" to military practice was very muted. The alliance between the church and militarism reached a zenith in the Crusades in the Middle Ages.

Long before the church was involved in the barbaric slaughter that accompanied the Crusaders' conquests in Constantinople and Jerusalem, the church's complicity with armed force was established. The same Augustine who out of an ethic of love could reluctantly sanction armed defense eventually came to excuse the application of armed force against heretics. Crusades approved by the church were carried out against nonorthodox Christian groups but also against Christian peoples (e.g., the Norman Conquest of England in 1068). The church sought through the techniques of the "Truce of God" and the "Peace of God" to limit violence, but it was too involved in the use of violence to protect its own temporal interests to be an effective peacemaker. Similarly, in the European conquest of the world from the fifteenth century until the twentieth, the church complied with the imperial needs of the European powers. It had its own missionary interests, but these were vitally compromised with the worldly motivations for wealth and empire. Here and there a prophetic voice from within the church, such as Father Bartolomé de las Casas in Central America in the sixteenth century, would protest against the subjection and murder of the native inhabitants. But religious legitimacy in the name of Christ was bestowed upon the European conquest of others.

The uneasy alliance between spiritual and temporal authority that characterized the Middle Ages resulted in many struggles between the spiritual and temporal rules. But in the eleventh century, the pope could claim to be under God, the source of both temporal and spiritual authority. The claim could not hold, however, and far-reaching claims of the pope contributed to the conflict that exiled Hildebrand, even from Rome. Secular rulers were limited by custom, by law, and by the power of the church. The church was at least coequal, if not the rightful sovereign, in this long, complex period of Western history. The legal thought of Thomas Aquinas (1225–1274) laid the grounds for much of Catholic constitutional theory limiting the role of temporal authority. His claim that positive laws are dependent on divine law and natural law has, in our own time, been the grounds for Christian resistance to unjust positive laws.

The Protestant Reformation tended to pit the new religious movement against the old order. Martin Luther (1483–1546) justified the refusal to obey the commands of the sovereign when they violated God's will ("We must obey God rather than any human authority," Acts 5:29). His high view of scriptural authority also led him to avoid resistance on the grounds of Rom 13:1 ("There is no authority except from God, and those authorities that exist have been instituted by God"). Disobedience to the authorities? Yes, when their commands violated God's law. Resistance to the authorities? No; at least, he avoided resistance until very late in life. Finally, he was persuaded that the emperor's move into Germany to destroy the Reformation was illegal, and on the advice of lawyers, he agreed that resistance to illegal action of the emperor was constitutionally legal. Then he could justify armed resistance to the emperor. Later, Calvinist-armed resistance to the sovereign often borrowed from theological arguments developed on Lutheran ground.

John Calvin (1509–1564) tried to restrain his followers from revolution. He also taught that impious commands of the sovereign were not to be obeyed. The authorities were constituted by God and were to be honored, though civil servants had a duty to resist their princes if they acted in a manner contrary to the law. Calvin's followers in the Netherlands, France, and Scotland were to push the implications of his positive attitude toward government much further. In all those lands, historical forces pushed Calvinists into revolution, and they succeeded in the United Netherlands and Scotland. The early Protestant revolutionaries acted out of a need to defend the true or Protestant faith against blasphemy and idolatry. But by the 1570s in the French Protestant political theory, the grounds of revolution were the supposed original freedoms of the people and their rights under natural law.[11]

Calvinist political theory developed in subsequent centuries until its positive view of the state, grounded in covenantal language of its Old Testament roots and founded in revolution, could be expressed in the U.S. Constitution. It underwent substantial change on its way to supporting popular revolution in John Locke's book *Two Treatises of Government* from John Calvin's disobedience to the sovereign in *The Institutes of the Christian Religion*.

The Reformed view of the emerging states was positive. The leaders of the states were, of course, sinners and often foolish, but the state was the dike of God against sin. Order was precious, and the vocation of a public office holder was in John Calvin's thought to be respected above all other vocations. There was no romantic anarchy or idealistic perfectionism in Calvinist political wisdom. Still, in its beginnings it recognized the duty to disobey on religious grounds. Soon it was driven in honoring that God is Lord of the conscience to resist and then overthrow tyrannical-idolatrous regimes. The conception of a covenant between the people and God for the ordering of their lives led to the idea that the sovereign could be overthrown if the ruler violated the covenant. The covenant's meaning was grounded both in the constitutional history of the realm and in the natural rights of the citizens. So the grounds were laid not only to resist unjust laws but to depose sovereigns. George Buchanan (1506–1582) carried the right to depose sovereigns as far as any Calvinist thinker, and, of course, he did it for Scotland, where Calvinists succeeded in deposing the Queen in 1567.

The historical material reveals only that Protestant Christians, like their Catholic counterparts, are free morally to resist or to replace governing orders that act against the purposes of the constitution or religious faith.

3. A Recent Example

Resistance to the U.S. war policy was well exemplified by Clergy and Laity Concerned about Vietnam (CALCAV). The organization, born in John C. Bennet's living room in the mid-1960s, organized, wrote, lobbied, and demonstrated against the war in Vietnam for a decade until U.S. participation in the war ended. Though dominated by mainstream Protestants, it also incorporated Catholic war resisters, including Daniel Berrigan as cochair until he was exiled by his bishop to Latin America. The organization provided an expression of protest for Jewish anti-war activists with Rabbi Abraham Heschel serving as co-chair and offering a consistently prophetic voice. Its leadership often drew from Niebuhrian realistic ethics; Richard Neuhaus, Robert McAfee Brown, and William Sloan Coffin encouraged radical actions against the war, including resistance to the draft and many nonsymbolic actions while CALCAV tried to read the American middle and organize the churches against the war.[12]

None of the CALCAV's leadership could be regarded as disloyal, though right-wing opponents, including J. Edgar Hoover, did so characterize them. John C. Bennett was a consistent leader of CALCAV throughout its decade of work, combining its responsibilities with his editorship of *Christianity and Crisis* and presidency of Union Theological Seminary. Some students at Union were drawn into demonstrations against the U.S. role in the war as early as the fall of 1963. CALCAV's role in reaching the middle of American public leadership undergirded the students' activism, whether in draft resistance and arrest or in political organizing in various campaigns. Reinhold Niebuhr, though too ill to actively lead the movement, had participated in its predecessor organization in September 15, 1963, as the Minister's Vietnam Committee condemned American tactics in the war as immoral. His 1966 address to Union Theological Seminary, arranged by John Bennett and myself, empowered the student opposition to the war. Political philosopher Hans Morgenthau contributed his political realism to the writings and thought of the group, while Martin Luther King Jr.'s participation represented its commitment to nonviolent tactics of resistance.

Though CALCAV was unable to end the war, its expenditure of millions of dollars and the organization of tens of thousands of anti-war supporters contributed to the undercutting of U.S. policy and the nomination of more dovelike candidates and also persuaded foreign policy elites to seek to deescalate and eventually abandon the war effort.

King's association with CALCAV symbolized the alliance between the civil rights movement and the antiwar movement, which generally was more natural for whites than for blacks. King led the civil rights resistors to anti-Vietnam war conclusions, but many black civil rights activists did not follow. The civil rights movement, led by black clergy through the Southern Leadership Council of Martin Luther King Jr. from the mid-1950s until King's assassination in 1968, is an important, successful example of Christian resistance to evil in our time.[13]

The clergy, fed by decades of oppression and a generation of theory of Christian social change, were able, when inspired by the resistance of Rosa Parks, to mobilize masses to change society. In a decade, official segregation was broken and black access to political power was opened. Economic opportunity would remain illusive for millions, though other millions of blacks would gain entry into the middle class.

Leaders of the opposition to the Vietnam War had learned tactics, organization, and theory in Christian social resistance in the civil rights movement. The synthesis of many streams of thought and action in King and the movement gave it an unusual brilliance.

CALCAV represented mainline, white-dominated resistance, and SCLC represented black clerical-led resistance, with both drawing on broad ecumenical sources for support and participation. Both movements defined clear evils to resist, and both expressed religiously passionate community while taking risks to influence society. Neither movement abandoned mainstream politics or American civil society while engaging in tactics of resistance that challenged that society to change.

Peacemaking and Resistance

In the 1990s mainline Christianity articulated theories and paradigms of just peace or just peacemaking. These emerging concepts, combined with international interventions to stop genocide, captured Christian thinking in the United States. After the Cold War, military budgets declined as a proportion of gross national product at home. The focus seemed to be to reduce U.S. nuclear weapons while helping to disarm Ukraine, Kazakhstan, and even Russia. Both nuclear weapons and the dangers of militarism in the United States seemed to decline. Globalization, democracy, and human rights were in the minds of some moving toward more international peace. Even Marxists such as the authors of *Empire*[14] seemed to think big wars were a thing of the past and imperial power would reduce international clashes to police actions. But the hopes and fears of both liberal and Marxist theorists proved illusory. The arming of the world continued, and India and Pakistan, with new nuclear weapons, replaced the denuclearized nations of Ukraine and Kazakhstan in the doomsday club.

Then, with the atrocities of September 11, 2001, the world, led by the United States, lurched back toward militarism and new uses for nuclear weapons. The realism of Christian neoorthodoxy seemed more relevant again than liberal optimism[15] or Marxist pessimism. The realism about violence in international relations[16] and awareness of imperialistic tendencies suggests the need for both resistance and increased political participation to oppose militaristic trends.

While exercising its approved right of self-defense against its attackers, the administration of the United States unwisely tried several other policies. A New Office of Strategic Influence in the Pentagon was shut down in 2002 as legislators protested its reputation for mixing untrue reports with information about Iraq. Military tribunals, policies overriding the civil liberties of Middle Eastern immigrants in the context of releasing studies of new uses for nuclear weapons, abandoning the treaty limiting missile defense, rejecting the landmine treaty, the comprehensive test ban treaty, and pursuing the largest-ever military budget suggest the need for resistance to militarism.

While public criticism drove the "crusade" language and the Office of Strategic Influence off stage, the other more potent militaristic emphasis remained in place. Minimalist gains toward recognizing the importance of multilaterialism, nation building, and peacemaking diplomacy seemed to have prevailed over the hard realism of the administration. Recognition of the need for resistance against nuclear weapons and militarism, and the extraordinary use of ordinary means of changing policy, seems once again appropriate.

Resistance, of course, means opposition to the development of threatening new military systems through political action, demonstrations, teaching, preaching, noninvestment, and divestment. It calls for occupational withdrawal from and noncooperation with the military when it is used destructively or for domination beyond legitimate self-defense and international order requirements.[17]

Resistance to militarism requires participation in and rebuilding of peace movements within churches and civil society. Clergy and Laity Concerned about Vietnam is a model; more recently the ecological movement's organizations, from Greenpeace to the Sierra Club, suggest what needs to be undertaken. One of the more recent studies emphasizing the junction of ecological and antimilitarist concerns on the landscape of the American West is Rebecca Solnit's *Savage Dreaams*.[18]

Moral realists, just peacemakers, traditional peace organizations, and churches all have a stake in the never-ending struggle to keep U.S. policy rational and sometimes benevolent. Barbara Green describes well the long-term struggle against militarism and excessive armament in her essay in *Church and Society*: "There are some significant characteristics of U.S. military policy that are neither ending nor beginning, but that cry out to be changed. Foremost among these is U.S. over investment in military spending and under investment in alternatives."[19]

The demonstrations against U.S. policy in Iraq were the most significant antiwar protests since the Vietnam War. Peaceful demonstrations around the world were accompanied by some acts of nonviolent civil disobedience leading to thousands of arrests. There were also violent protests against U.S. policy. Many of the demonstrators were mobilized by the churches. However, the elected officials and their advisors could refuse to heed the demonstrators and the civil disobedience.

Domestic dissent and even world dissent can be overridden in foreign policy defined as national security. Therefore, the resistance activity needs to be directed toward the desired political goals of winning elections. The policy toward Iraq was decided by an identifiable group of actors who took prerogatives of office under George W. Bush. A different result in the Supreme Court would have produced a different foreign policy. So the church and other nongovernmental peace organizations must plan for positive results at the election booth. The churches can promote parachurch peace movements that take direct action, while local churches can study the issues, participate in denominational peace activities, support peace-seeking pastors and leaders, and raise financial resources for peace movements. Finally, for changes in foreign policy election results are determinative. Of course, election results are then subjected to bureaucratic politics and the rise and fall of competing ideologies. George W. Bush's opinions on foreign affairs were changed by his team after September 11, 2001. The competition of ideas, bureaucrats, and lobbyists never ends. And in a violent world, the church's role of seeking peacemaking never ends either.[20]

Notes

1. "Consultation on Militarism," World Council of Churches, Montreux, Switzerland, 1977, quoted in José-Antonio Viero Gallo, ed., *The Security Trap* (Rome: IDOC International, 1979), 127.

2. Ibid., 117.

3. Dana J. Blackstock, *Trembling Like Trees in the Wind* (Louisville: Presbyterian Church [USA], 2003).

4. Paul Tillich, *Theology of Peace* (ed. Ronald H. Stone; Louisville: Westminster John Knox, 1990), 159. In addition to the quotation, the preceding two paragraphs represent Paul Tillich's ideas.

5. Ibid.

6. Ibid.

7. "Resolution on Challenges to Global Security," *Church and Society*, July/August 2002, 80.

8. Thom Shanken, "U.S. and Russia Still Dominant Arms Market," *New York Times*, August 30, 2004, A7.

9. Quoted in Ronald H. Stone and Dana Wilbanks, *The Peacemaking Struggle: Militarism and Resistance* (Lanham: University Press of America, 1985), 6.

10. Roland Bainton, quoted in Richard W. Baur, Carol Meier, Richard E. Moore, and Henry Carter Rogers, *A History of Civil Disobedience: In Defense of the Reverent Maurice McCrackin*, n.d., mimeographed, 14.

11. Quentin Skinner, *The Foundations of Modern Political Thought* (London: Cambridge University Press, 1978), 338.

12. For the history of Clergy and Laity Concerned about Vietnam, see Mitchell K. Hall, *Because of Their Faith: CALCAV and Religious Opposition to the Vietnam War* (New York: Columbia University Press, 1990).

13. The debates about Martin Luther King Jr.'s leadership continue, but there is widespread recognition that the movement for civil rights was clearly at its peak when inspired by King and led by black Christian clergy. See Taylor Branch, *Parting the Waters: American in the King Years 1954–1963* (New York: Simon & Schuster, 1988).

14. See Michael Hardt and Antonio Negri, *Empire* (Cambridge: Harvard University Press, 2000).

15. Glenn Stassen, ed., *Just Peacemaking: Ten Practices for Abolishing War* (Cleveland: Pilgrim Press, 1989), 133–55.

16. See Reinhold Niebuhr, *Moral Man and Immoral Society* (New York: Charles Scribner's Sons, 1952), 83–112.

17. For further discussion of the pros and cons and means of resistance, see Dana W. Wilbanks and Ronald H. Stone, *Presbyterians and Peacemaking: Are We Now Called to Resistance?* (New York: Advisory Council on Church and Society, 1985), 48–57.

18. Rebecca Solnit, *Savage Dreams* (Berkeley: University of California Press, 1994).

19. Barbara G. Green, "Militarism and Arms Control," *Church and Society*, November/December 1999, 59.

20. A section of this chapter contains edited material previously published in Ronald H. Stone and Dana W. Wilbanks, eds., *The Peacemaking Struggle: Militarism and Resistance* (Washington, D.C.: University Press of America, 1985), 1–11.

Index

action, 99–103
Acts
    5:29   175
Afganistan, 21, 154, 155
    British failures, xi
    intervention, x
    war, 94
Alexander the Great, 13
Allah, 93
Al Qaeda, xi, 151, 154, 156
    suppression of, 158
    war, 169
America, 94
    church and state, 126
    freedom, 170
American
    foreign policy, 48
    people, 145
Americans for Democratic Action, 59
Amos, xii, 3, 7, 61, 120
    4:11   4
    5:18   5
    5:21–24   8, 159
    14:25   4
    human rights, 134, 135
    justice, 159
    radical monotheism, 5, 134
apocalyptic, 5, 63
Aristotle, 10, 12–15, 181
    justice, 107
    in Morgenthau, 62

Armageddon, 97, 98
Aron, Raymond, 49, 50
Association of Theological Schools, xiii
Augustine, 15–19, 62
    Christian realism, 16, 80, 158
    Christian rulers, 17
    defense, 176
    dualism, 78
    politics, 18
    purpose, 78
    virtue, 91
    Wills, Gary on, 17

Barth, Karl, 123, 124, 128
Bennett, John C., 27, 28, 40
    arrest, 105
    changes in realism, 53
    Foreign Policy in Christian
        Perspective, 51
    human rights, 57
    realism, 109
    resistance, 178
Bhagavad Gita, 86
Bible, 2, 7, 10
    realism of, 10
biblical, 1, 22
    heritage, 172–75
    perspective, 94
    realism, 1–8
    sources, 57
Bill of Rights, 137

bin Laden, Osama, ix, x, xi, 118, 154, 160
Britain, 5
Brown, Robert MacAfee, xi
Burke, Edmund, 24
Bush, George, ix, 169
Bush, George W., , 150, 169, 181
     administration of x, 155, 171, 172
     policy, 116–119

Calvinist, 144, 177
Calvin, John, 2, 18–21, 158
     politics, 20
     realism, 20
     resistance, 173, 177
Carter, Jimmy, 133
     human rights, 141–44
     Niebuhr, 144
     test ban, 170
Casas, Bartolome' de las, 176
Central America, 89, 148, 176
Central Intelligence Agency, ix, 162
character, 124, 125
China, 5
Christ, 23, 58, 96
Christ and Culture, 78
Christian East, 92, 136
Christian faith, 97
Christian life, 122
Christian purpose, 77–80
Christian West, 92, 136
Christianity, 57, 103
Christians, 101
     act, 103
     and resistance, 167, 175
Christology, 123
church, 11, 18, 23, 122
     churches, 54, 150, 164
          Federal Council of, 111
          Mennonite, 123
          National Council of, 110, 112
          peace, 122
          Roman Catholic, 18, 21, 123, 127
civil rights, 24, 27, 100, 179
Clinton, Hilary, 129
Clinton, William, x, 155
cold war, 34, 40, 54, 122
     human rights, 138, 146
common good, xiii
Communism, 25, 27, 36, 38, 39, 116
     conflict with, 56, 58, 143

myth of, 64
optimism of, 65
power against, 72
Communist, 92
community, 120
     Christian, 96
     conscience, 33, 54
     Constantine, 18, 25
     Constitution, 13, 19
I Corinthians
     13:13   91
courage, 105–106
covenant, 1, 2, 34
     human rights, 133, 135
     government, 177
covetousness, 97
crusade, 157, 180
Crusades, 34, 163, 175, 176

Daniel, 2, 98
David, 2, 17
democracy, 30, 56, 170
     Israel, 164
     liberal, 80
     purpose of U. S., 80
deterrence, 5
     Deuteronomy, 2
diplomacy, 8, 12, 31, 34, 48, 49
     conduct, 62
     and negotiations, 104
     work of, 160
Doyle, Michael, 12, 45, 58, 151
     critique of 59, 60
     typology, 48, 59
Dulles, John Foster, 24, 30, 54, 59
     moralism of, 63

ecclesiology, 123, 127–129
ecological movement, 180
education, 14, 15
     American higher, 128
eirene, 85
elites, 119–20
emergency situation, 149, 150
empire, 116, 157, 170, 175
     American 25, 77
     Empire, 179
enlightenment, 24
equality, 103
     under law, 107

eschatology
  biblical, 101
  Christian, 99
  Hebrew, 99
Esther, 2
  4:16   173
ethical dualism, 30, 36
ethics, 23, 30, 31, 99
  ambiguity, 138
  Christian, 11, 16, 91
  political, xi, 53
  social, 28
  defined, 74
  dualism, 76
  and foreign policy, x, 11, 40, 122
  of peacemaking, 84–104
  Protestant social, 27, 124
  social, 30
evil, 38, 69, 101
  lesser, 117
Exodus
  1:15–22   173
  2   103, 104, 173
  20:2–3   91

faith, 91–97
  hope and love, 102
Fascism, 25, 72
fear, 101, 154
Federal Bureau of Investigation, 6, 100
Fellowship
  of Reconciliation, 29
  of Socialist Christians, 27
feminist
  critique, 96
  perspective, 57
  theory, x
foreign policy, 32, 33, 36, 51, 157
  American, 56, 82, 164
  human rights, 132–154
  immutable nature, 52
  prophetic realism, 84
  temperance in, 106
  United States, 57, 154–165
Fox, W.T. R., 45, 47
freedom, 147, 170
fundamentalism, 58

Galatians, 101
Gandhi, 133, 134

German
  government, 63
  power philosophy, 27
  refugees, 27, 61
  weapons, 172
Geyer, Alan, 113, 114
Gilkey, Langdon, 64, 66
God, 2, 77, 95
  City of, 16, 17
  control, 7, 10
  grace, 166
  judgment, 42, 68, 89
  justice, 135
  Kingdom of, 77
  law, 3, 5
  love, 3, 166
  obedience of, 64
  power, 20, 79
  transcendence, 64
  will, 23, 28, 35, 101, 134
  worship of 80, 88
  wrath of, 61
government, 46, 77
  Great Britain, 80
  Hobbes on, 22, 23
Greed, 94
Green, Barbara, 180, 181

Hauerwas, Stanley, xii, 11, 122–131
  critique of Niebuhr, 125–29
  critique of Wesley, 124, 125
  on love, 130
  on New Testament, 129, 130
Hebrew, 159
Hebrews, 174
Helsinki Final Accord, 133
Heschel, Abraham, 27, 28
  The Prophets, 6
Hindu, 92
  human rights, 133
history, 123, 126
  contingency in, 62
  human, 103
  philosophy of, 105
  power, 63
  violence, 124
Hitler, Adolph, 61, 63, 72, 123, 149
Hobbes, Thomas, 21–24, 63, 89
Hoffmann, Stanley, 45, 47–53
Hoover, J. Edgar, 6

hope, 43, 54
  not Armageddon, 97–99
  love, 102
Hosea, 2, 7
  10:13–14   95
  13:2   5
  13:4   5
human
  being, 65, 96
  development, xiii, xiv, 58
  doctrine of, 29, 30
  foreign policy, 132–135
  freedom, 88
  history, 1, 103
  life, 23, 65
  nature, 10, 23, 37, 87, 112, 151
  possibilities, 38
  rights, 25, 57, 80, 104, 132–52
humanity, 103
  doctrine of, 37
  freedom, 64
Humphrey, Hubert H., 40
Hussein, Saddam, 117, 119, 160, 168
  Kurds, 172

idealism, 48, 49, 147, 148
ideology, 143
ideals, 143
idol, 93
idolatry, 91–97
immoral, 160
imperialism, 25, 62, 116, 151
  neo-imperialsim, 168–169
India, 89, 91, 92, 114, 134, 170
injustice, 135
interest, 160
  national, 31, 34, 35, 40, 50, 80
international
  affairs, 57
  Criminal Court, 104, 107
  institutions, 103
  law, 4, 30
  organization, xi, 21, 57, 120
  politics, xii, 21, 28, 52
  theory of, 45–55, 58
intervention, xiv, 179
Iraq
  Baathisist regime, 155
  invasion of Kuwait, ix, x
  war in, 151, 160, 168, 170, 181

Isaiah, xiii, 4, 5, 7, 61, 84, 90
  1–5   88
  2   111
  5:8–10, 5:29   90
  evils, 89
  justice, 88
  lawgiver, 104
  oracle, 89,
  United Nations, 87
  vision, 87
Islam, xi, 93, 159
  humiliation of, 120
  faith, 95
  peace, 95
  war with, x, 154
Israel, xi, 1, 7, 89, 162
  Amos, 135, 159
  defense of, 63, 72
  as pawn, 6
  reappraisal, 162–64
  realists and, 84

James, 2:26, 4:1–2   97
James, William, 62, 123, 128
Jeremiah, xiii, 61, 70, 98
  and Ezekiel, 85
  shalom, 99
Jerusalem, 3, 4, 98, 164
  saints of, 102
Jesus, xiii, 7, 8, 73, 95, 134
  Christ, 166
  ethic of 29, 74, 101, 112, 113
  love, 8, 126, 129
  political power, 8
  words, 85
Jews, 163, 164
  defense, 164
  as refugees, 163
John XXIII, 103
John Paul, II, 128
Johnson, Douglas, 154
Joint Vision 2020, 149
Judaism, 4, 61, 102, 159
  love, 102
  as prophetic, 70
justice, 23, 69, 73
  biblical, 3, 107
  fairness, 103
  Niebuhr, 102, 103
  ontology, 63–66

and prophets, 3
rough, 28,
social, 140,
Tillich, Paul, 3, 102
of war, 11
just peace, 102–4
movement, 104
just peacemaking, 104, 109–21, 159
just war, 41, 110
Augustine, 15
Presbyterian Church, 161, 162

Kagan, Robert, 83
kairos, 58
Kant, Immanuel, 62
Kaplan, Robert D., 158
Kennan, George, 40, 50
Kennedy, John F., 65, 82, 126
administration, 170
King, Martin Luther, Jr., 3, 100, 133, 134, 179
Kingdom of God, 77, 79, 99, 101, 103
I Kings
12   173
22   173
Kipling, Rudyard, x
Kissinger, Henry, 72

land, 89, 90
law, 20, 102, 158
of God, 20
international, 117
natural, 20, 23
in United States, 149
League of Nations, 49, 84
Lefever, Ernest W., 132–52
Leviticus
19:18   102
liberal
institutionalism, 151
optimism, 180
thought of, 61
values, 61
liberalism, xi, 48, 54, 65
myth of, 64
liberation, 104, 136
ethics, 41
liberty, 20
Lilly Faculty Fellowship, xiii
Lincoln, Abraham, 36
Little, David, 149

Locke, John, 22, 24, 59
optimism, 24
Two Treatises, 177
Long, Edward L., Jr., 104, 113
Lord, 4, 5, 88, 90, 91, 95, 98, 99, 107
Lord's servant, 6
love, 37, 175
Augustine, 16
of God, 3
hope, 102
human, 65,
ontology of, 63–67
Niebuhr on, 66
and power, 65
Luke, 113
10   102
14:31–32   8
Luther, Martin, 16, 18, 123, 176

Machiavelli, Niccolo, 19–21, 58, 59, 89, 129
The Prince, 72
realism, 89
theory of, 47
Machiavellians, 72, 73
Madison, James, 25, 50, 129
Mark
12   102
Martyrs, 23
Marx, Karl, 48, 62, 120
Marxist
pessimism, 180
philosopher, 91
Marxism, xi, 140
Matthew, 113
5:9   85
21:46   8
22:37–40   102
25   6
McCarthy, Eugene, 41
Mennonite, 102, 127
Messiah, 174
Micah
6:8   107
Middle East, 154–165
immigrants, 180
militarism, 41, 122, 166–181
Mollov, M. Benjamin, 60, 61
monothieism, 159
radical, 135
moral

ambiguity, 73, 74, 132
consensus, 33
law, 6
principles, 36
moralism, 38, 39, 49, 62
of John Foster Dulles, 63
morality, 28, 31, 35
decline, 32–34
international, 33, 50
and politics, 20, 40
prophetic, 68
and religion, 158
morals, 132
More, Thomas, 73
Morgenthau, Hans J., 10
on Aristotle, 13
on Hobbes, 59
human nature, 37
Judaism, 3
Machiavelli, 58, 59
moralism, 30, 38
Niebuhr, 39–41
Politics Among Nations, 39, 50, 68,
74
power, 56–70
prophets, 3
realism, 27–43
sin, 37
Thucydides, 58, 59
Vietnam War, 178
Moses, 1
Muilenburg, James, 4, 65

National Council of Churches, 109
national interest, 40, 50, 118
concept of, 81
and morals, 52
and peace, 164
nationalism, 30, 34, 35
national security, xiii, 95
Nazism, 53, 84, 116
neoconservative, 72, 162
neoimperialism, 151
New Testament, xiii, 7, 8, 18, 85, 125
Anticipated war, 111
resistance, 174
Niebuhr, H. Richard, 78
Niebuhr, Reinhold, 27–43
Augustine, 15–16
The Democratic Expereince, 65

Federal Bureau of Investigation, 6
Gilkey on, 64
God, 42, 64
hope, 43
injustice, 88
The Irony of American History, 51
Kingdom of God, 41–43
Locke, 24
Love, 66
Moral Man and Immoral Society, 52
Morgenthau, 39–41
The Nature and Destiny of Man, 42
Nixon, 6,
ontology, 64
perspective,7, 62
pessimism, 5
power, 56–75
prophets, 3
social theory, 10
*The Structure of Nations and
Empires*, 50
utopianism, 42
Nietzsche, Frederick, 62, 120
Nixon, Richard, 72
Novak, Michael, 139, 141, 142
Human rights Commission,
147–148
nuclear
destruction, 101
terror, 104
test ban, 170
war, 5, 57, 85
weapons, 101, 156, 170

Old Testament, 1, 4, 7, 17, 84
resistance, 174
ontology, 64–66
optimism, 29, 109, 114, 180
Orthodox Chruch, 136

pacifism, 8, 31, 110, 122–31
Christian, 29
Palestine, 164
Palestinians, xi, 155, 162
Patriot's Act, 157
Paul, 8, 85, 95
law, 136
love, 101, 102
peace, xii, 8, 15, 23, 84, 85
Augustine, 16, 78

of God, 16, 67
human nature, 23
just, 102–3
just peacemaking, 109–121
universal, 57
peacemaking, 84–107, 181
  action, 99–103
  just, 109–121
  realism, xii, 109–121
  resistance, 166–181
  task, 56
Pentagon, ix, xi, xii
pessimism, 5, 180
philosophy, 124
  and human rights, 134
  political 10–25
  social, 140
Plamenatz, John, 20
Plato, 13, 107
policy, 47
  U.S. foreign, 50, 62
political philosophy, 10–25
  international, 37, 47, 68
political science, 160
politics, xii, 2, 10–25, 35
  absolute ends, 25
  comparative, 11–15
  international, 35, 114
  philosophy of, 68
  Politics Among Nations, 39, 50
  Politics of Aristotle, 11–15
  responsibility, 25
poor, 4
  interests of, 103
  in Isaiah, 88
  oppression, 91
  provision for, 106
postcolonial, 46
postmodern, 155
postmodernism, 56
power, xii, 35, 38, 50, 56–70, 160
  balance of, 54, 67, 107
  concept of 51, 54, 66, 74
  defined, 76
  lust for 37, 38, 63
  in Morgenthau, 74
  political, 74
  politics, 77
  seekers, 37
  soft, 119

typology of, 77
pragmatism, 36
prayer, 61, 99
Presbyterian Church (USA), 130, 160
  United Nation's Office, 132
pride, 68, 89
  American, 94
progress, 29
prophet, 7
  biblical, 163
  and international relations, 3, 8
  Niebuhr, Reinhold, 3
  prophetic books, xiii, 84
  prophets, 102
  sociological use, 61
  Tillich, Paul, 3, 61
  Weber, Max, 61
prophetic realism, 119, 120
  attacked, 105, 122
  contribution, 62, 63
  Israel, 163
  Mollov, 61
  peacemaking, 84–107, 109–21
  perspective, 62, 159
  wisdom, 105
protestant ethics, 123
Protestantism, 19, 69
Protestant Reformation, 176
protestant tradition, 134
prudence, 105, 122, 160
purpose, 72–82
  Christian, 77–80
  national, 80–82, 118
  political, 77

Quaker, 122

Ramsey, Paul, 40, 41
Reagan, Ronald, 97, 133
  administation of, 138, 148
realism, xii, 73
  American, 27, 28
  amoral, 19
  Aristotle, 15
  Augustine, 16
  biblical, 12, 59
  Christian, 16
  complex, 12, 59
  Constitution, 24
  criticsm, 50–53

democratic, 24, 25
evaluative, 48
German, 25
historical sources of, 10–25
moderate, 40
moral, 19
neo-Orthodox, 180
political, xii,
prophetic, xii, 6, 17–43, 48, 56, 60
school of, 48, 57
and theory, 46, 50
realists, 40
democratic, 24, 25
forgiveness, 114
moderate, 106
moral, 180
pessimism, 119
writing, 52
realpolitik, 19, 25
Bush administration, 119
religion, 33
and ethics, xi
and morality, 158
and politics, 6, 56, 159
and realism, xii
resistance, 69, 77, 107
Bible, 172–75
Calvin, 173
defined, 168, 180
to militarism, 167–180
Revelation
16:16   97–99
revolution, 53, 93, 177
Glorious, 24
myth of, 64
Rice, Condoleeza, 151
Roman Catholic Church, 18, 19, 23
human rights, 134
Roman Empire, 8, 16, 18, 113
Christian resistance, 175
destruction, 98
Romans
8:22–24   99
12   113
12:18   8, 85, 112
Rousseau, Jean Jacques, 22
Russia, 5, 149, 179

Sabine, George H., 13
sacrifice, 96, 97

salvation, 85
Samuel,
I, II   2
Saudi Arabia, ix, x
Schweitzer, Albert, 124
scripture, 134, 173
security, 170
Sermon on the Mount, 113
Shalom, 84, 85, 98
Shanksville, xi, xii
Shinn, Roger, 65, 109
sin, 116
Six Pillars of Peace, 111, 112
slaves, 14
slavery, 137, 138, 155
social gospel, 27, 28, 41
socialism, 50, 59, 61
Israel, 104
Socialist Party, 114
social theory, 18
Society of Christian Ethics, 109, 120
South Africa, 145, 146, 148
sovereignty, 22
of God, 23
Iraq, 117
unified, 23
Soviet Union, 34, 46, 63, 72, 140, 141
collapse, 91
human rights
USSR, 54, 116
Spegele, Roger D., 45, 48
Stackhouse, Max L., 136
Stassen, Glen, xii, 104, 109–21
Just Peacemaking, 111, 114
Just Peacemaking: Ten Practices for
Abolishing War, 110
on Reinhold Niebuhr, 112
Stoessinger, John, 45, 47, 48
superpower, 69, 77
hegemony, 107, 109
solitary hegemonic, 116

Taliban, xi, 154, 156
terror
nuclear, 68, 104
religious, x
terrorism, 154–158
terrorist, 77
actions, 84, 155, 164
theologian, 60, 67

theology, 53, 54
  liberation, 57, 88, 89
  Niebuhr, 64
theory
  Covenantal, 136
  international relations, 45–55, 58
  social contract, 136
Thomas, Aquinas, 13, 18, 20, 134, 136, 158
  law, 176
Thomas, Norman, 27
Thompson, Kenneth, 45, 47–49, 109
Thucydides, 10–12, 58, 59
  The Peloponnesian War, 11, 22
Tillich, Paul
  on Augustine, 15, 16
  *Biblical Religion and Ultimate
    Reality*, 65
  kairos, 58
  Love, Power and Justice, 64
  nuclear weapons, 171
  political philosophy, 10
  power, 56–70
  and prophets, 3
  realist, 39
  The Socialist Decision, 61
torture, 161
tragedy, 40

unilateralism, xiii, 116, 117
United Methodist Church, 123
  polity, 129
United Nations, x, xii, 33, 34, 154
  Charter, 160
  human rights, 132, 137
  Human Rights Commission, 147,
    148
  Isaiah, 87
  Niebuhr, 63
  supporting, 121
  world government, 49, 50
United States of America, xi, 5, 46
  Al Qaeda, 158
  demonstrations, 181
  economy, 81
  ethics, 36
  government, 6
  and human rights, 132–52
  influence, 107
  militarism, 41, 166–68
  military, x, 156, 164, 168

policy, 21, 38, 57, 80, 109, 154, 180
power, 34, 68, 76
purpose, 82, 119
responsibilities, 67, 68, 118, 142
torture, 161,
Vietnam, 76
in world, 157
Universal Declaration of Human Rights,
  133, 137
utilitarianism, 35, 36
utopia, 104
utopian
  dream, 91
  plans, 63
  thought, 53
utopianism, 57
  in *Pacem in Terris*, 69
utopians, 73

values, 32, 82
Vietnam war, 6, 21, 100, 181
  Clergy and Laity Concerned About,
    27, 178, 179
  and power, 75, 77
  realists, 41, 61, 105, 122
  students arrested, 106
violence, 32, 88, 120
  Girard, René, 120
  Suchocki, Marjorie, 120
virtue
  Christian, 91
  classical, 91
Vision 2020, 157, 169

Waltz, Kenneth, 45, 46, 61
  categories, 89
  Man, the State, and War, 87, 104
  realism, 112
weapons
  biological and chemical, 171, 172
  nuclear, 170–72
  small arms, 172
Weber, Max, 5, 25, 61
War, 11, 12
  abolition, 37
  against terrorism, 155–158
  Cold, 40
  Gulf, 155
  Iraq, 151
  just, 161, 162

nuclear, 5, 85
origins, 86
Peloponnesian, 11
theory of, 46
Vietnam, 21, 41, 77, 141
work of gods. 86
World War I, 11, 29
World War II, 11, 67, 72, 114, 151
Wesley, John 24, 123–25
Whitehead, Alfred North, 88, 89
Wilson, Woodrow, 39, 158
Witherspoon, John, 24, 25
World

community, 55
Court, 104
government, 49, 54, 63, 104
World Council of Churches, 99, 137
World Trade Center, ix, xi, xii, 120
World Trade Organization, 39

Yoder, John, 113, 122, 124, 127, 128
    The Politics of Jesus, 129

Zecheriah, 84
Zionist, 162